THE Challenging Child

PHOTOGRAPHS BY BILLIE D. VINCENT

A MERLOYD LAWRENCE BOOK
LIFELONG BOOKS ● DA CAPO PRESS
A Member of the Perseus Books Group

THE
Challenging
Child

UNDERSTANDING,
RAISING, AND ENJOYING
THE FIVE "DIFFICULT"
TYPES OF CHILDREN

Stanley I. Greenspan, M.D.

WITH JACQUELINE SALMON

Many of the designations used by manufacturers and sellers to distinguish their products are claimed as trademarks. Where those designations appear in this book, and Da Capo Press was aware of a trademark claim, the designations have been printed in initial capital letters (e.g., Cheerios).

Library of Congress Cataloging-in-Publication Data

Greenspan, Stanley I.
    The challenging child : understanding, raising, and enjoying the five "difficult"
    types of children / Stanley I. Greenspan with Jacqueline Salmon.
        p.   cm.
    Includes bibliographical references and index.
    ISBN 0-201-62647-0
    ISBN-13: 978-0-201-44193-2
    ISBN-10: 0-201-44193-4
    1. Problem children.   2. Parenting.   I. Salmon, Jacqueline.
    II. Title.
    HQ773.G74   1995
    649'.153—dc20   95-8645
                                                                              CIP

Da Capo Press is a member of the Perseus Books Group.

Jacket design by Suzanne Heiser
Jacket photograph © Elizabeth Hathon
Text design by Karen Savary
Set in 12-point Monotype Baskerville by Weimer Graphics, Inc.

21   22   23   24   25   10   09   08   07   06

*To all the
wonderfully challenging children
and their families
who have allowed me to participate
in their growth*

Contents

Acknowledgments

I WISH TO THANK ALL THE COLLEAGUES WITH whom I have had the honor of collaborating in both clinical work and research. I also wish to express special gratitude to my wife Nancy, the late Reginald Lourie, Serena Wieder, Stephen Porges, Georgia DeGangi, Diane Lewis, and Valery Dejon for discussing with me many ideas that are part of this book.

THE
Challenging
Child

1

YOU'RE NOT THE CAUSE, BUT YOU CAN BE THE SOLUTION

EIGHT-YEAR-OLD JESSICA WASN'T AN EASY CHILD. A bossy, fussy girl with only a few friends, she frustrated and alienated even the people who loved her most. She threw tantrums over seemingly minor issues—"These socks hurt my feet!" or "This juice tastes yucky. I won't drink it!" She became angry when her parents tried to leave her with a babysitter, often throwing herself down on the ground and screaming furiously. At bedtime, she demanded that her parents stay with her. Her teachers reported that she seemed overwhelmed, unable to concentrate.

After school, she came home complaining that "Katie and all the other girls hate me. And my teacher thinks I'm a dummy. I can just tell." Yet Jessica was bright and articulate. At times, she could be a warm, funny girl who loved to giggle at knock-knock jokes, cuddle on the couch with her mother or father, and indulge her passionate interest in horses. But most of the time she was an unpredictable "tyrant," said her weary parents.

The most frequent complaints I hear from parents fall into roughly five patterns, one of which is a personality like Jessica's, often described as "fussy," finicky, and oversensitive. The others, also described in depth here, are children who are self-absorbed, defiant, inattentive, and aggressive.

When confronted with one of these patterns, parents, understandably, may feel confused, overwhelmed, and, not infrequently, infuriated. What worked for an older child may not work now. Advice from friends, family, and parenting books often sounds good at first, but in the day-to-day battles somehow loses its effectiveness. Talking out your feelings, finding compromises, and setting firm limits is easier said than done with a defiant four-year-old who has been screaming for a half-hour and screams even louder when you try to talk to him or help him quiet down.

Over the years, our thinking about children who face challenges in controlling their feelings and behavior has swung from one extreme to another. At one point, the accusing finger was directed at parents—somehow it was *their* fault that their children were impossible. If parents were more rigid, less rigid, more tolerant, or less tolerant (depending on the expert), then their children would be "good." This view didn't make sense to many parents, although it did provoke their guilt. Parents were further confused because they could see that their parenting worked for one of their children but not for another. Many parents had an intuitive sense that one or another of their children was especially challenging but were stymied when it came to helping that child.

The pendulum then swung to the other extreme: experts came to believe that children are simply born this way. A great deal of recent research on "temperament" assumes that key personality traits are mostly fixed, grounded in biology. In this view, we are for the most part destined to be extroverted and confident or inhibited and introverted. Irritability, aloofness, aggressiveness, or fussiness in children is seen as part of one's nature, and parents, while an important influence, have no choice but to learn to live with such characteristics in their offspring. Adjusting their own behavior and trying to fit in with their child, so as not to make the situation worse, was certainly helpful, but this strategy left many families believing that they were limited in the ways they could help a child become more emotionally flexible.

Such extreme views polarized "nurture" (it's mostly the parents' doing) and "nature" (it's mostly biological). Not only are such views unable to account for all behavior, they are of little use to parents.

While many people studying child development recognize that biology and upbringing work together, this recognition has not been sufficiently applied in advice to parents. I would like to propose a potentially more optimistic way of thinking about dealing with challenging children. This new approach focuses on how "nature" and "nurture" work in tandem. It recognizes that even seemingly fixed characteristics, such as a child's tendency to be fearful when presented with a new stimulus, can be significantly altered by early, and even by later, caregiving experiences. Early care, in fact, not only can change a child's behavior and personality, but can also change the way a child's nervous system works. For example, we now know that early in life certain experiences can actually determine how some cells in the nervous system will be used—for example, for hearing, vision, or for other senses. In the same way, certain experiences can enhance a child's emotional flexibility while others may increase rigid tendencies. We can look at a child's emerging personality traits and pinpoint to some degree the types of experiences each youngster may require. Children, in this view, *can* change. They *can* become more pleasant, flexible people. They can become easier to live with—less rigid, more trusting. Life with an initially challenging or "difficult" child doesn't have to be a perpetual battleground.

Why are some children more difficult than others? Our research, as well as research by many others, such as Jean Ayers, T. Berry Brazelton, Sybil Escalona, and Lois Murphy, has shown that children come into this world with individual differences in physical makeup. Some children, for example, have bodies that just don't feel comfortable, and so they tend to be fussy, irritable, negative, or withdrawn. Even in the early months of life, we have found, babies can reveal unique traits in specific sensory perceptions and in the workings of their motor systems. Contrary to the belief that all of us experience basic sensations similarly, we have found that children vary considerably in how they perceive sights, sounds, touch, odors, and movement patterns. A child may be overly sensitive and overreactive or undersensitive and under-reactive to a given sense. One may be best at taking in and decoding information through a certain sense, while another may have difficulty in comprehending information through that sense. We have observed that some children are gifted in their ability to plan complex behaviors and movement patterns, while others find even the most elementary sequencing of motor acts, such as putting their fingers in their mouths, a most perplexing task.

Imagine driving a car that isn't working well. When you step on the gas, the car sometimes lurches forward and sometimes doesn't respond. When you blow the horn, it sounds blaring. The brakes sometimes slow the car, but not always. The blinkers only work occasionally, the steering is erratic, and the speedometer is inaccurate. You are engaged in a constant struggle to keep the car on the road, and it is difficult to concentrate on anything else. Needless to say, you would probably be irritable!

That's how some challenging children feel much of the time. Because their bodies may not work the way they're supposed to, they are constantly striving to keep their "car" on the road. They may feel out of control, frustrated.

Let's look again at Jessica. As a baby, she was highly sensitive to touch, sound, and smell. Every time her mother stroked her, she squirmed and cried. It didn't feel good. When anyone tried to brush her hair, give her a bath, or change her diaper, it hurt. She didn't like new clothing because it felt too stiff. Wool sweaters felt too scratchy. Clothes washed with certain detergents had a chemical smell. She wanted only soft, old cotton clothes. Even sounds could be painful. Daddy's deep, melodic voice saying, "Hey, my little angel!" sounded like a fingernail on a blackboard.

What was her experience with the human world? Pretty unpleasant. Her reaction was to cry, as if to say, "Leave me alone!" These difficulties played out at every stage of her development. As she got older, she was at times inattentive and easily distracted because she was so sensitive to the array of sounds, sights, and smells coming her way. When she found herself in a busy classroom for the first time, where kids bumped up against her sensitive skin, startled her with yells and screams during recess, and sometimes intruded into the well-defined, protective space she had set out for herself, her reactions ranged from tantrums to fearful avoidance. Jessica, everyone agreed, wasn't an easy child.

While with Jessica and many other children, biology is important, it isn't destiny. We have found that how parents relate to their children *can* make a huge difference in how youngsters feel about themselves and respond to their world. Imagine, for example, that because of her sensitivities to touch and sound, baby Jessica was easily overloaded and, therefore, fussed much of the time. Her mother, having similar tendencies, reacted to Jessica's long tantrums with irritability and, more often, with anger and intrusiveness. When Jessica's mother was very frustrated, she sometimes withdrew emotionally. Jessica's father also felt frustrated. When his attempts at even gentle play overwhelmed Jessica, he began staying at work longer because he found it hard to face feeling so unsure of himself and his parenting skills.

On the other hand, imagine that her mother and father had been able to "read" Jessica's physical makeup and signals and helped her learn new ways to cope. They found the right voice tone and rhythm, the most soothing touch. They discovered just the right way to hold her to give her a sense of security. Even when Jessica was upset and overwhelmed, they could console her by using firm pressure on her back, arms, and legs, for example. As she got older, they helped her comfort herself by verbalizing her feelings and engaging in certain activities, such as jumping and rhythmic games. Most important, they gradually showed her how to take charge of her own environment. By introducing new experiences in small increments, providing extra security, and encouraging Jessica's initiative, they helped her gradually become more confident and outgoing. Slowly but surely, Jessica was able to explore her world and the people in it. She moved from being easily overwhelmed and cautious to figuring out ways both to calm herself and to master new experiences. She even learned skillful ways to lead her peers into games that she enjoyed and which were not overwhelming for her. Eventually, her own emotional sensitivity became a basis for a developing sense of empathy and compassion for others as well as leadership abilities. For many children, as they learn to deal with their physical tendencies and become more assertive, empathetic, and flexible, their own physical tendencies may change. Certain types of touch or sound, for example, may become more comfortable.

Parents can make a dramatic difference in how children use their wonderfully different natural abilities. Children vary considerably in the ways they use their senses and bodies and the ways they respond to the world. For each unique pattern, however, parents can create experiences that promote flexibility.

The types of physical differences we have been discussing have been described throughout this century. In recent times, these types of differences have been identified in children with severe psychological problems by researchers such as Sybil Escalona and Lois Murphy; in newborn infants by T. Berry Brazelton; in children with a variety of learning and sensory integration problems by Jean Ayers; in parental descriptions of temperament by Stella Chess and Alexander Thomas; and in a particular temperamental type, the "inhibited child," by Jerome Kagan. In our own research, which included colleagues Serena Wieder, the late Reginald Lourie, Stephen Porges, Georgia DeGangi, Diane Lewis, and Valery Dejon, we found that there were differences in the way infants and children took in, perceived, and responded to sensations for each sensory system. We also found that these differences could be assessed and were present in both at-risk and not-at-risk groups of infants and children. We further found that certain physical and physiologic profiles put children at risk for specific types of learning and psychological problems. We have thus far identified five types. Most importantly, however, we have found that these traits can be influenced significantly by early and later experiences. Furthermore, these traits are only a part of larger personality patterns critical for intellectual and mental health, such as relating with intimacy and empathy, modulating behavior and impulses, using one's imagination, and thinking creatively and logically.

Therefore, whenever you hear that a child's temperament or traits may be fixed, remember that not only are these traits *not* fixed, the personality characteristics we are most concerned with are "bigger" than any one trait. The capacity to love, to empathize with others, to be confident and assertive, and to think creatively are complex products of many of our traits; indeed, they are the result of our relationships and experiences over many years. For example, does being sensitive and fussy as a baby mean you can't be a warm, loving spouse and parent? Does being fearless and assertive mean that you will? Hardly. In fact, it may be a little easier for the sensitive child to learn empathy and caring. But most types of children can be emotionally healthy individuals and can become wonderful parents.

A child's personality, therefore, is not simply a product of both "nature" and "nurture," or even a product of how nurture adjusts to nature. It is a product of the unique and continuous interplay *between* nature and nurture. And this interplay happens in your relationship with your child. Your child brings his or her "nature," and you bring warmth and love wrapped up in a particular pattern of caring. In the last ten years, we have learned a great deal more about this interplay. It operates a little like a lock and key. Finding the right key creates new patterns of interactions. Out of this new relationship, a child can often develop the warmth and confidence he or she needs.

Furthermore, each stage of development, as will be described in the next chapter, has its own goals, which are in turn associated with new ways for nature and nurture to work together. For each stage of development, then, there is a special "key." I believe that this knowledge about how to find the "keys" that will help any child, even those with difficult challenges, needs to be in the hands of each and every caregiver and parent.

This knowledge does not mean instant solutions, however. With time, you can learn how to influence favorably this interplay of nature and nurture in your child. This *doesn't* mean that you are to blame for any continuing challenges. One common myth that puts pressure on all parents is the belief that just because we are able to become a mother or father, we should be able to mother and father all of our children under all circumstances. Yet, if we're reasonably modest, we quickly become aware that, other than having had parents ourselves, we have had little preparation. Most of us learn on the job. Many of us rely on our children to teach us as we go along. Children who are especially challenging, however, are often unable to teach us in a way that makes us feel successful. They often overload us with too many challenges so that we are always either frantically trying to catch up or actively considering dropping out of "parenting school." The information in this book, on how we can work with children who have special challenges, will take time to put into action. It is intended to offer the understanding that parents and caregivers need—to learn from, and help, their challenging children.

In this book, I describe five different basic personality patterns and some of the physical and emotional characteristics that go with these patterns: sensitivity, withdrawal, defiance, inattention, and aggression. In the extreme, each of these personality patterns can be very daunting for parents.

But we can also think of the five personality patterns as characteristics that appear in different proportions in many individuals. Not all of us (or our children) neatly fit into one type or another, of course. Some of us are combinations, so we fall into more than one of these five profiles; others tend to be shaped by just one or perhaps a different pattern entirely. As you read, you will see that for each characteristic, certain ways that parents behave enhance the flexibility, creativity, and potential of a child showing that pattern of behavior. We also explain how some approaches taken by parents are almost certain to compound the problems presented by a given characteristic.

While many of the examples that follow feature children with difficult challenges, most parents will also recognize some aspects of these traits in nonchallenging children (although in milder and less obvious forms). My goal in this book is to provide both a general philosophy that parents can use to gear childrearing to their son's or daughter's unique characteristics and also specific approaches and strategies for the more extreme challenges that, as many parents know, arise more frequently than they wish.

2

STAGES OF CHILDHOOD:
A NEW WAY OF THINKING
ABOUT YOUR CHILD

EACH CHILD MASTERS MANY DIFFERENT DEVELOP-
mental challenges. For instance, early in life, babies must learn
to pay attention and be part of a relationship. Later on, children
learn to use their imagination and think logically. For each of
these stages, or challenges, a different mix of inborn characteristics and outside influences may produce the desired result. For
example, a sensorily overloaded, easily distracted infant will
have a hard time learning to pay attention to a mother who is a
highly verbal, veritable whirlwind of activity. On the other hand,
if this child is fortunate enough to have a soothing, comforting
father or grandmother who can help him through the early
stages until he is a more confident, curious preschooler, his

dynamic mom may be just what the doctor ordered at that stage of his development. In our new way of thinking, a child's personality emerges from the dynamic interplay of his or her interactions with key caregivers. These interactions are influenced by nature *and* nurture. A child brings nature into the interaction with his or her unique traits. Does she love light touch or avoid it? Does he enjoy loud vacuum-cleaner noises, or is he easily overwhelmed by them? Family members and caregivers bring personality, cultural, and family patterns into the interaction. Does a mother feel rejected when her baby turns away from her attempts at wooing? Or does that rejection motivate her to try even harder? Does a father react angrily when his tired, overwhelmed twelve-month-old flails out and hits him on the nose? Or does he redouble his efforts to be soothing? These interactions have a life of their own, and go far beyond the initial contributions of nature and nurture.

At each stage of development (described later in this chapter), a child has different needs, and there are certain experiences that can promote mastery of that particular stage and certain experiences that may create hurdles. This means that *many opportunities* arise for parents to influence a child's personality favorably. And at each of these junctures, nature and nurture can discover a new partnership. For example, when a sensitive child is learning to use her imagination, even if we feel we weren't so perfect in comforting her when she woke us up at 2:00 A.M., 3:00 A.M., and 4:00 A.M. night after night (and who could remain soothing under those circumstances?) we get another opportunity to help her develop flexibility with her feelings. As this little girl learns to use her imagination, she begins to understand her own and other people's feelings and explore ways to feel more protected and secure. For example, her mother doll may comfort and empathize with a crying baby doll, in the same way that you comfort her in daily life. I discuss these approaches more in chapter 3; the main point here is that the complexity of a child's development gives us numerous *windows of opportunity*. Throughout this book, I will show how every challenge faced by your child provides a wonderful new opportunity to help him or her find new ways to cope, new skills, and a growing sense of humanity.

DIFFERENT WORLDS OF SENSATION

Let us briefly discuss how your child's biological endowment and the family and community environment interact.

First, let's look at a child's physical capacities.

To many parents it may seem obvious, particularly if their children have had very different physical makeups, that children differ in the way they respond to sound, touch, or sights. Yet, historically, it's been thought that most humans are similar in the way they respond through their senses to expected, basic experiences of life. In other words, we usually assume that a loud noise sounds loud and a soft noise sounds soft to almost everyone except those with a severe hearing loss. A light, feathery caress feels nice and tickly to most of us and is perceived as quite different from firm, deep pressure. Yet, as discussed earlier, both our own and other studies of infants and children reveal that sensory perceptions may vary.

Infants and young children express their differing physical makeup (whether from genes, prenatal experience, early life experiences, or other factors) in certain ways, especially the manner in which they react to different sensations, the way they interpret different sensations, and the way they plan and organize their motor behavior. We sometimes call these "constitutional and maturational patterns."

For some children, a light, feathery touch feels like someone rubbing sandpaper over sunburned skin. For others, it simply feels nice. For some children, a vacuum-cleaner noise is ordinary or perhaps exciting. For others, it seems like a volcano is erupting in the room. In fact, for each sense—touch, sound, sight, smell, taste, and reaction to one's own movements—children can be hyperreactive, or *overly sensitive*. Alternatively, for each sense, children can be hyporeactive, or *undersensitive*, meaning they require a lot of input before they are even aware of certain sights or sounds.

Such children may be relatively impervious to pain and keep running into people and things. They may also love to rough-and-tumble and wrestle in order to get more tactile sensations because they are so underreactive to ordinary touch. Parents notice this in the way that some children love to be tossed in the air—the higher the better—and other children are very cautious about their bodies in space.

Some researchers have suggested that certain children, such as those who are shy or inhibited, have a lower threshold to sensations in general. My colleagues and I have found, as part of our studies of children with regulatory challenges and problems, that children may be oversensitive in one sense (such as touch) and undersensitive in another sense (such as sound). Therefore, it does not appear that children necessarily have a general stimulus threshold for all sensations. Each sense, we believe, needs to be looked at individually. We have also found, as discussed earlier, that these sensitivities in themselves do not make a child shy or inhibited. Rather, it is the way in which the caregivers and other key individuals interact with the child that significantly influences the child's personality. In this model, there are many kinds of over- or undersensitivities, interacting with many different caregiver, family, and cultural patterns, making for a variety of personalities. We describe some of these variations in the following chapters.

Through each sense, children not only react to the world, they also *comprehend* their world. Different sounds come together into a pattern. We have noticed that some babies as young as four months can decode (or comprehend) complex rhythmic patterns, such as "bum bum BUM bum bum BUM BUM." Other babies look confused when presented with such a complex pattern and focus and attend only when presented with a far simpler rhythm, such as "BUM bum, BUM bum." Similarly, some children already follow two-step requests from their parents ("Please pick up your truck and put it by the toy box") by the age of two, while other children have a hard time comprehending even one simple request ("Please give me the apple").

Less obvious to many parents is that children comprehend

what they *see* very differently also. Some babies can easily take in and read the expressions on their mothers' faces. Other babies can barely figure out what the changing expressions of their mothers' mouths mean. Some toddlers can go into a new house and quickly figure out where all the rooms are and how to get back, while others get lost easily, cry, and need their mothers to come and get them.

Equally important is how a baby communicates *back* to caregivers and the world at large. To do this, infants use their motor systems to produce a variety of purposeful actions and behaviors. These include pointing, walking in a certain direction, and facial expressions to convey emotion and communicate intentions. More developed skills include piecing together a series of behaviors into complex communication, such as taking mother's hand, walking her to the fridge, banging on the door, and, when it is opened, pointing to the juice. Making sounds into words, and sequencing phrases and ideas require more advanced aspects of the nervous system.

As most parents already know, even children within the same family vary considerably in the types of skills I have just described. Some babies have an easy time getting their fingers into their mouths to soothe themselves, for example, while others keep touching noses or eyes in an effort to find the mouth and get that soothing experience. One toddler may cry helplessly, hoping his mother figures out that he is hungry, while another points to the fridge or even pulls her mother down to sit on the floor so that she can climb on her shoulders to get the food she wants! Some children effortlessly engage in complex socializing, which involves a series of subtle steps in certain sequences, while others have to think out each step consciously.

The way children organize their responses or actions with others can be summarized as involving a broad range of skills called "motor planning." This involves the child's ability to "sequence" movements and behavior into patterns. As the previous examples suggest, it has implications for almost every kind of communication a child might use and goes far beyond simply learning to tie shoes or copy shapes. Later in life, motor planning

involves many things we do on "automatic pilot," such as greetings, good-byes, or wriggling through a crowd at a cocktail party.
It may involve such complex social sequences as making friends,
cooperating with teachers, and dealing with many of the complexities of family life. This individual profile for reacting to, taking in, and giving out information is often an expression of the
child's physical makeup, which is in turn shaped by genetic, prenatal, perinatal, early experiential, and other factors.

Similarly, each family, caregiver, and community has a
unique communication profile. Some families and caregivers, as
I have noted, are high-energy but chaotic. Some communities
have this quality as well. Other caregivers and families have a
laid-back, passive, or even depressed quality. Some caregivers
and families read a baby's cues sensitively and respond supportively and empathetically. Others may misinterpret the baby's
signals and, for example, take a baby's playful reaching for a
nose as a sign of aggression. Or they may see a school-aged
child's healthy assertiveness as a rejection of the family. Such
misperceptions can then lead families and communities to behave in inappropriate ways that undermine, rather than support, a child's development. Some families tune into a child's
creativity and initiative. Others favor cooperation and conformity. Some enjoy a child's exuberance, some admire quiet concentration. Others are alarmed by too much emotional intensity.
Just as a child's unique traits can be profiled, so, too, caregivers
and families can come to know their own natural patterns.
Caregivers and families need to recognize that they, too, have
been influenced by their own earlier experiences and genetic
makeup. The more they can be aware of their own patterns, the
more they can use those natural abilities that support their
child's development and watch out for reactions that might undermine the child.

The child's traits and family patterns don't simply interact at
one time. Rather, nature and nurture come together continually
to help or hinder a child in mastering a number of developmental
tasks: to be calm and attentive; to be loving and intimate; to

be communicative, imaginative, and thoughtful. How does this occur?

STAGES OF DEVELOPMENT

Over the years, I have developed a kind of road map that lays out the core emotional milestones through which every child must pass on the way to healthy, mature personality development. This goes beyond simple and one-dimensional measures of development (such as behavior, physical development, or the way children think) and looks at the types of experiences that children need at each particular stage of their life in order to grow emotionally and intellectually.

Each stage builds on the previous one. At each stage, children learn basic abilities that carry them forward developmentally into the next stage. Their abilities to think, to reason, and to feel become more sophisticated as they pass these key emotional milestones. As we'll see in this book, once these milestones are achieved the experience stays with children for the rest of their lives. They are the foundation upon which children build a sense of themselves and their most important capacities. If for whatever reason that foundation is shaky—if these milestones are not reached—the effect can reverberate through a child's life and even into adulthood. I explore the problems that can develop in the sections that follow.

Security and the Ability to Look, Listen, and Be Calm

One of the first abilities that all babies need is to be calm and regulated. This makes it possible for a baby to be interested in and attentive to people, things, sights, sounds, smells, movements, and so on.

If, however, a baby is highly sensitive even to routine noises and to unexpected hugs and cuddles, he may get overwhelmed and be unable to interact quietly with his parents. A little girl may cry for hours and scream angrily whenever her parents try to play with her. Parents can help such highly sensitive children by showing them how to soothe themselves. These infants can learn to explore their world if parents are exceptionally gentle and empathetic, using gentle but firm pressure to calm them. Parents can protect their son or daughter from loud, motorized sounds and use gentle, high-pitched voices in their play. Through a series of small steps, avoiding intrusive gestures, they nurture confidence. They can lead a baby to take the initiative, simply by urging the baby to reach for a toy rather than handing it to him or her.

Relating: The Ability to Feel Close to Others
The inner security that makes it possible for a child to pay attention also gives the child the capacity to be warm, trusting, and intimate, both with adults and with peers. Normally, we see this ability reaching an early crescendo between four and six months. An infant studies his parents' faces, cooing and returning their smiles with a special glow of his own as they woo each other and learn about love together. We see it later in a seven-year-old, working independently at her desk, who greets her teacher with a grin and proudly shows off her work. We see it in a twelve-year-old who strolls over to a group of his friends at recess and begins to joke and talk with them, casually draping his arm around one friend's shoulders, playfully punching him in the ribs.

But children who are overloaded by other people's voices, who find others' touches frightening, or who have a hard time decoding what people are saying or communicating with their gestures or facial expressions may have special challenges in learning to enjoy relationships. For example, think of all the touching, vocalizing, gesturing, and subtle multiple-level communications that go on in a group of nine-year-olds during recess! It's not surprising that children whose senses provide them with uneven information find the challenges of complex relationships difficult.

Children who aren't able to relate to people in a warm, trusting manner—children who are aloof, withdrawn, suspicious, or who expect to be humiliated—can become isolated. They may decide that it's best to be a loner or to treat people as things, hurting others because they don't expect to get what they want. They may also decide that they can relate only in terms of their own thoughts or experiences. Distrustful of others, they effectively "march to their own drummer." While this kind of independence can be good in other circumstances, a child who is lost in his own sensations, feelings, and thoughts can become—to some degree or another—alienated from external reality and the world of logic and objectivity.

Children who can't get along well with other children or with adults, who can't negotiate one-on-one relationships or group relationships, have a fundamental challenge to meet before they can accomplish other developmental tasks. This is because in the early years of life not only intimacy and self-esteem but also most learning—insights, intuition, and principles—comes from what we learn from relationships. For example, "a lot" is, for a preschooler, a little more than he expected his mother to give him. The sense of quantity or time, as well as the meaning of words, are very much tied to the child's relationships and the emotions and experiences that are a part of them. All abstract, intellectual concepts that children will master at later ages are based on concepts they learn in their early relationships. If children haven't the fundamental ability to relate, much of their learning is in danger of being undermined and sabotaged.

Intentional Two-Way Communication

The next ability builds on the first two, and involves two stages. One has to do with learning to read body posture, facial expressions, and the like. The second stage involves understanding and communicating with nonverbal patterns.

From an early age, children learn to use and read signals that are expressed, not through words, but through behavior. This includes facial expressions, body language, and the like. Their ability to communicate unfolds in a sequence of stages, starting between about six months and eighteen months of age. At first, infants communicate only nonverbally, but they can carry on a rich dialogue with smiles, frowns, pointing fingers, squirming, wiggling, gurgling, and crying. By twelve to eighteen months, children are entering the second stage of nonverbal communication, in which they abstract patterns. They can take you and point to a favorite toy and gesture for you to get it for them—a pattern of communication with many parts. They can also figure out your patterns. For example, when daddy and mommy come home from work, an eighteen-month-old will know by their facial expressions or their posture whether they are going to get down on the floor and play or whether they are in a bad mood. Before infants can talk, they can communicate and understand most of life's basic emotional themes—approval, praise, love, danger, anger—through gestures, facial expression, body language. They can readily size up a new adult and respond to him or her either as someone who seems safe, secure, and approving or as someone who is dangerous, critical, or rejecting.

Later on, of course, words enhance this fundamental method of communication. Words, however, must build on this more basic sense of our own personhood and understanding of the world. In a sense, we learn about what we want and who we are even before words are available. Words provide us with a shorthand way of communicating our wishes and intentions as well as providing a vehicle for our future development. This ability, then, to size up situations quickly and intuitively without, or in spite of, words, obviously is a critical skill later in life.

Children who have difficulties understanding other people's facial expressions or rapid changes of vocal tone or the sequences of other people's behaviors, perhaps because they have difficulty recognizing patterns in what they hear or see, will have a difficult time making these quick and intuitive judgments. In fact, an element of what we commonly call intuition is, in reality, an early learned method of figuring out patterns or clues that we all more or less learn preverbally.

Children who can use and understand nonverbal communication comprehend the fundamentals of human interaction and communication much better than children who can't. They tend to be more cooperative and attentive in school. They are able to pick up on unspoken cues and figure out situations that might baffle other children. Boys and girls who have a hard time with nonverbal communication are likely to have a hard time in school and with friends. If a teacher warns his class in a serious but not angry tone of voice, "You kids had better shape up today because I'm in no mood to fool around," a child who isn't able to read and respond to nonverbal cues may hear those words as an aggressive challenge and start throwing erasers, duck under her desk, or in other ways behave inappropriately. Another child who is able to read these cues may think, "Oh, Mr. Gerber means business today. I'd better pay attention."

Emotional Ideas

Children next learn to form mental pictures or images—to form ideas about their wants, their needs, and their emotions. A child who says, "I want that pencil," instead of just grabbing it, is using ideas or symbols. We see this capacity when children say, "Give me that" or "I'm happy" or "I am sad." They begin to substitute a thought or idea ("I'm angry!") for an action (kicking or hitting). They not only experience the emotion, but they are also able to experience the *idea* of the emotion, which they can then put into words or into make-believe play. They are using an idea, expressed in words, to communicate something about what they want, what they feel, or what they are going to do. This ability opens a whole new world of opportunities and growth. Children can begin to exercise their minds, bodies, and emotions as one. In the school years, emotional ideas and symbols become the basis for understanding not only relationships and playground games but also the story the teacher is reading, principles in math, and the basic logic involved in arguing one's own point of view.

We can see evidence of children using emotional ideas in make-believe play; for instance, dolls may be hugging or fighting, or they may be explorers searching for a rocket ship. The ability to use fantasy and imagination underlies much of creative thought. When children are asked to make up a story or to figure out how another child might feel or to understand the meaning of a story, they are being asked to make certain creative leaps based on this ability to use their imagination.

But if a child has difficulty with motor planning—that is, putting his own actions into a sequence—even if he has the idea of putting a puppet on his hand and talking for it, for example, he may not be able to carry out the required actions. Instead of squawking in the "puppet's voice," the little boy may sit in frustration, unable to express his ideas in pretend play. Or the pretend play may occur in fragments because a little girl can't create long sequences of ideas. This ability, therefore, can remain undeveloped or it can even be lost before it gets organized. Alternatively, if a child is especially sensitive to visual images and to changes in voice tone, a make-believe drama with animal faces and strange voices may be frightening and overwhelming. Ideas, rather than being soothing, come to be scary. Such a child will be timid about entering into the wondrous world of fantasy and tapping into imagination that lead to higher-level thinking. Similarly, if a child has been overreactive to sensations for some time and is already quite frightened of new experiences, the capacity to create mental pictures may be fueled by scary, rather than adventurous, images. Daydreams of witches and nightmares of robbers and thieves may occupy such a youngster's mind, crowding out other ideas.

Many children (and adults) never fully master this stage of development. They equate feelings or thoughts with action: "If I think it, I will do it." In general, I've found, children who have problems controlling their aggression often have difficulty acknowledging feelings to themselves and then expressing the idea of those emotions through words. Instead, they plunge right into action, discharging their feelings through their motor system—hitting, biting, pushing. Children who can't identify their intentions and feelings and who have an action-only approach to life use aggression as a way to cope with all challenging situations. Sometimes children who are very rigid also have difficulty using emotional ideas. Rigid rules and patterns take the place of more flexible thinking about feelings.

Emotional Thinking

At the next stage, children go beyond labeling a feeling; they become able to think with these images. Between the ages of two and a half and three and a half, children take the emotional ideas that they have elevated from the level of behavior to the level of ideas and make connections between different categories of ideas and feelings: "I'm angry today because you didn't come and play with me," or "I feel happy because Mommy was nice." If you think about it, that is a rather sophisticated viewpoint—it means connecting an idea and a feeling across time and recognizing that one is causing the other. Again, we see this in make-believe play: children start to develop plots—one event leads to another. A child's soldiers will fight—not just randomly, but for a cause, because a princess was stolen by the bad soldiers and now the good soldiers are coming to save her.

At this stage, children also link all those ideas that pertain to "me" and all those ideas that pertain to "not me." In this way, they begin to make the distinction between fantasy—things that are inside "me"—and reality—things that are outside "me." They are also able to use this me/not me distinction to control their impulses and to concentrate and plan for the future. "If I do something bad to someone else, I may hurt the other person, and I may get punished." They begin to understand that the world works in this logical way; actions have consequences.

But consider a child who, because of difficulties with figuring out or processing the information he hears (that is, auditory processing difficulties) finds it much easier to live in his own private world. He plays out elaborate dramas, and his parents view him as enormously creative. But every time you ask him a difficult question about school, perhaps, or even try to find out why his Power Ranger wants to chase the bad guy, he ignores your questions and retreats further into his own fantasies. Without experience in two-way dialogues using ideas, he doesn't learn to create bridges between his own ideas and the ideas of others. Without linking his own ideas to an external idea, his ability to get feedback from outside reality is compromised, and his ability for emotional thinking becomes compromised. Because of this, as creative as he is, his ability to abstract and formulate higher-level logical categories of thought will also be compromised. It's often not well understood that higher-level thinking depends on experience with emotional interactions in which there is a great deal of give-and-take using ideas. This give-and-take using ideas provides emerging concepts with multiple experiential reference points. When an adult, for example, understands a concept like love, he understands it because he is abstracting the many different types of experiences—joy, devotion, empathy, excitement, and so forth—that make up something as complex as love.

Understanding the complexities of life, as well as something as basic as reading comprehension, is based on the capacity for emotional thinking. While no one would disagree that emotions are important for confidence and the capacity to love, the fact that emotions are critical to thinking has not been self-evident. Since the 1970s, as outlined originally in my 1979 book *Intelligence and Adaptation*, we have been exploring the connection between emotion and intellect. We have found that most experiences are double-coded. An infant or child experiences sights, sounds, touch, and the physical aspects of things and simultaneously registers an emotional reaction. These emotions organize the information and then are used in later thinking.

Thinking almost always has an emotional, generative aspect and a categorizing aspect. For example, when we asked children about "bosses," the highest quality response began with personal emotional responses: "I don't like it when they boss me when it's not needed" followed by an attempt to put these subjective emotional reactions into a larger frame of reference: "I guess sometimes bosses are necessary, sometimes not." Emotions seem to create the ideas which are then categorized. Emotional interaction using ideas is therefore an important contributor to creative and flexible thinking. Tendencies to use rote ways of teaching young children, especially those with processing problems, should be minimized and dynamic, interactive approaches increased.

The Age of Fantasy and Omnipotence

In the first stage of the grade-school years, which I have called "the world is my oyster," children develop their abilities to relate, communicate, imagine, and think. To children immersed in this stage, which tends to run from about four and a half to about seven years of age, all things are still possible. There is a sense of grandeur and magic. They have a curiosity about life, a bold expressiveness ("I am the best!"), and a deep sense of wonder about the world. In our culture, little boys may imagine themselves to be a Ninja Turtle, a Power Ranger, or Super Mario, while little girls may see themselves as Cinderella, Belle from *Beauty and the Beast*, or Barbie—or, of course, also as a Power Ranger or a Ninja Turtle.

As you probably know, this stage is commonly called the "Oedipal" stage: boys, it is suggested, have romantic fantasies about their mothers and girls about their fathers, and children develop strong rivalries toward the parent of the opposite sex that coexist with loving feelings. This phase ushers in a new type of relationship: the triangular relationship. Mother and father no longer easily substitute for each other, as they could when the child was younger, when the basic needs were security and trust.

Having three people in a system gives a child greater emotional flexibility. The child doesn't have to look at the relationship with each parent as an all-or-nothing situation. A triangle is an efficient system of emotional checks and balances, allowing children to work out complicated feelings without volatile outbursts. All sorts of rivalries and intrigues are played out.

At the same time, "the world is my oyster" years can be a time of great fearfulness. Children's sense of grandeur and rich fantasy life constitute a double-edged sword. They are easily frightened by their own power. They may fear witches under their bed, and ghosts and crooks who are going to come in and kidnap them. They want to hop into mommy and daddy's bed to be protected.

In a child who is oversensitive to sound or touch, the fearful side of life can overwhelm the power and feelings of omnipotence of these years. The expansive "I can do everything" may turn into "I'm scared of everything." In a child with visual-spatial processing difficulties, it may be harder to picture how a three-person system works because this requires holding in mind three different images all interacting. She may cling to one-on-one relationships, avoiding life's complexities but robbing herself of important coping strategies.

If all has gone well, children emerge from this stage with certain capacities: their grasp of reality begins to get firmer, though they still have an active fantasy life and a degree of grandiose omnipotence. They are able to grasp more complicated relationships and, in this way, become more emotionally stable. They begin to develop a capacity for more "adult" emotions, such as guilt or empathy (although empathy is easily lost when they are feeling jealous or competitive). And they can experience a wider range of emotions and emotional dramas—revolving around dependency, rivalry, anger, love, for example. All of these abilities equip children to move out from their families and into the wider world.

The Age of Peers and Politics

As children move through their seventh and eighth years, their horizons expand. Their world, as I have pointed out elsewhere, is other kids. They begin to move from the family-oriented stage of development out into the rough-and-tumble world of peer relationships. They move away from the intrigues of triangular relationships at home and enter the multifaceted world of their peers, into the politics of the playground.

Children now define themselves a little less in terms of the way their parents treat them and more by how they fit in with classmates. Their self-image begins to be defined by the group— by the pecking order that prevails on the playground—instead of being determined solely by their parents and immediate family. In everything from athletic ability to popularity, appearance, brains, and clothes, children rank themselves against others. They tend to be tied to the opinions of others in defining who they are.

Children get big benefits out of moving into the group and defining themselves as group members. For example, they gain an enormous ability for complex thinking. To negotiate the intricacies of multiple relationships within a group, they have to learn to reason on a very sophisticated level. They learn, "Nora might want to play with Emily, not because she hates me or because I'm a turkey, but because Emily is her best friend today, and I'm her second-best friend today, and Joey is her third-best friend. But that could change, especially if I invite Nora over to my house a few times and let her play with the new toys I got for my birthday."

This ability to diagnose group dynamics helps children to develop cognitive and social skills that will be very valuable in school—and beyond school into the real world, since much of the world they will eventually operate in will involve these dynamics. They learn that most of life operates in shades of gray, not in all-or-nothing extremes. Sizing up these subtle shades of gray requires understanding that feelings and relationships can exist in relative terms. A child begins to learn that "I can be a little mad one day, a lot mad the next day, and furious on still another day." Or "Tasha likes me better than Maria but not as much as Eva." Or, at an even more complex level, "Bethany, Joel, and I are on one team during recess, and Sally, Rajan, and I are on another team in math. But when both teams want me on their side during kickball in gym, the best move for me might be to raise my hand and ask to go to the bathroom!"

At this age, competition can be very intense. Games are taken very seriously ("You cheated, I know it!"). Children may be intolerant of anyone (other than themselves) changing the rules, and they may take a loss personally. At this stage of life, humiliation, loss of respect, and disapproval may be a child's worst fears. "No, I won't play with David," you may hear. "He wins all the time." or "Dad, it's no fair for you to win! You shouldn't play your hardest!" They haven't yet fully learned to experience loss and disappointment.

In order to carry out these complex social and cognitive operations, children must react rapidly to multiple sensations that come at the same time. They are also trying to comprehend what they see and hear and, as anyone who has been around youngsters knows, the subtle grin, the glance out of the corner of the eye, or the tinge of humor in a voice may be far more important than spoken words. Therefore, any of the challenges I have discussed (in a child's capacity to react to sensations or process what he or she sees and hears or in his or her ability to carry out different actions requiring complex motor-planning skills) will make mastering this stage even more challenging.

During these years, school-age children gradually learn about their position in the group and, to some extent, in the larger culture. Then, if all goes well, they rise above these exterior definitions and integrate them with their own developing internal values and ideas. A stronger sense of self, based on a combination of external reality and internal ideas, begins to emerge.

An Inner Sense of Self

After years of being dependent on what others think about them, children from about the ages of ten to twelve begin to develop a more consistent sense of who they are. They are gradually more able to develop an inner picture of themselves based on their emerging goals and values, and on who they feel they are as people, rather than on how other people treat them from day to day. As a result, they become a little less influenced by the issues of the moment, and begin to shape their world from inside themselves.

These years can also be a scary time, when children begin to contemplate moving even further away from their families. Rocked by strong feelings, they may feel caught between their childhood longings for closeness and dependency and their desire to grow up and be teenagers and young adults. They may vacillate between these two desires. Sometimes they are defiant— "Who needs you?" or "I know better than you!" At other times, they are fearful of their independence—"I don't want to go to school. I just want to stay home!" Only an emerging sense of themselves can help them resolve their ambivalence. Without it, they may slip back to depending even more on their parents or, conversely, they may try to deny their dependency by taking more risks or becoming even more rebellious.

During this phase, children begin to be able to hold in mind an emerging sense of their inner self at the same time that they are still buffeted by their relationships within their peer groups.

They begin to embrace their own beliefs and to develop their own set of internal values ("I want to be a good student" or "I shouldn't be mean"), and they begin to be able to think about the future ("I want to be a fireman" or "I want to be a teacher some-day"). They can now hold on to two realities at once: their peer group reality and their emerging inner reality of values and attitudes.

This ability to form two realities requires a good deal of intellectual and emotional competence, which builds on the abilities described earlier. For example, a boy who is extremely reactive to sensations and, therefore, who reacts strongly to a minor emotional challenge by a friend may become so glued to the emotions in his peer relationships that he can't nurture his potential for an independent inner self. Or a girl who is having a difficult time abstracting patterns from what she hears or sees may find it especially challenging to create larger categories of experience. She now needs to create one category of experience that deals with peer relations and another category that has to do with her own emerging inner beliefs. On the one hand, she has to keep these two patterns interrelated and, on the other hand, keep them somewhat independent from each other. "Yes, I know Bobby was mean to me, and I do feel bad because it seems like nobody likes me. But I'm still a pretty good kid. I was nice to my brother today and I'm doing OK in school and Bobby will probably get over it in a few days."

BUILDING ON STRENGTHS

As you can see, we now have a road map of the abilities that children need to master as they negotiate their preschool and grade-school years and the challenges they may encounter along the way. These stages are described in more detail in my books *First Feelings* and *Playground Politics*.

I have briefly described how certain challenges in a child's physical makeup, such as being overreactive to sight or sounds or having trouble comprehending verbal or visual images, can make negotiating this developmental road map far more difficult. In the remainder of this book, however, I will show how each of these seeming challenges can create *opportunities* for new and healthy growth and development. For each type of child, I will show how to build on the strengths that his or her personality offers. For example, parents and educators could provide certain types of experiences to help an overly frightened child or youngsters who seem stuck in defining themselves only through what others think.

Just as families have many different ways of helping children negotiate these emotional milestones, different cultures often have their own unique approaches to helping the younger generation form core capacities. We can observe many children and families around the world learning to relate to others, use their imaginations, think creatively, and communicate logically. The subtleties of peer relationships are negotiated by generation after generation, in different ways and perhaps with different values or rules.

In facing the challenges of raising a child, some families, and even some cultures, find solutions more effortlessly than others. For example, a family or culture with a long tradition of offering care to others may find a child who is irritable and overly reactive easier to help; they teach self-soothing and confidence with ease. Throughout this book, I will attempt to describe how families can build on their natural strengths and tailor their approaches to each child's unique set of characteristics and changing developmental needs. In this way, at each stage of your children's development you can assist them in becoming more emotionally healthy and also easier to live with.

3

THE HIGHLY SENSITIVE CHILD

A HIGHLY SENSITIVE CHILD IS OFTEN BRIGHT, ARTIC-ulate, creative, and insightful, easily able to tune into other people and their feelings. She may display a deep sense of empathy and compassion for other people. Perhaps she is a budding artist, a future novelist. And yet, she is also clingy and whiny, sometimes bossy and demanding. Sometimes she's all of these at the same time! She throws long tantrums over seemingly minor issues— shoes that feel "funny," familiar cereal that suddenly tastes "different." She shrieks furiously when you leave her with a babysitter, even one she knows well, grabbing desperately at your legs as you leave. Her teachers complain that she is "scattered" and seems to pay attention to too many things at once. It's no wonder that parents of such youngsters feel frustrated, helpless, angry— under the thumb of a mercurial, moody "prince" or "princess," as some describe their children to me.

To help you understand this child, let me walk you through how she may look and behave at different stages of development.

You may recognize many features of your child. Of course, every child is unique, and you may see only a few similarities. If you are feeling discouraged, rest assured that I will soon discuss ways to approach your child's challenges.

THE SENSITIVE BABY AND TODDLER

A sensitive infant is often colicky, finicky, irritable, demanding. She may cry almost constantly for the first year of her life (or so it may seem to an exhausted parent) and want to be held continually. The normal activities of infancy—sleeping, eating, diaper changing—can become early battlegrounds between parents and baby. One seven-month-old girl I saw screamed in fury if her mother put her down for the briefest instant. She fell asleep only when her mother or father rocked her for an hour or longer. Several times each night she woke up crying and needed to be rocked back to sleep. She hated having her clothes changed and would even squeal indignantly when her parents removed a dirty diaper. Breastfed, she furiously resisted taking a bottle, and she angrily pushed away spoonfuls of rice cereal and bananas when they were first offered. She cried when the vacuum cleaner made noise or if her older siblings were loud. When she learned to crawl, she simply used her newfound skill to scurry over to her mother and cling to her leg, rather than venturing out to explore the world. She fussed when her mother tried to interest her in toys and threw temper tantrums when her parents tried to put her in her playpen. "I feel like the prisoner of a tyrant in my own home," the baby's weary mother told me.

These sensitive infants find the emotional skills that we expect them to master in their first year more difficult to learn than do other babies. Ordinarily, babies begin learning to calm and regulate themselves in their first few months and, at the same time, remain interested and engaged in their environment. They also learn to relate to people in a warm, trusting manner—by gurgling and cooing as they study their parents' faces, for example. Especially gratifying to most babies is the ability to let their parents know what they want through vocalizations and gestures (reaching up to be picked up, pointing at a desired toy, and so on). But such goals can be elusive for a baby who is overly sensitive. New people, sights, sounds, smells, and the results of her own exploration and initiatives (touching daddy's rough beard, for example) easily overwhelm her and make her cry.

As a toddler, the very sensitive child often continues to be demanding and clingy. Once she has mastered a few words, she may resort to whining. "Mama, mama, mama," she may say over and over again as her exasperated mother tries to untangle her arms from around her legs so she can work. She throws monstrous tantrums if her parents try to leave her at daycare or with a babysitter. Now, her parents' sleep may be disrupted by her shrieks as she wakes up at night feeling scared. New situations upset her, and she may avoid playing with other children, shaking her head stubbornly and bursting into tears if a parent tries to lead her over to a group of other toddlers who are happily rolling toy trucks and banging toy drums. She may act aggressively, but more out of fear than defiance: she may bite or hit other children who come too close, for example, or pinch a child who tries to take away a toy. She may not like to be held or carried in a certain way.

Rather than become more assertive and organized as she grows, by taking her father's hand, for example, and leading him over to the cracker box, she may whine and passively expect daddy to guess what's on her mind and get it for her.

As she approaches the ages of two and three, when children ordinarily start to engage in lots of pretend play with each other and begin to expand relationships beyond their parents and siblings, the overly sensitive child may be cautious, fearful, and clingy. She may not be comfortable in expanding her fantasy life, even though a full fantasy life is very important at this stage of development. She may feel cautious about exploring certain themes in her pretend play, such as coping with aggression. Her dolls or action figures may always kiss and hug, but never fight or tussle with each other, for example. Or the dolls or action figures may fight, but then the story line may disappear: she may simply bang her dolls and toys together in what looks less like pretend play and more like a direct discharge of energy.

As she learns more words, she may start talking about her fears, telling you about the witches under her bed or the monsters in her closet. Fear and shyness inhibit her from making friends, and she is very frightened of children who are more assertive than she is. When parents leave for work or an evening out, she may shriek hysterically, "Mommy, no go!" or "Daddy, come back!" even though she is familiar with her daycare center and acquainted with her babysitter.

THE SENSITIVE PRESCHOOL CHILD

As she learns to string her emotional ideas together into emotional thinking, which we ordinarily begin to see at about the age of four or so, the highly sensitive preschooler may have elaborate explanations for some fearful or scary feelings.

"I know the robbers are going to come get me as soon as you put out the light, and I won't stay in my bed," she may argue. "Leaving the light on will only let the robbers see where I am!"

The sensitive child's fears appear to be growing because she is able to use logic to build bigger sand castles in the sky. With enhanced logic, she may seem even more tyrannical, insisting that she will be safe only if you do everything she wants.

As your sensitive preschooler begins to approach the school-age years and becomes even more articulate, her bossy, demanding behavior takes new forms (the sensitive child is, after all, usually very verbal). "You didn't buy the right cereal!" she may yell indignantly as she glares at her bowl of Cheerios from the newly opened box on the breakfast table.

"Honey, it's Cheerios, the same as always," the parent replies.

"But the box is a different color! And they taste different. I want the *old* Cheerios like you always get!"

And so it goes. "My new dress feels yucky!" she may say. Or, "These socks pinch my feet!" "This sandwich hurts my mouth!"

New experiences may cause her all kinds of concerns, and she may be quite articulate about her fears. "If I go to nursery school," your four-year-old may argue, "that boy Kim will hit me and he will take away my teddy bear until you come get me!" She may worry that "bad things" will happen to her parents and may threaten and whine if she is taken to a babysitter's house. "If you go to work and leave me at Mrs. Farwell's house, I will be sad forever!"

As you can see, infants, toddlers, and preschoolers each convey their sensitivities in their own special way. Seemingly in no time at all, the clinging, fussy baby turns into the passive, avoidant, fearful toddler who, as she acquires the "gift of gab," develops ideas, stories, and plots that elaborate this same sensitive core.

At this point, some readers are undoubtedly saying, "I've had enough. What can I do about it?" But let's continue our journey through the school years. It will give you a fuller picture of our sensitive child—a picture that will enable us to discuss strategies to help her overcome her special challenges.

THE SENSITIVE SCHOOL-AGE CHILD

At the ages of five and six, children ordinarily move through the "world is my oyster" phase, experiencing a sense of grandeur about themselves and a bold expressiveness. A highly sensitive child may immerse herself in the rich fantasy life of this phase, but then constantly scare herself. As a result, she can seem moody, self-centered, and demanding, throwing lots of tantrums. She may imagine herself as powerful as daddy, for example, but later convince herself that a thief is going to come into her room and hurt her. So she demands that you stay with her for the night. Or, after pretending to be Ariel saving the underwater world from the mean witch, she may refuse to go to bed, saying that she is scared of the dark. She may even begin to develop new fears, of escalators or high places, for example.

At this stage, a sensitive child may try to avoid fantasy and feelings of power altogether. She may be too fearful to elaborate or even create fantasies and be passive, scared, and shy. She may be obedient in many ways, clearing her dishes off the table and putting away her toys, but she may then put up a fuss at going to a new playground or making new friends.

In school, the sensitive child may be a quick and eager learner, absorbing with her keen attentiveness everything the teachers, say, do, or expect. Or, on the other hand, the sensitive child may be overloaded at school because of the number of people, the variety of sounds, and the complexity of beginning to learn so many new things.

As this child turns seven and eight, if she is secure enough to take her family for granted, she moves more fully into the rough-and-tumble world of peer relationships. But she may become overwhelmed by the complex "politics of the playground." Unable to negotiate these, she may feel defeated. "Katherine hates me! She won't pick me for the kickball team!" Or, "My teacher doesn't like me. I put my hand up and she looks at me funny and the answer goes right out of my head, and then she thinks I'm just a big dummy."

Some sensitive children may choose to avoid playground politics altogether. They may stay on the periphery, watching the recess-time basketball games and jump-rope competitions from the sidelines of the playground. Such a child doesn't participate in the jockeying for friends that other seven- and eight-year-olds engage in. She becomes very distressed when a child she particularly likes won't play with her or makes fun of her, and she sometimes feels so hurt that she decides it is better to be done with the whole thing. She may talk to her parents about her loneliness, or she may hold it in. For many parents, watching their child in such a situation can be very painful!

Sensitive children are unusually vulnerable to feelings of embarrassment and humiliation. They may feel very angry at people who make fun of them. Mild teasing that other children take more or less in stride ("Jeffrey wears goofy shoes!" or "Ashley's hair is funny") is intensely painful to some sensitive children. "No one likes me," one eight-year-old told me sadly. "Everyone hates me. I'm a bad person."

As they get closer to the age of ten, children become more able to balance the peer group pressures with an emerging sense of themselves. But the overly sensitive child may have had such a hard time negotiating the politics of the playground that she is still focused on her peer group, struggling with the hurts or embarrassments, or finding a better way to sit on the sidelines and not jump in.

In order to be able to develop her own internal values, a child needs first to master the issues of the peer group. As the child moves ahead intellectually, dealing with the more abstract issues of what she is like and what other people are like, we may see the struggles she is undergoing very vividly. The sensitive child may wrestle with a desire to be more independent and yet be so wrapped up in the day-to-day squabbles of the peer group that she has little opportunity to explore the world inside her.

One moment she may say, "I shouldn't care what someone thinks of me. I know I'm a good person—lots of people like me." And the next minute she is saying, "Mommy, will you talk to Vanessa's mother and make her play with me?" or "I know what I'll do. I'll ignore her and she'll have to come talk to me!"

Even when the sensitive child is making progress in negotiating the many stages of development, parents may find it especially baffling that their child varies so much in day-to-day mood and outlook. That is because sensitive children, like all challenging children, have a wider range of behavior than more easy-going children. One moment, they can appear mature, respectful, empathetic, compassionate. Then, later that day or the next day, they are crawling under tables, whining, clinging, throwing tantrums, and bossing everyone around. Parents often feel that they are on a roller coaster with their child in an unpredictable "ride" of shifting moods and behavior.

Parents might find some reassurance in the realization that while they can't predict how their child will act from one moment to the next, they *can* predict that there will be a large variation in the child's mood. They might remember the old story about the king who told his wise men that he would cut their heads off unless they found him something that would make him happy when he was sad and sad when he was happy. After struggling for months, their lives hanging in the balance, the wise men presented the king with a ring with a message. "This, too, will change," it said.

This insight will be reassuring when a sensitive child is in one of her more infantile moods, but not reassuring when she is being mature and helpful! But the awareness and expectation that her mature mood will also change can help parents avoid being too shocked or disappointed when, once again, they see that their child hasn't "gotten over it," or they realize they haven't mastered "the problem."

Over time, this range of behavior *can* gradually shift to higher and higher levels. Her "best" behavior, over time, can become better and her "worst" behavior can become not quite so difficult. But keep in mind that this is usually a slow and gradual change.

HOW IT FEELS TO BE A SENSITIVE CHILD

Think about all the ways that our senses can give us pleasure and open us up to the world. We are soothed by soft strokes on the cheek, cheered by a friendly arm around the shoulder, uplifted by the exhilarating sound of a marching band. We enjoy the clean scent of freshly washed clothes, smile at the bright face of a clown.

These sensations, however, are entirely different for the highly sensitive child. A friendly touch might feel harsh to her. Certain sounds may seem to come out of a bullhorn. Certain smells seem oppressive. Even bright colors can overwhelm.

Imagine how you would feel if, for example, you attended a rock concert after staying up the previous night consuming cup after cup of strong coffee. The sound would probably grind right through you, while the flashing lights and crowded bodies would be bewildering, overwhelming. Many overly sensitive children feel this way every day, as if they have little barrier between themselves and the rest of the world. They feel as if things are happening *to* them, rather than feeling that they have much control over their life.

These physical sensitivities take many forms. The sensitive

child may dislike being tickled or cuddled. Walking through a crowded school hallway or playground is daunting because it means brushing up against so many bodies. Deep voices or loud machines can set a sensitive child's teeth on edge. Even a mother's voice can be irritating.

Some children are sensitive to movement in space. They may dislike sensations that children ordinarily love—the fast rush down a slide, pumping higher and higher on a swing, whirling around a merry-go-round.

Some children are oversensitive to certain sights, although this particular sensitivity isn't as common as sensitivity to touch or sound. These children almost see too much: they are so aware of what they see that they become frightened or overwhelmed. They sometimes react to just part of a visual image, rather than the entire image. For example, they may be frightened by a clown's face or a cartoon figure because they focus on just part of it—the big red lips or nose, for example, or the bright orange hair. They are unable to view those features as part of something that others see as comforting and funny.

Because sensitive children are so tuned into sensations, they tend to experience the world in little pieces. They see the details but miss the big picture. Such a child may, for example, look at a picture and describe the details first. "I see a tree with pink flowers, and another tree that doesn't have any flowers," she may say, "and a red-and-white tablecloth on the ground. And four people are sitting around the tablecloth." In such a manner, the child pieces together what the picture is about—four people having a picnic in the woods.

In school, these children may do well in subjects that involve grasping details, such as vocabulary, spelling, and language skills. But subjects that are more abstract, such as scientific concepts or math, may cause them difficulties. Sometimes they may feel so confused and overwhelmed in class that they appear to be learning disabled, although they may be quite capable of grasping the material.

The highly sensitive child tends to be very perceptive, sensing every nuance and subtlety of her world. "Molly looked at me funny today," eight-year-old Fanny may inform her parent about a friend who threw her a quick glance during social studies. This child is also very sensitive to the feelings of others; she can "read" other people through their expressions, their body language, the voice tone. However, because she is so perceptive, she can sometimes be too affected by the moods and feelings of others. Adults who have such traits often say they wish they had "thicker skin."

A tendency to get lost in the details further intensified by a challenge they have in dealing with spatial concepts may mean that certain children get lost easily. Not being able to figure out distances easily, they feel less secure than other children and panic easily when their parents leave them. An ability to picture spatial concepts is also an important component of any "big picture" thinking—seeing how the pieces fit together in a particular situation (or life in general).

In addition to spatial difficulties, the overly sensitive child can also experience motor-planning challenges—that is, the skills that are required to carry out a series of action sequences, such as putting on socks or remembering a nighttime routine of brushing teeth, putting on pajamas, and kissing mom and dad goodnight. This challenge can be very perplexing to parents because their son or daughter otherwise seems so bright. The problem may be so severe that a teacher may raise questions about attention problems or even the possibility of medication.

So if your child has a "gift of gab" and can stay on the subject while talking but gets lost when she has to do anything that involves a sequence of movements, the difficulty may be a very circumscribed part of a motor-planning problem. Your child is well organized when operating in an area of strength but may appear disorganized when dealing with an area of vulnerability.

Some sensitive children are overstimulated not only by outside sensations, but also by internal forces as well, that is, their own emotions. They experience their feelings very intensely. Such a child may throw herself on the floor sobbing when she is sad, jump up and down and scream when she is happy, and shriek and pound the walls when she is angry. Never is there a middle ground: no pleasure is merely mild, no irritation is slight, and sadness is felt as despair. She may also complain of sore muscles, stomach aches, and other pains. Because of her sensitivity to internal experiences, puberty may be especially troubling because of all the new sensations and stirrings of her body.

The foregoing profile is a broad cluster of ways that sensitivity commonly manifests itself in a child. Not every boy or girl who appears cautious and fearful has these sensitivities. And not every child with these physical sensitivities comes across as cautious and fearful.

PARENTING PATTERNS TO AVOID WITH SENSITIVE CHILDREN

A very sensitive child is not an easy child to raise. Fortunately, certain parenting patterns can help this child mature into a creative, insightful person; and parenting patterns that intensify this child's challenges can be avoided. With especially supportive parenting, highly tuned "antennae" on the world could become a valuable tool. A sensitive child can easily become the kind of person who can tune into other people and their feelings, and she may develop a deep sense of empathy and compassion for other people.

It is all too easy to get drawn into reacting in certain ways that, unfortunately, only dig the hole deeper for you and your child. It's very easy for parents of sensitive children to swing from one extreme to the other. They may be quite empathetic, but not very disciplined about setting limits or giving their children structure. When this fails, they become rigid and strict, but not very empathetic. This pattern is understandable, of course. A parent may assume that if he or she were a "better" parent—more nurturing, more understanding, more patient, more responsive— then the child would be easier to live with. And so, the parent begins to indulge and overprotect the child. A mother may try desperately to calm her angry, crying seven-month-old with hugs and offers of juice and toys. Parents may carry her around constantly, afraid to put her down for fear she will burst into tears again. They play with her continually and won't leave her with a babysitter for fear she will get upset. The parents of a sensitive three-year-old may find themselves spending hours trying to get her to go to bed—reading to her, playing with her, singing to her, rubbing her back. The parents of an eight-year-old who is upset at being rejected by a friend may respond by arranging play dates with other children, and offering a constant stream of unsought-after advice. When an eleven-year-old complains over the amount of homework he has, his parents may step in and do part of the homework and then call the teacher up to complain about the volume of schoolwork.

Unfortunately, such actions may only teach a child to be more helpless and dependent. As a result, he or she may respond with even more whiny, demanding behavior. When that occurs, after the poor parents have exhausted themselves with trying to "fix" things for their child, the parents' indulgent, protective attitude begins to fade, to be replaced with anger and impatience. After all, they had assumed that indulging their child would make their child "better." But, after all their work and worry, she isn't better! They may begin to yell at the child constantly and per-haps even spank her, and react with irritation to anything she says and does for a time. Some parents withdraw instead of get-ting angry. They relate less to their child, play less with her, in an attempt to stay emotionally distant from her. But the effect is the same. Then the cycle begins all over again. The parents revert to trying to protect and indulge the child before their anger kicks back in again. Depending on the parents and the family, these moods can occur over a few minutes, a few hours, a few days, or a few weeks.

Sometimes parents unknowingly split up the roles. One par-ent, often the mother, will be indulgent, while the father is angry and overbearing, thinking he can shout his troublesome child into submission. While the father yells, the mother may feel sorry for what now seems like her vulnerable little baby. Sometimes the mother is the one who gets angry and frustrated, while the father is the protective one. While each parent's approach may be con-sistent, the child is aware of the vacillation between the parents' approaches. When parents are divorced or separated, the vacillation may be even more intense. One parent may feel guilty about the divorce and become even more indulgent, while the other parent responds to the "spoiling" with anger at the child. Sometimes parents in this frame of mind will behave in a punitive manner; for example, in addition to yelling at the child, they may handle the child in a physically intrusive way. They may grab her, restrain her more firmly than needed, or order the child around ("You come here right now, or else!"). A thicker-skinned child would be affected by such behavior but be able to minimize the effects. But to the sensitive child, a loud voice, a rough grab, may feel like a major calamity.

Vacillations between anger and overprotectiveness only worsen the situation. The child feels anxious and unsafe as she tries to cope with her parents' unpredictability. It's yet another way she gets confused by her world. At one moment, she is being fussed over and treated with kid gloves and the next minute she is being harshly scolded or ignored. She may withdraw or rebel further.

Parents, for their part, feel responsible for their child's behavior, and therefore incompetent and inadequate when they can't "fix" their child. Because they can't stand hearing that constant inner voice telling them they are incompetent, and the guilt it invokes, they may respond with anger or by withdrawing from the child. Some parents may also feel disappointed and sad that the child isn't the easy-going sweetheart they had expected. Rather than acknowledging the disappointment to themselves, they may cover it up by blaming the child. They begin to see the child's behavior as one big manipulation. "She's just trying to get attention" is a comment I hear frequently from parents of overly sensitive children.

Parents may respond to these inner feelings by getting very rigid. "That's the only cereal you're going to get," an exasperated mother may snap at the child complaining about the Cheerios. "So eat them. You don't get anything else until lunch!"

Or they may attribute malevolent intentions to their child. "My child wants to break up our marriage," I have heard parents say. Or "He's just doing that to make me feel bad." Or "I think my child is evil. He's out to get me!" In the extreme, parents can even become physically abusive.

Some parents fall into what I call an "escape pattern" with a child who clings constantly. The child stays wrapped around the parent so much that the parent feels suffocated and perhaps even angry by her presence. "I can't get a moment to myself," a mother or father says in despair. So the parents "escape" every chance they get: they talk on the phone, read a magazine, busy themselves with chores—anything to give themselves a moment's peace. But this "escape pattern" only confirms the child's worst fears—that the parent is trying to run away from her. So she may get even more vigilant, hanging on even more, causing her parents to feel even more suffocated and angry and increasing their desire to want to run away even more. And so the cycle continues.

HOW PARENTS CAN HELP THE SENSITIVE CHILD

The goal for the parent of a sensitive child is to work around the child's sensitivities in order to provide the basic psychological experiences that she needs for emotional development. But it takes a special kind of parenting to cope successfully with a child who is drowning in a sea of sensations. Even though she may be a gifted, brilliant child, her sensory system isn't quite under her control.

Parents of such a child need to work together as a team. They need to create a parenting atmosphere that has four basic elements: (1) empathy, (2) structure and limits, (3) encouragement of initiative, and (4) self-observation.

Empathy

An extra-sensitive child needs more empathy, compassion, and flexibility than most kids. At the same time, she requires more firmness and structure than many other children. In other words, I am suggesting here that you use *more* of both the carrot *and* the stick.

"Why do I need to be more empathetic and compassionate

with a child who is already so whiny and demanding?" parents often ask me. That is because such a child is feeling overloaded, ruled by the sensations constantly assaulting her. She feels her emotions more intensely than other children and is more disturbed by them. She needs parents who can react compassionately to her plight—just as they would to an adult friend who was having a difficult time.

That compassion takes different forms, depending on the age of the child. For example, let's look at an eight-month-old who has been crying for hours, unable to fall asleep because she is so overstimulated. Her parents have rocked her, walked her, fed her. They know she's tired, but she's unable to cuddle down and drift off to sleep. How do you empathize with the baby? Of course, she can't understand your words. But you can tell her how you feel by the way you talk to her, look at her, and hold her. "I know it's hard to fall asleep, sweetheart," you could say in a warm, soothing voice. "You want to fall asleep, but you just can't." Resonate with your child's feelings. Hold her firmly but carefully. Let her feel your warmth and understanding. Use her sensitivity to touch and emotions: she will pick up on your soothing demeanor. Remember that her behavior is rooted in her physical condition: she isn't doing this deliberately or maliciously. You may also want to experiment with different rhythms of rocking as well as firm pressure on her back as a way of calming her.

Of course, maintaining a warm emotional tone when you're exhausted isn't easy! But keep in mind that reacting with anger ("You better stop that right now!") is simply going to prolong her crying by overloading her even more.

An eighteen-month-old who is overexcited by noise and touch may fly into long tantrums whenever she doesn't get her way. Let's assume she is being greedy with her three new toys, and she won't let her older brother play with any of them. She has thrown herself on the floor and is rolling back and forth, screaming furiously. Here, you need to walk a fine line between dealing with her extra need for comfort and security and helping her learn to cope with her greed. You can be empathetic, but with a firmer tone. "I know you're mad," you might say. "And I know you want to keep all the toys. But your brother just wants to play with one of them," and you point to her brother. Then, in a firm, but supportive tone of voice, you can try to negotiate some trades. Maybe big brother will let little sister play with one of his toys in exchange for being able to play with one of the new toys. Again, you are empathetic, recognizing your child's anger. But you aren't rushing in with an overdose of hyped-up sympathy ("Oh, my poor little baby!") and you don't rush in with a punitive "police approach" either—grabbing one of the toys and saying angrily, "You can't be so greedy!" In negotiating the trade, you are respecting her special needs, and at the same time you are teaching her to cope with selfishness. Again, your child may not understand all your words. But she can hear both the empathy and the resolve in your voice and read it in your face and posture.

To some parents, this attitude comes naturally. But, many of us have to work consciously at adopting it, especially when the child's extra neediness, on the one hand, and greediness on the other hand pull us in the direction of either overprotectiveness or being too punitive.

What about a four-year-old who wants all the treats on the dessert table at the party, but has been told she can have only one? "I don't want just one!" she begins to wail. "I want more!"

"Oh, I bet you could eat all the cake and candy on the table," you might say. "I bet your eyes are telling you that your stomach is big enough to have every single thing at the table." As the child gets angrier, your tone continues to be empathetic but gets firmer. The key is to empathize with a child's feeling even if it is a feeling you don't like. Often parents think that if they empathize with a child's feeling, they will somehow encourage that feeling in the child's mind or intensify it. But recognizing what a child is feeling will help *her* recognize and label that feeling rather than experience it as a vague sensation. Keep in mind that empathy creates closeness between you and your child. That is the important part. You don't have to guess accurately each time which particular emotion to empathize with. The goal is compassion for how she experiences things—to create that atmosphere of closeness between the two of you.

When that four-year-old grabs for an extra piece of cake, father has to intercede, blocking her rapidly advancing hand with a firm tone of voice and stern look as she begins to fly into a tantrum. Father quickly says, "I know it's hard with so many good things at the table." And he puts his hand on her back and rubs it a bit as she whimpers. What father *didn't* do was to yell and overwhelm his daughter. Nor did he patronize or overindulge her by giving her three extra pieces of cake. Father was firm, yet warm and compassionate. Easy to say, but hard to do!

As the sensitive child enters the school-aged years, her sensitivity may express itself in clinging and terror at leaving your side. You may want to empathize specifically with her uncertainty about where you are going to be while she is in school.

"I know you don't want me to walk out that door," you could say gently, "because you don't know just where I will be." You can then help her picture where you will be. One strategy would be to use pretend play to help you in this. You could re-create her school with blocks, for example. Using toy cars and buses, you could act out how mommy and daddy travel to and from work, home, and school. You could also take her to your work and then to school so she can begin to grasp just how far away you are. This will help your child picture her parents when they are separated from her.

Sometimes you may feel like escaping from your clinging child. However, your child will sense this urge in you, and she'll only watch you more vigilantly, holding onto you with a tighter grip and watching you with an eagle eye. Compensate for your wish to escape by providing your child the security she desperately needs. Spend *extra* time with her to reassure her that you are willing to be with her. A very useful way to spend extra time is in what I will describe later as "floor time." Sympathize with her need to be close. After that, having relaxed and compensated for your own desire to escape, you have essentially "earned" the right to set limits, teaching your child that sometimes mommy and daddy need time for themselves.

Empathy can be especially hard with a child who has an angry clinginess ("Don't you dare leave me!"). Some children, for example, are quite willing to be separated from their mother or father if they themselves are going off with a friend and her parents for ice cream or a visit to the park. However, they become enraged if the parents dare to go out for fun and leave them with the boring babysitter. But parents can still empathize. In their words and emotional tone, they need to direct their empathy at the child's predominant feeling. When this is outrage rather than fear, it's helpful to try to empathize with that rage. "I know you *hate* it when we go off to have some fun," you could say. "But, you know, mommy and daddy need to go out sometimes also."

As your sensitive child advances in the school years, the politics of the playground—that is, peer relations—will be a challenge to her many sensitivities. A nine-year-old who, in growing up, had been sensitive to touch and easily overwhelmed by her feelings, may now feel exceedingly disappointed because she has just learned that she is only the number two best friend of someone she considers her number one best friend. Many parents have an especially hard time when their children are feeling sad and disappointed. Since these feelings are some of the hardest human feelings to cope with, parents hate to see their children suffer through them. It's an especially hard situation for parents of sensitive children and the children themselves because these children feel emotions so strongly. But parents can help their children come to grips with these difficult feelings, learn to tolerate a sense of loss and disappointment, and move on.

No matter how extreme or unrealistic your child's feelings may seem to you, try to empathize with them.

"I feel empty—like no one will ever like me again," she may sob.

As you see your child going from a feeling of emptiness to overgeneralizing with "No one will ever like me," try to help her examine the emotion for a moment. You might, for example, comment that you've had times when you've felt "empty" inside, too, and you know that feeling seems like it will never go away. This may help your child go on and describe related feelings, such as "I just can't stand it. I feel so lonely. I feel embarrassed, too, when everyone else is with their friends and I'm all by myself."

As you help your child express her plight, you may see her go back and forth between feelings of being "ugly," embarrassed, enraged, and empty. Don't try to analyze the feelings, instead, just help her become a "poet" of her feelings, particularly ones that to you seem associated with loss, such as "emptiness."

A child may not be able to reveal much of her feelings the first time. The next day, perhaps, a little more may emerge. The key is to help your child experience your warmth and acceptance alongside her own painful feelings of emptiness, humiliation, and rage. Just hang in there. Don't try to say too much. Just maintain a soothing, comfortable presence. This lets your child know that feelings of loss and emptiness are part of the human drama. Eventually, as your child begins to talk about new friends or different groups that she is beginning to get to know, you will be in a position to support her and the beginnings of more positive feelings.

Some emotions are painful, there's no doubt about that. But if those feelings are experienced as part of a *relationship*, then the child no longer feels alone in trying to cope with them. She learns to tolerate the feelings and not be devastated by them.

If your child were to tell you "No one will ever like me," and you were to change the subject too quickly, or give your child a pep talk too soon, flooding her with practical suggestions ("That's too bad about Alicia. But you have lots of other friends. There's Beth and Stacy and Leah. I'll call them up and invite them over!"), you could deprive her of a valuable opportunity. The message becomes "I don't want to hear those sad, lonely feelings." The emotion then gets pushed down and becomes more a private feeling, to be endured alone.

Structure and Limits

While sensitive children need a strong dose of empathy, as we have seen, their whiny, clinging, demanding, sometimes aggressive behavior also needs to be dealt with in a firm, loving manner. You need to couple warmth and compassion with a big helping of structure and limits. Remember, these are children whose bodies feel out of control at times. They especially need a sense of limits and structure in order to feel more in control of their lives. Giving structure in a calm way is not easy. Some parents tend to fall apart themselves when their children lose it. They scream, yell, and cry, which simply adds fuel to their child's raging fire. Other parents are intrusive—blowing up at their child and threatening him ("You better cut that out or else!"). Sometimes they threaten rejection or abandonment (I overheard a mother say, "If you don't shape up, I'm going to lock you in the car!"). Other parents shut down emotionally, ignoring the child or becoming aloof and distant. Some people hit their children.

While all of us who are parents have felt out of control ourselves and, because we're human we can all get overloaded, we need to keep reminding ourselves that two frantic people can only make the situation worse for each other. As adults, we may be in a better position to observe ourselves, calm ourselves down, and begin the soothing process.

When parents want to know how best to set limits with a sensitive child, I tell them to think of Smokey the Bear—the big, gentle bear with his firm message of individual responsibility ("Only you can prevent forest fires."). The idea is to be like a teddy bear—firm, but always warm and gentle. Your overall message to the child is "I'm on your side." It's not "I'm only doing this because I love you." You convey love with firm, teddy bear–like limit setting.

For example, your eight-month-old is sitting in the middle of the living room floor wailing uncontrollably. You have some chores, but she expects you to entertain her nonstop. She won't pick up a toy. She wants you to put it in her hand. She won't crawl over to you, but expects you to pick her up. Think of that big bear. You put an attractive toy two inches in front of her hand and say, "I know you can get it. I know you can get it" in a firm but loving voice. You convey resolve through your voice tone and facial expression. Of course, she won't understand your words. But she can interpret your loving, but firm, tone of voice.

With an eighteen-month-old in a tantrum who is trying to hit and bite you and her older sister, you need to be even firmer.

Again, she won't understand your words so much as she will comprehend your tone, posture, gestures, and facial expressions.

"No," you could say firmly, shaking your head, positioning yourself in front of her. "No hitting."

If (or when!) that doesn't work, raise your voice slightly and use a little more emphasis. "No! No hitting!"

And if she still hasn't responded, use more emphasis. "NO! No hitting. Now, I mean business!" Your voice is getting tougher and deeper. Your facial expression is getting more serious, and your hand is reaching to stop her blows.

The goal is to go "up the scale" of emphasis, getting more forceful as you go and showing through your body and your voice that you are determined to get her to understand that she cannot bite or hit. Imagine this on a scale of one to ten, where you start off at a one or two and gradually work up to an eight (similar to a sergeant with his undisciplined recruits). If necessary, restrain her physically. But remember that teddy bear stance: hold her firmly only to contain her, without inflicting pain or punishment. And while holding her, you are also talking in a firm, but soothing tone of voice, about calming down. With an older child, if she crosses a certain line that you have already discussed with her, such as hurting a sibling or destroying something precious, you will also want to further stress the importance of limits with some sanctions that you have already discussed with your child. That way, she won't be shocked that they are being implemented now, and she will have a reason to consider her actions. These sanctions should be strong enough to get your child's attention and get her to ponder her behavior and change her ways. But they should not involve practices that would undermine her development. For example, just as you wouldn't keep your child home from school as a punishment, you don't want to take away opportunities to play with peers, which is a developmentally necessary experience. Losing television or access to a special toy or an activity or having to do extra chores around the house will not deprive your child of developmentally needed opportunities.

Such sanctions are likely to make the child angry. Yet you want to maintain a positive, soothing relationship despite her anger at you for punishing her. This doesn't mean you give her a big hug right after you punish her, because that will feel contrived. But as she is pouting and refusing to look at you, you might make a few comments about knowing that she's mad at you. You can say that she also has to realize that she must work with you to control or limit some of her behavior. You could tell her that you want to help her become better at setting limits so she won't get into all this trouble. With the sensitive child, you convey this with an extremely soothing yet realistic tone of voice that recognizes her anger at you and the seriousness of the situation. But you continue to convey the message that her behavior and her anger at you won't undermine the fundamentally supportive and reassuring nature of your relationship.

Keep in mind that rapport and limit setting go hand in hand. As you increase the limit setting, you need to increase your empathy. Let's look at a five-year-old girl who is angry because a friend wants to share her toys. You have pointed out that it's polite to share toys with visiting friends. "But she's gonna break all of them into little pieces!" she wails. This is a little girl who is extremely sensitive to touch; she feels fragile, thin-skinned, easily breakable herself. So it's understandable that she would worry that her toys will break easily, too. Of course, knowing this doesn't mean you have to tolerate a temper tantrum. You can use the same steps as you did with the eighteen-month-old, going "up the scale" of emphasis, but this time explaining your position as well—"You need to share."

But you can also empathize with her fears. "It's hard to share toys if you think they're going to get broken." (You can also put away, with her help, anything especially fragile.)

As soon as possible, a child should be involved in setting limits. This is especially important for sensitive children, since they already feel out of control at times. An eight-year-old, for example, can collaborate with you in choosing sanctions. For example, your child won't do her homework. "The teacher hates me and he's only going to give me a bad grade anyway," she says grumpily. "So what's the use of doing my stupid homework?" You and she can discuss some automatic punishments (such as losing TV time or doing more household chores) when she doesn't complete her nightly assignments. At the same time, you can empathize with her feeling that the teacher dislikes her and how bad she must feel when she has these feelings.

Encouraging Initiative

Passive, helpless feelings are uncomfortable for a child (or for anyone, for that matter). When they continue, a child can end up feeling angry at herself and despairing for not being more assertive. In some children, I see adultlike depression or even suicidal-type thoughts (wishing they weren't alive).

One of the antidotes to this attitude is to help the child find ways to feel more secure, lovable, self-sufficient, and independent. With a child like the eight-year-old just described, if you listen and empathize with her feelings, even the negative ones, and help her figure out ways to be more assertive in class and master the work, over the long haul, this will lead to positive feelings. You can even help her figure out ways to handle the teacher when he is being controlling, or less than understanding. For example, help your child see that the teacher's disgusted looks happen when she tunes out and stops listening. Since that annoys the teacher, it can lead to a cycle where the child and the teacher are upsetting each other. Helping your child to ask the teacher, perhaps, to slow down and go over things carefully may create a more positive atmosphere. You could give the teacher the same message during private conversations.

There are no magic cures. Quick reassurances, such as "Oh, the teacher really likes you because you're such a nice girl," won't change the child's picture of herself, because her self-concept has formed gradually from experiences with her teacher and an attitude that was already forming inside of her.

Encouraging initiative can begin early. With an eight-month-old who wants you to hand her toys instead of picking them up for herself, you could put the toy a few inches from her hand and gently encourage her to reach for it. Cheer her on from the sidelines. "You can do it!" you tell her as she stormily asserts with a few tears and shrieks that it's too hard.

With a two-year-old who clings constantly to your leg and expects you to wait on her with toys, food, and attention, you could expand her assertive side through pretend play. For example, you and she are playing tea party with her dolls and you notice that two of her dolls begin to squabble with each other but then kiss and make up quickly. You could ask what they did about their mad feelings. Or you could start talking for one of the dolls. "I'm not ready to make up," one doll could squeal.

In essence, you are trying to help the child elaborate her angry or confrontational feelings more fully. If the child keeps running away from conflict into the kiss-and-make-up stage too quickly, you can guess that perhaps anger is scary for the child. By helping the child stay a little longer (even if it's only a minute or two) with her angry side may, over time, begin to let her know that angry feelings aren't so scary. The security of your presence will help this process. The child can start to learn that, just as love is a part of life, so, too, are anger and conflict. Knowing that anger and love can go on together will help her solve her problems as she gets older rather than run away from them.

Parents' attitude plays a large role in encouraging initiative. Are you inadvertently overprotecting your child? The parents who take over encourage their child to become even more passive. That is an easy trap for many of us to fall into. We think we are helping our children by protecting them from conflict or stepping into their squabbles. But our actions only aggravate their passivity and feelings of helplessness. Avoid taking complete charge, or telling your child how to feel. Your goal is to help your child learn to take charge herself. This will be a gradual process.

Be willing to tolerate some challenges from your child. A sign of true assertiveness is when a child is willing to take on his or her parents. So if your child wants to argue with you about bedtime ("C'mon, Dad! It's only nine o'clock!"), let her try to persuade you to stay up later. She may say, "I don't have school tomorrow and I want to watch the rest of . . ." Sometimes, if her argument seems good enough, let her persuade you.

When you are flexible, you are teaching your child flexibility. Being flexible about an extra half-hour of TV on a nonschool night doesn't mean you are going to let your child do something dangerous or skip her homework or hurt another child. Flexibility in the parent tends to lead to flexibility in the child. Rigidity in the parent tends to lead to rigidity in the child—either a rebellious and negative type of rigidity or a passive and cautious type of rigidity. Maintaining a flexible attitude with your child can go a long way toward helping her become more assertive and independent.

Encouraging Self-Observation

Helping sensitive children become aware of their feelings and sensitivities fosters their coping capacity. Since extra-sensitive children are often overwhelmed by their feelings, and may experience emotions more intensely than other children, they need help in differentiating and labeling emotions. The sensitive child needs to become a "poet" of her feelings—able to give them symbolic form so she doesn't feel as if she were drowning in a sea of sensations. (We often see adults who haven't moved past this stage. They complain of being "overwhelmed" by their feelings, but they can't be more specific about what they feel—happy, frustrated, angry, or disappointed.)

Start by helping your child elaborate on her feelings. A child who is more sensitive needs to be better than other children at labeling her feelings. Take a child who comes home from school clearly upset. When her mother asks her what happened, all she can say is "I feel bad. I feel awful."

With a little encouragement from her mother, the child may reveal that a group of children wouldn't play with her. "I was all alone at recess—all by myself." But she may be unable to articulate feelings of being lonely or sad or furious that the kids were mean to her. Her mother could continue to empathize with how hard it is when other kids aren't nice and also keep the conversation going by talking about similar experiences when she was a child.

"Sometimes I would feel really lonely and lost, and sometimes I would get so mad I would want to just scream and scream at those mean kids!" With that kind of empathy and encouragement from a parent, a child may feel able to describe her own feelings in more detail.

Parents may wonder why it's helpful to encourage their child to go from more defuse feelings to more specific feelings, such as sadness, loneliness, or anger. After all, you may think, that didn't solve the school problem! The child may still be excluded at the playground. I have found, however, that children, as well as adults, who are aware of their feelings *in very specific ways* and can express them to someone they trust are generally able to develop better coping strategies and better solutions. Being aware of specific emotions gives you valuable information about yourself and how to proceed in particular situations.

A child who experiences loneliness, sadness, or anger only as "awful" and "bad" feelings may be more likely to blame herself for her plight and get stuck in a pattern of self-defeating behavior. If, on the other hand, the child is more aware of her sad, lonely, or angry feelings, she is more likely to, in some circumstances, let go of a relationship, or relationships, that aren't working and look for other relationships. She could, for example, find another group of girls to hang out with. In addition, a child who is aware of her anger is more likely to take assertive action to change her situation.

As parents, you can also help your child develop a "reflective" attitude toward herself and her tendencies. If she refuses to eat certain foods, you could start by observing, "Gee, it's hard for you to eat those things, isn't it? Maybe they don't feel good in your mouth?" Or if she has trouble wearing certain socks because "they hurt my feet," you could empathize. "I guess socks with big seams across the toes bother your feet," you could say. "Your feet seem to be very smart in figuring out what they like. And you seem to get very mad and sometimes have a tantrum when someone even suggests that you wear these socks. Maybe people don't always know how your feet feel."

Your goal is to help your child do more than *react* to her sensitivities with avoidance, anger, or controlling behavior. You need to help her become aware that she has sensitivities *and* that she has *feelings* about these sensitivities and certain ways of trying to cope with them.

Don't be embarrassed about your child's unique features; learn to talk about her sensitivities in a light-hearted way. And always be respectful of your child's behavior. If you are respectful, your child will feel it and become more confident and comfortable in the long term. Respect and even admiration for your child's individual differences doesn't mean your child will turn into a tyrant who expects the world to cater to her special needs. The shared respect that you and your child have for her physical makeup (after all, she has to live with those feet!) will create a collaborative attitude. From this, you and your child can then work together on increasing emotional flexibility. Because, while she has to live with those feet, she will sense over time that it's also in her interest to be flexible and not let them get in the way of her goals and pleasures.

Small Steps toward Mastery

Sensitive children dislike surprises and sudden transitions. Adding pressure will only make them feel overloaded. The extra-sensitive child needs to get one toe wet at a time. Take the clinging three-year-old who won't let her parent go into a different room without a tantrum. But you have to cook dinner in the kitchen. As a first step, you might bring her with you. But instead of having her cling to you, she could serve as your assistant chef. She could stir her own pots and pans at your feet while you cook dinner. Then, as the next step, she could play at the kitchen table while you talk to her and cook. In the following days and weeks, she could gradually move into the next room while you talk to her and cook. Eventually, she could play in the next room with you calling out to her or checking on her every now and then. This way, you gradually help your child become more independent. She goes from needing to see and touch and smell you to just needing to hear your voice occasionally. Eventually she won't even need that as often. Through this gradual process, she will learn to picture you in her mind even when you are away from her, rather than needing you in front of her all the time.

•   •   •

To sum up, we have seen that our sensitive child comes by her finicky behavior honestly. She has special physical sensitivities— to touch, sounds, sometimes to movement or even different sights, which can make routine events overwhelming or scary. Being a smart little person, she wants either to control or to avoid sensory overload. When she does get overloaded, naturally she wants immediate relief. Your goal is to understand these natural tendencies and use your understanding to help her find better ways to cope. As she learns to be more flexible, as she learns to gradually try new things, to soothe herself more effectively, to observe her own feelings and sensitivities, to be more assertive and confident, and to see you as a respectful collaborator in her efforts, rather than as a protector or underminer, she will have initiated the processes of her own growth.

HANNAH'S STORY

Hannah Weitz's parents brought her in to see me after running out of energy and solutions for handling their little girl, whom they described as being "scared and fussy all the time." New situations frightened three-year-old Hannah a great deal. When her parents left her with the babysitter or dropped her off at nursery school, she would scream hysterically, clinging desperately to them. She seemed frightened of the other children and avoided them for the initial part of free play. When she did play, she would burst into tears if another child approached her while she was playing with a toy. "Mine, mine!" she would say, clutching the toy and running to the teacher.

At times, she became panicky and acted as if she were seeing something scary, or having something scary happen to her. Her face would freeze in terror, and she would cry uncontrollably for up to a half-hour.

Her temper tantrums were long and loud—she would throw herself on the floor at home, screaming and pounding the floor, leaving her parents helpless and angry. The outbursts were particularly pronounced during transitions in Hannah's day—when she was leaving the house for nursery school, when her parents left for work, or when she had to leave a store or a park where she was having fun.

Situations or sights that other children enjoyed terrified Hannah. At the sight of lively cartoons on television, she would run to her mother or her babysitter, burying her face in their arms as a giggling Bugs Bunny was chased by Elmer Fudd or when Wile E. Coyote took off after Road Runner.

She enjoyed some kinds of music, but loud drums or motorized sounds, from such kitchen gadgets as a food processor or a disposal, frightened her. She would put her hands over her ears, yelling, "Mommy, hurts!" Busy rooms with lots of children, or parties with chatter and loud background racket would also cause her to hold her ears and want to run out.

Nighttime wasn't any easier. Hannah never slept more than three hours at a time, and fell asleep only when one of her parents was with her. If she awoke and they were gone, she would cry out "Mommeeee, Daddeeee" until one of them came in and stroked her forehead until she fell asleep again.

For all this difficult behavior, Hannah could also be a warm, delightful child. She loved trips to the zoo, giggling delightedly at the perky prairie dogs as they popped in and out of their holes and stretched up on their hind legs to sniff the air. She loved reading with her parents, snuggling contentedly in her mother or father's lap to hear *Good Night Moon* and *Green Eggs and Ham.* She had a wonderful sense of humor and would shriek with laughter when her daddy made funny faces and squeaky noises. She enjoyed fingerpainting with her babysitter Miriam or her mother and would lavishly apply thick swirls of deep purple and pink and proudly tape the artwork to the refrigerator.

She was extraordinarily insightful and observant, constantly surprising her parents by what she noticed. She had a steady stream of original questions about the world. After passing a herd of cows by the side of the road while in the car, and later seeing a car go by with a pizza sign on the roof, she thought for a moment and then asked her mother, "Mommy, can cows ride on the roofs of cars?" Another time, after spending time with the infant of a family friend, she asked, "Who took care of the babies before there were mommies and daddies?"

When Hannah's parents brought her in to see me, I found her to be an intense, friendly, and eager child. She was small for her age, I noticed, with intense brown eyes and soft hair that curled around her head in wispy tufts. When she first arrived, she curled up on her mother's lap, resting her head against her mother's chest, her legs draped over the arm of the chair. She eyed me warily. Soon, bored by the adult conversation, she wiggled down and surveyed the room, but still kept one hand hanging on to her mother. The dollhouse in my office caught her eye.

"Mommeeee," she implored, tugging at her mother, demanding her mother's attention. "Play with me."

Her mother shushed her gently, smiling tightly at me. "Honey, I'm talking to the doctor. Just a minute—." But Hannah persisted. "I want you to play with me *now*," she insisted, a slightly petulant tone creeping into her voice. Sally sighed, looking at me as if to say, "See what I mean?" She was a tall woman with dark hair and anxious eyes.

"Go ahead," I said, nodding to Sally and her husband, Bruno, who was looking slightly exasperated at the interruption. Hannah headed happily for the dollhouse, her mother in tow. After a moment's hesitation, Bruno swung himself out of the chair and down to where his wife and daughter were. This was his second family, he had told me during our initial interview; he had two children by a previous marriage who were now in college. Starting a family had been Sally's idea, and he clearly preferred to leave most of the parenting to her.

Watching Hannah play with her parents as she absorbed herself in moving furniture from room to room in the dollhouse and setting up the dolls in various rooms, I was impressed with how focused and attentive she was to people and to things. She was very animated and demonstrative with her gestures.

"Mommy, put the bed in that room. It's for the baby," she ordered, pointing to the baby doll. "And the mommy goes in this room and the daddy is playing outside with the doggie. . . ." As Hannah played, Sally crouched over her, staying close—an inch or two away, rather than a more usual three or four inches. Sally's movements seemed jerky, tense, her face strained, as if she were trying very hard to please her daughter without quite knowing how to do it.

"Honey," she quickly broke into her daughter's monologue. "I think the baby might like to be with the mommy, don't you think?" Sally looked over at Bruno, smiling nervously, trying to draw him into the play. "Daddy, where do you think the baby should be in the dollhouse?" she asked him.

Bruno shrugged and didn't move, but he winked at his daughter. "How about on the roof?" he said. Hannah giggled and leaned over to take a playful swat at her father. "Silly daddy! Then she would fall off and hurt her head!"

It was also clear that Hannah was very sensitive to her parents. As they played, she turned eagerly in their direction, seeking to pull them into her game. Her pretend play was rich but had a fragmented quality to it. After a few minutes with the dollhouse, she found a toy car and quickly wheeled a teddy bear around in it before coming upon a baby doll that she dressed and undressed, all the while chattering away and ordering her mother to help her get the teddy bear out of the car or help her dress the dolly. Sally complied, while Bruno watched. He seemed a little tense and distant.

A few minutes later, as she continued this type of play, the baby doll got scared while sleeping. At this point, Bruno jumped in and said, in his gruff, Germanic voice, "I'm the scary nightmare that the baby is scared of. I'm a monster and the baby is scared about having a bad dream about me." He then picked up a Transformer toy and made deep growling monster noises with the same type of low pitch that her parents had earlier told me usually scared Hannah. I observed Hannah momentarily freeze with what Bruno thought was a playful overture. Sally protectively encouraged her daughter to "Hit the monster. Make him go away!" As Hannah's doll stood motionless and speechless, Sally handed the doll a stick and said, "Here, hit the monster! Hit the monster!" While some children might thoroughly enjoy the permission to be aggressive and would start hitting and perhaps even jumping on the daddy monster, Hannah took the stick and hit the doll, saying, "Bad girl for waking up! Bad girl!" She clearly showed her discomfort with the theme of aggression.

Seeing Hannah hit her doll, Sally quickly shifted gears and started nurturing Hannah's little doll, saying, "No, no, she's a nice doll. She just got scared and woke up. Nice doll!" Bruno, somewhat impervious to the drama unfolding in front of him, was still huffing and puffing in his monster role. At an earlier point in the play, when Bruno had tried to engage her in some rough-and-tumble play Hannah had twisted away.

Hannah also showed a lot of sensitivity to her environment. At one point, when a car went by outside my office and beeped its horn, her head jerked up and her eyes widened. She looked scared by the sudden noise and scrambled over to her mother, grabbing at her legs. She also seemed very sensitive to the sunlight and the dust particles streaming into my office. I noticed that she blinked a lot and, at times, seemed to be trying to bat away the dust.

As Hannah busied herself with puzzles for a few minutes, her parents filled me in on her infancy and early childhood. This continued in a follow-up session where Sally and Bruno came in on their own.

Sally said her pregnancy and Hannah's birth were healthy and normal. But she did note that Hannah had been a fitful sleeper from the beginning, waking up easily, and startled by loud noises. Hannah had seemed to prefer firm holding to light touches.

Sally praised herself for her ability to calm baby Hannah. She would carry Hannah around the house for a half-hour or longer in order to help her calm herself and go to sleep during the day. Sally also prided herself on finding the right way to talk and sing to Hannah, using a high-pitched, slow, gentle rhythm, coupled with very slow rocking.

By three or four months, Sally said, Hannah would smile, coo, and move her arms and legs in rhythm with her mother's smiles and sounds, showing a deep level of warmth and affection for her mother. Hannah had been slow to warm up to her father and initially seemed frightened by him. She would cry if he came into the room suddenly or if he picked her up when her mother wasn't present. But, starting at about four months, Hannah began to relax in his presence, giving him warm smiles, although saving her brightest smiles for her mother.

Sally told me that Hannah related well to her babysitter (Sally had returned to work part-time as a sales representative for a hotel chain when Hannah was six months old and was working three to five days a week by the time Hannah was eight months old). The babysitter was an older woman with a lot of experience with babies.

By eight months, Hannah could pick up small objects by scooping them up into her fist. She babbled a lot and smiled warmly at her parents and the babysitter. But if they talked too fast (particularly in a loud voice) or played with her too long and vigorously, or if she was presented with too many choices (three or four toys, for example) she seemed to fall apart. She would cry, scream, or simply flail her arms in all directions. She displayed sensitivities in other ways as well. When her mother stroked her head while trying to cuddle her, Hannah would squirm and cry. Loud noises made her burst into tears. Hers was a loud, piercing cry that sounded as if she was in pain.

As a toddler, her parents recalled, Hannah communicated very well and was skilled at picking up on what they were trying to tell her. She would take her mother's hand and guide her around the room as she searched for her favorite doll. "Baby?" she would say with a big shrug and a smile. "Where baby?"

Her sensitivity to loud noises and touch, as well as to bright lights, continued. She twisted and screamed when her mother tried to comb her hair or clean off her face after eating. She was terrified of clowns; Sally was careful not to take her to birthday parties where there would be clown entertainment.

She also seemed to have sensitive skin. "She hates socks and shoes," Sally said with a sigh. Sally was constantly going back and forth to the shoe store trying to find shoes that Hannah would wear. Hannah cried furiously and frequently threw tantrums when she had to put them on in the morning. Hannah also preferred old clothes to new ones and often would turn up her nose at the pretty dresses and sweaters that Sally bought her, much preferring the worn hand-me-downs that came from friends and relatives. It had sparked many power struggles between Sally and her daughter. "I try not to make a big deal out of what she wears," Sally said. "But sometimes she looks so shabby that I can hardly stand it!"

Now that Hannah was a little older and more verbal, she could express her concern at things she saw that were less than perfect. "Bread broken, bread is broken," she sobbed one morning after pulling a piece of bread out of the package and having part of the crust break off.

She was easily overwhelmed by too much excitement and stimulation. Many times her parents had carried her kicking and screaming out of the grocery store or the local department store. On one recent visit, for example, after she was promised that she could pick out one treat, she had become dazzled at the rows and shelves of bright objects and threw herself on the floor of the store, banging her fists into the floor. "I want *two* treats!" she shrieked. "*Two* treats!"

"It's like that all the time," said Sally, relating the story. "I can't take her *anywhere*. She screams, cries—it all seems too much for her." Sally paused. "I keep wondering what I could be doing differently. I keep trying to figure out what I'm doing that's so wrong." Her eyes filled with tears. I sensed that she loved her little girl a great deal but was feeling hopelessly lost about how to cope with her.

In an effort to control the situation, Sally and Bruno had attempted different approaches. They had tried "cracking down on her," as Bruno put it, drawing up lists of sanctions they would impose when Hannah misbehaved. Any time she threw a temper tantrum, she wasn't allowed to watch TV or play with her best friend Leah, for example. But that didn't work. In fact, they noted, Hannah simply became more defiant, screaming, "No! No!" or "Go 'way! Go 'way!" constantly. So Sally and Bruno had tried to adopt a more laissez-faire attitude and permitted Hannah to have her way as often as possible to avoid any struggles. They'd even tried occasionally to let her bite and pinch Sally when she was out of control, hoping she would give up if her mother showed no reaction. But this didn't work; it only seemed to increase Hannah's frustration.

This vacillation between different approaches showed in other ways. At times, Sally worried about Hannah so much that she hovered over her, as I had observed during their play time in my office, and reacted to virtually every breath that Hannah took. Sally was somewhat aware of her hovering, protective stance, and commented, "I so worry about her, I sometimes cry for hours to myself. I don't know what will happen to her when she gets older." At other times, Sally said, she just felt she had to get away from Hannah. "I can't stand it," she said, "particularly when she is ordering me around." She would install Hannah in front of the television and retreat to another room. But then Hannah would shriek furiously, "Mommeeee," and follow her from room to room, desperately grabbing at her. "Don't leave me!" she would cry.

Whereas Sally vacillated between hovering protectiveness and escaping, Bruno vacillated between being aloof (working late or bringing work home and secluding himself in his office or, as Sally said, simply "tuning out" while sitting in the room with them) and intrusive discipline, where he would yell back at Hannah when she was having a tantrum. He would threaten her with different punishments, often only escalating her outrage and disorganization.

In a subsequent meeting where I had an opportunity to go into their personal backgrounds more deeply, I learned that with both parents there were understandable reasons for the way they related to Hannah. While I won't go into Bruno's and Sally's background in this discussion, it's important to note that the more parents understand the basis for their own reactions to their children, the more flexibility they will have in finding approaches that meet their children's unique needs.

Hannah's parents had taken her to several specialists.

Medical, allergy, and neurological examinations had turned up nothing wrong.

After hearing about Hannah's current behavior and history, and after observing Hannah myself, my initial impression was that Hannah was an extremely bright, articulate, warm, and loving child with creative flair and imagination and a capacity for experiencing many emotions very vividly. She was clearly able to relate and engage with others, use nonverbal gestures to communicate, size up situations, and call on ideas to explore her own imagination and communicate with her parents. She was able to communicate at both the level of make-believe and the level of logical discussion and negotiation. She, therefore, had many of the capacities we like to see in a three-year-old.

At the same time, however, she showed that she didn't quite have the flexibility in her personality to adapt to the routine challenges of each day. While she had a rich capacity to engage warmly with each parent, she could not easily extend that to peers or in different settings. She was often cautious and withdrawn in unfamiliar situations. While she could size up social expectations when she was calm, she became easily overloaded and then could not adapt her behavior to routine situations—shown by her tantrums in stores, school, and at parties. While her imagination was rich and creative, in fantasy she also tended to be overextended. While playing, she flitted from one theme to another in a fragmented way, rather than remaining organized and going into greater depth on one theme. While she could use her cleverness and natural abilities to debate her father, she had trouble in applying logic to the world of scary feelings, which were present a good deal of the time, not just once in a while. Her lack of flexibility and ways of coping showed up in her rapid transformation from bright, cheerful three-year-old at one moment to a demanding, frightened, fragmented, inconsolable little girl.

Contributing significantly to these difficulties were Hannah's extreme sensitivities. These had been present since early in her life and were in evidence during the play I observed with her parents. She overreacted to certain types of touch, visual experiences, and sounds. For Hannah, routine sights, sounds, and touches were not routine at all.

Her parents' coping patterns were in many respects very typical. They loved their little girl very much and were trying their best under difficult circumstances. And yet, inadvertently, they were digging the hole deeper for Hannah. Sally's vacillations between overprotecting and then trying to escape left Hannah feeling only more insecure. Sally's overprotectiveness undermined Hannah's ability to be assertive and learn to calm herself, to cope with her environment on her own. Sally's escapism then further pulled out the rug from under Hannah by making Hannah feel that there was no one to turn to.

Bruno's shifts between aloofness and overintrusiveness also only made life harder for Hannah. When he withdrew, she felt a lack of affection and security. His less-than-sensitive monster play only overwhelmed her further.

Her parents and I agreed that our prime goal for Hannah was to help her develop better self-soothing capacities to offset her overreactivity and also to improve her assertive coping skills so that she could take charge of her world rather than feel helpless. We wanted Hannah to be less overwhelmed and to improve her ability to tolerate a wide range of feelings and situations and remain organized and secure. At the same time, our goal was to work directly on her sensitivities so that over time, she would not be so overreactive to routine sensations. Obviously, the approach would involve both Hannah and her family.

Even as I was learning more about Hannah and her parents in subsequent visits, we began to carry out a five-step process: "floor time," problem-solving time, empathy, progress in small steps, and limit setting. As with the other children we will visit in this book, our goal was to help Hannah renegotiate, or negotiate for the first time, the stages of development that she had not fully mastered. We also wanted to help Hannah learn to use her unique strengths—her insight, her intelligence, her focus on detail, and her intense responsiveness—to her own advantage rather than allow them to become liabilities that make life more difficult. We wanted to help her establish a strong inner sense of competence. The five-step process is described in the following sections.

FLOOR TIME: ESTABLISHING TRUST AND SUPPORTING INITIATIVE

The first step in the five-step process is meant to establish a sense of involvement, security, and warmth between parents and child. The parent simply joins the child at her level, playing or engaging in the child's chosen activity for about twenty minutes each day. This is an essential foundation for a child who is feeling physically overwhelmed by the world. The idea is to follow the child's initiative.

With Sally, we focused on helping her express warm encouragement and develop a more positive, respectful relationship with her daughter. We wanted her relationship with Hannah to be characterized by less tension and anxiety and by neither overprotectiveness nor escapism. Since Sally worked in a fast-paced world with lots of worries and anxieties, it was understandable that she would relate to her daughter in that way too. She tended to focus on down-to-earth concerns with Hannah—feeding her, telling her what to do, trying to control her fussiness—rather than sharing feelings and ideas with her. She didn't take the opportunity to engage in pretend play with her daughter—to transcend their everyday existence and soar in the rich, imaginative world of a three-year-old. Sally wasn't taking the time to visualize "not what is, but what could be."

With encouragement, Sally began to get down on the floor to play with Hannah. She tried to follow Hannah's lead in a warm, empathetic, and respectful manner, helping Hannah to broaden her pretend play. Sally tried to do this for at least twenty or thirty minutes a day and more on the weekends. Initially, true to her personality, Sally started directing the drama. "That doll doesn't belong in the bedroom," she would say. "She's the mommy doll. She belongs in the kitchen." Or "No, that car can't go through the window. It has to go into the garage." Sally even grabbed Hannah's hand at one point, showing her how to brush the doll's hair. When Hannah rebelled with a tantrum, Sally grew exasperated. She told me later, "See, she doesn't want to play with me. I'm no good at this anyhow." She used this as an excuse to escape from playing with her daughter. With empathy and encouragement, however, Sally was helped to identify her overprotectiveness and escapism. She was also encouraged to relax and let Hannah's creative imagination do most of the work. All she had to do was to amplify and occasionally challenge. She was to be a plot thickener, not a plot developer.

Behind mother's anxieties, fortunately for Hannah, there lurked an imaginative playmate. As Sally relaxed and let her own childhood emerge, she and Hannah shared tea parties, pretend cookouts, and other fun make-believe dramas and experiences. Over time, Hannah began experimenting with what she was most scared of—aggression. For example, after a few months of rich pretend play, when angry toy dogs barked and tried to ruin the cookout one time, Sally was flabbergasted when Hannah's doll shouted "Bad dog!" and pretended to strangle the stuffed dog. Sally wondered whether to permit this kind of aggression, but I assured her that it was only pretend play. Perhaps, I told Sally and Bruno, the aggression was helping Hannah learn to be more comfortable with some of the angry feelings that we all imagined lay just beneath Hannah's enormous frustrations and irritability.

With her mother's compassion, warmth, and acceptance, Hannah's dramas gradually became richer in their emotions. She didn't just have tea parties. Now there were confrontations, scary feelings, and outright rage. There was also a lot of love and protectiveness displayed in her pretend play. Equally important, Hannah began experimenting with a larger range of sensory and motor experiences. Hannah both initiated and invited more touching and louder sounds, and she tackled greater physical challenges in her play (dolls clung to tall towers, hid in closets, and the like). As Hannah's play broadened and blossomed, so did her ability to engage in life's routine experiences. She tolerated such sensations as touch and a larger range of sound, and more frustration.

Floor time was very hard for Bruno. Having already

fathered two children, he had only reluctantly agreed to have another child. Sally, ten years younger than he, had expressed a strong desire to have children of her own, which made him feel that raising Hannah was her responsibility. In working hard and in paying the college bills for his two older children, he felt he had done his share. After coming home from the office, he usually had a quick dinner and then settled in front of his computer for a few more hours of work, leaving Sally to bathe Hannah and put her to bed. When he tried floor time with his daughter, he was always wandering off to make a phone call that seemed particularly urgent right then. Or he would try to do floor time on a Sunday afternoon while keeping one eye on the football game on the television. Hannah got frustrated that she had only part of her father's attention, and would become even more demanding ("Daddy, you dropped my teddy bear! Pick him up or he will be hurt! Right now!"), causing him to retreat even further.

At other times, however, when Hannah got to him, he would respond to her demands with a punitive yell. "You and that bear are too damned spoiled," he would shout. "When are you going to learn to behave?" His gruff, loud voice terrified Hannah, and she would usually fall apart with a tantrum, screaming for her mommy.

"I'm not good with young children," he told me with a shrug and a smile. "Sally is much better with this kind of thing than I am." I had to work hard to persuade him that Hannah needed *both* her parents to do floor time with her. I suspected that, deep down, the various emotional themes that Hannah played out were too much for Bruno. Other people's emotions were a bit overwhelming to him, and his self-absorption was probably his way of remaining emotionally uninvolved with other people.

So Bruno compromised. He would try to do floor time every other day at first. He could consider the time a success if he could simply lie on the floor for a full twenty minutes, remaining warm and supportive and not leaving or losing his temper. If the only thing that happened was that Hannah jumped on his tummy or made him into a horse or a teddy bear, that would be great. If

Bruno felt confused or anxious, he could always simply smile and lie there. I had noticed early on that Hannah was so pleased to have some of her father's attention that she was quite delighted even if he wasn't the active play partner that her mother was. From this humble beginning, Bruno found that with the football game and the telephone turned off, his daughter's imagination was quite interesting. He could lie there, and she could make him into a bean bag chair, similar to one that she had missed when they had moved a few months ago. Hannah would stand on him and jump a little bit, saying, "You is my favorite bean bag!" Bruno commented later that he was getting a good workout for his stomach. Soon, after doing this for a week, Bruno got so comfortable, he started responding with "The bean bag is going to catch you and won't let you up!" Hannah giggled with delight and pushed, saying, "I got away! I got away!" and then would tempt him again by sitting on his stomach and scampering away when the "bean bag" came alive again. Many weeks later, she began getting even more comfortable, and made the daddy bean bag into a Venus flytrap, which she had seen on television. She delighted in outsmarting the "flytrap monster." As with her mother, against a backdrop of warmth, empathy, and security from Bruno, Hannah gradually broadened her emotional, motor, and sensory experiences.

Bruno also benefited from the floor time and began being more gentle and involved in his relationship with Hannah. He talked and reasoned with her more, and yelled, intruded, or avoided her less.

I've found that many parents find it difficult at first to engage fully with their child during floor time, for whatever reason (and they don't necessarily need to know the reason). This doesn't mean they are "bad" parents, just that they have no experience with that way of relating to a child. The goal in floor time is to establish some sense of warmth and some sense that you're responding with rapport to your child's interests. There are many ways to do this. One father I know who had difficulty spending an unstructured thirty minutes with his eight-year-old son found that both he and his son liked building complicated structures out of Lego pieces. So they could sit quietly, adding block after block to various buildings they were constructing. Gradually they began building a rapport based on this mutual love for creating structures. One mother I know found that her eleven-year-old daughter liked to read aloud to her. So she listened while her daughter read *Sweet Valley High* stories to her. Afterward, they talked about how they would have written each book differently.

As a special feature of floor time, for the sensitive child who is verbal and capable of pretend play, it's very important to learn how to elaborate different feelings in her pretend play. As the child learns to put feelings into words, she is mastering a critical coping capacity. When her body gets overloaded, she is no longer at the mercy of wordless sensations, but can identify which feelings are getting stirred up.

Since most adults can verbalize their feelings to themselves and others, it's often hard for us to realize what it must be like to be unable to describe strong sensations to yourself or others. To the child without such capacities, the overload often translates into physical behavior, either a tantrum, clinging, or aggression, or else avoidance and shutting down. Sometimes it just translates into fragmented, disorganized behavior.

Even more than the average child, sensitive children need to find ways to express their feelings. Therefore, as you get into floor time, try to become an actor in the drama and help your child imbue the characters with rich feelings—the horse and elephant can be scared or mad, the teddy bear can get worried and need a hug or time in the panda's lap.

PROBLEM-SOLVING TIME: COPING WITH FEARS AND ANXIETIES

Problem-solving time is a special period set aside to negotiate and discuss particular difficulties or challenges. For the sensitive child, this may mean simply describing her life—her likes, dislikes, excitements, fears, and trepidations. You can begin quite early—as soon as a child is verbal. As a child learns to describe her day, she will gradually get better at explaining how she felt, say, when another child was mean to her or when somebody inadvertently jostled her. Simply possessing the ability to translate each day's special sensitivities into words for an empathetic mother or father is in itself an enormous help to the child. Without this ability, solutions will not be attainable.

With any kind of challenging child, the key is to help the child foster a "reflective" attitude. That means to help her *anticipate* and *prepare for* situations that you both recognize are difficult for her. That way, she won't do things by reflex. Anticipating helps the child substitute ideas for action. As she becomes older, she can begin to understand the different outcomes of several possible actions. (Most adults meet challenges better when they have thought about and prepared for them in advance.) Anticipating helps children become better at monitoring their own thoughts and actions.

Let's illustrate problem-solving time with one of Hannah's big challenges. She was manifesting a great deal of anxiety about separation. When Sally left the house in the morning, Hannah would cry for forty-five minutes or longer. After Sally returned from a one- or two-day business trip, Hannah would at first behave coldly, ignoring mommy and continuing to play with her dolls when Sally bent down to kiss her. Then she would become quite clingy, grabbing at Sally's legs as she tried to unpack or make dinner, sobbing uncontrollably.

As we wondered about this, Sally and Bruno revealed, much to my surprise, that they did not prepare Hannah for their departures for work or trips at all. The babysitter would try to distract Hannah while they sneaked out the door to work. And Sally did not tell Hannah when she was leaving on a business trip until the last minute. "I'll be back in two days, honey," she would tell her as she headed out the door.

"If I tell her sooner than that," Sally explained to me, "I would have to suffer through hours of crying and whining."

But, of course, for a child like Hannah, a lack of warning is very upsetting. It was not surprising she reacted as she did every time.

We set up a new routine. Sally would take time to sit down

with Hannah and explore how she felt when separating. A day or two before a trip, Sally would use dolls to dramatize her departure. For example, a doll would fly to the place where mother was going to and Hannah would construct a scene of the room where mother would be staying, with one doll representing Sally. Sally would leave photos of herself in a special photo album for Hannah and call home frequently.

After getting the hang of problem-solving time, and the need to help Hannah start to develop a reflective attitude toward the inevitable short or long separations, Sally was able to help her daughter meet this challenge. We began to see results. One day while Sally and Hannah were doing some shopping, they ran into an acquaintance of Sally's. After greeting Sally, the acquaintance pounced on Hannah.

"She's cuter than her pictures!" the woman said loudly to Sally and leaned forward to grab Hannah by the chin to inspect her more closely. Hannah's lip began to tremble and she clutched Sally's legs, turning her face away from the intruder.

"Your little girl is rather clingy," the woman observed with a trace of disapproval.

Sally looked down at Hannah. "Are you clingy?" she asked.

Hannah looked up. "What's that mean, Mommy?"

"That means that you like to hang onto me a lot," Sally said.

Hannah's tears stopped and she thought for a moment. "Sometimes I like to hang onto you."

"When's that?" Sally asked.

Hannah peered up at the woman, who was beginning to look embarrassed.

"Oh," said Sally. "When somebody new is around?"

Hannah nodded.

"Are you clingy at home?" Sally asked.

Hannah thought for another minute. "Only sometimes."

"Oh," said Sally. "So you're only clingy sometimes. When there's somebody new around and you feel scared."

Hannah nodded. Sally turned to the woman, whose smile was looking strained.

"Hannah says she's clingy, but only sometimes, when she is in new situations." She turned back to Hannah. "Isn't that right, sweetheart?"

Hannah nodded her head again, a faint smile creeping across her face.

The woman hurried off, and Hannah's smile deepened.

Rather than tensing up when she sensed her acquaintance's disapproval of her daughter's clinginess and trying to untangle her daughter from around her legs, Sally turned the situation around and made it into a good problem-solving experience. She was able to help Hannah recognize that her reaction to new situations and to new people was to get frightened and to cling to her parents.

In talking about it in a matter-of-fact way, she helped Hannah both observe her reactions and to be accepting of them. Paradoxically, as a child begins to recognize and accept her own patterns of response, she is less likely to need to use them in the future. Conversely, the more guilty you make a child feel about her behavior and the more you pressure her to give it up without giving her a better substitute to handle the underlying feelings, the more likely the child will hold on to her habits.

As they talked together, Sally learned to be less embarrassed by Hannah's reactions and by her behavior. If parents are respectful of their child's unique features, that child will sense this and become more comfortable and confident in the long term. The goal, of course, is to avoid getting caught up in others' standards. Admire your child's differences and work with them.

With an older child (an eight- or nine-year-old, for example), problem-solving discussions can be quite direct and involve in-depth discussions of feelings and solutions. For example, a child who is afraid to raise her hand in a certain "mean" teacher's class can be helped to picture the situation, including the teacher in the classroom as it will occur the next day. She can then be helped to talk about the feelings, which may include fear, anger, humiliation. Then she can be helped to picture her routine response, which is probably avoidance and becoming quiet. She may even tell you her secret strategy—hitting and teasing the children next to her. She can also be helped to visualize some potential new strategies that might deal more effectively with the feelings she has already elaborated to you, including both fear and anger. For example, the night before the teacher will talk about a particular subject, the two of you might come up with some questions on the subject that your daughter doesn't think the teacher will ask. That would give her a safe way of preempting the teacher's questions, perhaps stumping her, and developing the gumption to speak up.

Of course, this solution might not work for all children. For many, it may be too scary. Often, however, the very act of brainstorming is helpful. Even if a perfect solution is not found, the child goes from being passive to planning a strategy and eventually acting.

Some solutions found in problem solving may address the child's particular physical makeup. Hannah, for instance, needed a lot of gross motor activity where she had a chance to feel assertive—such as running, chasing, or playing airplane and rocket ships. I also suggested that Bruno and Sally encourage Hannah to do physical activity that involved lots of joint compression, such as jumping rope, or jumping on a mattress or a small trampoline. They also could calm her with touch that involved deep pressure, such as bear hugs and back rubs (as opposed to light, tickly touches).

These kinds of activities at home and at school—sports like gymnastics and soccer, which involve these kinds of movement patterns—all appear to help a child become less sensitive and less overloaded by life's daily events. Noise, touch, and the like do not tend to tax a child who has recently engaged in these types of physical exercise.

IDENTIFYING AND EMPATHIZING WITH A SENSITIVE CHILD

As I have discussed earlier in this chapter, the sensitive child needs more compassion and flexibility than most children. (At the same time, as you may remember, she requires more firmness and structure than many other children, but we will talk more about that later.) The key is to empathize with how your child feels, even if it is a feeling you don't like. This will not plant that feeling in the child's mind or make it stronger, but will help her recognize and label that feeling. And, of course, empathy creates a closeness between you and your child.

The hardest part of this step for Sally and Bruno was when Hannah was both scared and demanding at the same time. For example, when she was clinging in a demanding way, they wanted to yell at her because they felt she was being manipulative. On the other hand, they remembered that at those moments, Hannah was frightened.

Bruno, in particular, was doubtful. "If we are nice to her and supportive and give in to her, that is just going to spoil her," he maintained. He had a hard time holding his temper when Hannah was in a clinging, insistent mood. "I know she's scared," he said. "After it's happened several times in a day, I just get sick of her behavior."

This is perhaps the most difficult thing in the world for all parents to do—to empathize with a set of feelings that are themselves somewhat contradictory (like anger and fear). With some support and practice, Sally and Bruno were able to be patient with their own annoyance and try to experience both sides of Hannah's feelings.

For example, as they attempted to identify with her when she was angry and frightened about a thunderstorm, they learned to say such things as "I know you must be so mad that you have this scary feeling from the big noise of the thunder. I know how scary it must feel and how much you want mommy or daddy to take away the feeling."

When Sally and Bruno broke down Hannah's feeling into its different parts, to their surprise, Hannah responded to their empathy and support. "Make the scared feeling go away," she said during a violent thunderstorm. And then, more frustrated, she pleaded, "Daddy, why can't you make it go away?"

Bruno finally understood Hannah's expectation. The more scared Hannah got, the more she wanted daddy or mommy to make her feel better and the angrier she got when mommy or daddy couldn't or didn't. Simply sympathizing and stating what came to be self-evident truths in a comforting way helped Hannah enormously. Bruno didn't agree with Hannah's assumption that he should be able to take all bad feelings away. But he could certainly understand why a child, particularly a sensitive child who needs extra protection, could feel this way.

The more sensitive the child, the more likely it is that her feelings will be intense and sometimes complex. Parents who haven't experienced these sensitivities themselves may not have a good reference point. "It's easy to empathize with one feeling," one frazzled mother of a highly sensitive child told me. "But when you have a barrage of feelings coming at you at once from your child, it's hard to think straight."

Sometimes simply encouraging your child to describe what it feels like helps the parent grasp what the child is going through. For example, one very sensitive child (a verbal seven-year-old), told her mother, "Mommy, it feels like somebody is sticking nails into me and I'm bleeding. It hurts so much." Mother, needless to say, was pained by such a vivid, frightening description. Yet a characteristic of very sensitive children is the vividness and, at times, almost earthy and physical descriptions that they use to describe their feelings. Parents sometimes have a hard time empathizing because it is too painful to hear these feelings, and it is natural to avoid listening to them, usually inadvertently. No matter how excruciating the child's descriptions, there is nothing more soothing for her than to share them with somebody she loves. Sometimes this shared understanding may lead to more practical solutions. Often it won't. Yet it will have been very helpful in its own right.

Another aspect of Hannah that made it hard for her parents to empathize, as it is with all sensitive children, is the way her behavior changed from moment to moment and from day to day. Sometimes Hannah was warm and sweet and cooperative, raising her parents' hope that all her difficulties were behind her. And at other times (sometimes on the same day) she was cantankerous, demanding, and clinging. On those days, Sally and Bruno were convinced that Hannah was never going to improve.

In such situations, I tell parents that if they think the unpredictability is hard on them, imagine how it is for their child. It is also helpful to view a child's progress not day to day but, instead, over several months.

Look back over the last three months. Is she better now than she was three months ago? While all children have a large range of functioning—that is, one day they can be mature and reflective and the next day impulsive and full of temper tantrums—children with extreme sensitivities have a range that is even greater. So the swings on a *day-to-day* basis may be quite wide. Recognizing and controlling the feelings that produce the negative behavior is a long, hard task. Parents need to continue to empathize with the child.

Looking at it from a longer perspective, Sally and Bruno said that they began to see some progress. Hannah was a little less apt to become frantic in busy places, such as shopping malls and grocery stores. Sally noticed that she hesitated less about taking Hannah shopping than she did three months ago. And Bruno noticed that Hannah was throwing fewer tantrums than she had earlier in the year. Her behavior changes weren't huge, but they were big enough to give Sally and Bruno reasons for hope.

BREAKING BIG CHALLENGES INTO SMALL PIECES

Since the sensitive child dislikes surprises and sudden transitions, she needs to approach mastery of her new skills gradually, rather than plunging in. We want her to learn new skills, of course, but with a sense of security. For example, at nursery school, which Hannah attended three mornings a week, Sally overcame her impulse simply to pull Hannah out of school and wait until another year. Instead, she met with her teacher to discuss Hannah's challenges. It turned out that group activities, such as circle time and group play time were especially stressful for Hannah. She seemed to enjoy quiet one-on-one time with a teacher, and she liked it when the children listened to a story read by a teacher.

The teacher agreed to help introduce Hannah gradually to playing with other children. At first, the teacher would play just with Hannah, rolling a ball to her. Then she brought in another child and served as a "buffer" between Hannah and the other child by allowing Hannah to roll the ball to her at first instead of to the other child. Soon Hannah and her partner were rolling the ball back and forth directly to each other under the watchful eye of the teacher.

Over several months, Hannah began reaching out to a few other children and, eventually, was able to get involved in pretend play with a few special friends. She would play dolls with another girl, for example. Each girl played a "mommy" taking care of a baby.

For circle time, which could get boisterous with eleven three-year-olds, the teacher let Hannah be in a little circle with just one other child for a while. Then a second child joined the circle, then a third until Hannah felt comfortable enough to bring her small group into the larger group. As with any highly sensitive child, the goal was to avoid throwing Hannah into new situations. At the same time, parents and teachers can't simply leave an overly sensitive child out of the action; she may never learn the skills to join in. So the goal is to find a comfortable middle ground—to draw the child *gradually* into challenging situations.

With some children, progress in this area won't be as quick as it was with Hannah. Parents and teachers need to work together so that some children who, for example, find circle time difficult, do an activity in another corner of the room.

Sensitive children learn flexibility from our flexibility. Anytime teachers and parents become too worried about whether a sensitive child is manipulating them, they should take that very feeling as a warning that they could be involved in a potentially undermining power struggle mentality. When children don't engage in activities that other children consider fun, perhaps by claiming that their "stomach hurts" or they're tired or would rather watch TV, their apparent "manipulation" is usually for a good reason. It's similar to a grown-up who acquires a sudden "headache" to get out of a concert she doesn't want to attend.

SETTING LIMITS GENTLY

The key issue when setting limits for the sensitive child is to be firm but in a very gentle way. The image of Smokey the Bear that we talked about earlier is a useful one. Don't be afraid to negotiate and compromise. But make sure that some outer boundary is firmly maintained.

For example, Hannah sometimes got scared and wouldn't want to go to sleep. It annoyed Bruno greatly. He often ended up yelling, which only led to nightmares and midnight awakenings for Hannah—hardly a good solution. The solution that worked much better on days that Hannah seemed a little apprehensive or in a frightened mood was to begin the bedtime ritual forty minutes earlier than usual. When Hannah started saying, "I don't want to go to sleep. I need another story," or "I need Mommy," Sally gently and supportively agreed that it was a good idea to have another story and a little more of mommy. If the routine was started early enough, Hannah could get three fifteen-minute extensions and still only be five minutes beyond her usual bedtime. In the back of Sally's mind the "outer boundary" was getting Hannah to sleep comfortably within an hour of her usual bedtime. So even if Hannah had managed to insist on yet another fifteen minutes, Sally was still well within the boundary she had set in her mind, which meant she was less rattled and upset if Hannah stayed up later than usual. Different families will have different outer limits.

When Hannah required limits because of aggressive behavior, which tended to occur when she was frightened, Bruno learned not to yell at her, but to get between her and the child she was about to poke, blocking her path and gently encouraging her to use words not fists. His large, reassuring presence, firm voice, and nonintrusive, nonscary demeanor helped Hannah settle down. If she managed to sneak through his legs and get in her poke or hair pull, and if he needed to use physical restraint,

Bruno learned to do it with a Smokey the Bear tenderness. He also made a point of sitting with Hannah for twenty minutes or so in another room, where they discussed her feelings and why it was better to use words rather than hitting. Missing some play-time was punishment enough for the hitting. Sally and Bruno sometimes had to make their point clearer by saying "No TV" for a couple of nights or cutting out desserts.

When a child is out of control, parents need to stay in con-trol. The more sensitive the child, the firmer the parents have to be, but also the gentler. As a special caveat, when sensitive chil-dren require lots of limits, make sure you also introduce more floor time. With the "carrot" as well as the "stick," the relation-ship never deteriorates.

After spending extra floor time with Hannah, Sally felt in a stronger position to say "no" to some of Hannah's more disrup-tive behavior, something that she had been unwilling to do before because she had felt so guilty.

Some parents don't want to do floor time when they are feeling so angry at their child. To be sure, you may need to calm down first before feeling much like spending any kind of special time with your child. But later that day or the next, look for op-portunities to do extra floor time so your sensitive child learns that the warm and loving part of your relationship continues even while she is losing her TV because of her aggressive behavior.

Hannah's story has elements that seem familiar to many parents. For reasons that are not entirely clear, more and more parents are being challenged these days by bright and, at times, adorable children who are excessively fussy, finicky, and demand-ing. Many such children have some of the physical sensitivities we described for Hannah and outlined earlier in this chapter. Chil-dren with these sensitivities find life's daily events more stressful and overwhelming. From the noise of a play group to meeting new relatives to trying a new food or getting ready for sleep, the highly sensitive child is being asked to climb mountains each and every day. But parents are in a position to instill in the sensitive child a sense of mastery based on the very attention to detail and empathy inherent in the sensitive child. By following the five principles outlined here, parents can teach the sensitive child to soothe herself, to become gradually more assertive even in new situations, and to use her feelings and imagination as a means of comprehending what at times is a confusing and chaotic world. Over time, the unusually sensitive child may become unusually sympathetic, creative, and competent.

4

THE SELF-ABSORBED CHILD

PARENTS OF A BABY WHO TENDS TO WITHDRAW OFTEN congratulate themselves on having such an "easy" child. Such babies usually don't cry much and seem content to lie in their cribs or strollers, playing with their fingers or staring at a mobile. Even after learning to crawl, the baby who withdraws may be content to sit and wait for his mother or father to hand him toys. If his parents make funny faces and noises, he glances at them briefly, but then returns to staring at his toys or into space. He may have a hard time making eye contact and seems to be looking inward, uninterested in the outside world—daddy's smiling face, a shiny new toy, the soft summer breeze against his skin. At first, parents may tell themselves that their baby is just more quiet and laid-back than other children. If his motor and language milestones are all as expected and he seems also to enjoy manipulating and figuring out how toys work, they do not worry. Perhaps he is just more of a "thinker" and not very sociable. Some self-absorbed children play elaborate fantasy games by themselves, and one can admire their creativity and imagination.

Sometimes a parent's worries do not begin until the child starts school and shows no interest in playing with other children. Perhaps the child sits alone in a corner of the playground while other children scream and laugh together. He seems to make few friends and is content to stay at home after school and play Nintendo until bedtime.

The parents may then worry or a teacher may become concerned and suggest a consultation for the child to help him become more involved with his peers. At that point, parents of some self-absorbed children come to see me. "I can't figure out what went wrong," they say. "He was such a good baby. But now, something about him just doesn't seem right."

Self-absorbed, passive, laid-back children are the Walter Mittys of the world—more comfortable spinning their own fantasies than functioning in reality. They find it easier to listen to their own thoughts and ideas rather than to focus on the workaday world. They don't fit into the popular image of a "difficult" child. Unbeknownst to us, they cut themselves off from interaction that could help them develop a sense of reality. This lack of communication makes it hard for them to reach the milestones described earlier and to achieve healthy emotional development. Even though some of these children may be articulate and good students, they miss out on some of the essential experiences in psychological development.

THE SELF-ABSORBED BABY AND TODDLER

Parents of a self-absorbed baby, especially a first baby, rarely find cause to worry about their newborn. He may sleep a lot, he doesn't fuss much, and he appears easily satisfied. But later he may be harder to engage. Starting at three or four months, when children ordinarily begin enthusiastically relating to people, carrying on a "dialogue" with gurgles, coos, and bright smiles, it may not be so easy to connect with the self-absorbed child. A mother and father may find they have to work very hard to get his attention. He rarely makes eye contact and, instead, seems to look past his parents. And, instead of objecting noisily to being left alone (as many children would), this child may be content to lie in his crib and stare into space or play with his fingers.

In the toddler years, when other children are beginning to explore their worlds (much to the delight and exhaustion of their parents!), the self-absorbed child may sit more passively. A little boy might finger toys that are placed close to him, but he usually won't busy himself with such toddler pursuits as crawling into cabinets and trying to scoot down stairs. He appreciates, more than most toddlers, a lot of familiarity. He likes to look at the same books over and over again, or to watch the same videos over and over.

While other children are learning to communicate through gestures and facial expressions (and also to understand such non-verbal communication), the withdrawn child may tend to drift off into his own world, playing with a favorite toy or seeming to ponder the mysteries of the universe. It appears to be a great effort for him to use gestures and facial expressions—a key form of communication for toddlers. He uses them intermittently, only when he really needs something.

Parents of a self-absorbed child may begin to notice some delays in their child's development between the ages of eighteen and thirty months. First, his language skills don't seem to develop as quickly as other children's. Instead of beginning to combine words with an already sophisticated "language" of gestures (for example, grabbing his foot and making kissing noises to signify he wants his stubbed toe kissed), this little boy may only look at you and then at his foot and cry. His receptive language skills also may be slow to develop: he may seem confused, or appear to ignore you, when you talk to him.

As I have noted, he may not show much interest in other children. While children his age are beginning to socialize (eighteen-month-olds giggling over a silly face, two-and-a-half-year-olds setting up a tea party or crashing trucks together), the self-absorbed child seems to be content to amuse himself. He may play with a few toys he is comfortable with but won't look at other children or even play side by side with other toddlers in what is called "parallel play."

Sometimes the self-absorbed child also shows little interest in his parents, ignoring them or seeming not to focus on them. This behavior is often what alerts parents to a problem. But, quite often, the self-absorbed child is warm to his parents. He may respond with a shy smile when mom or dad blows bubbles on his stomach. He may like to cuddle with his mother in a rocking chair and enjoy sitting quietly with his father while he watches TV or reads. It's easy for parents who have noticed his self-absorbed behavior around other children to reassure themselves that everything is fine because he relates well to them. But parents may not realize that while the child is indeed connecting emotionally with them, it is not in any kind of assertive way. He is responding to their actions, often physical overtures involving touch, but he isn't initiating the emotional involvement.

Beginning at the age of eighteen months or so, when emotional ideas begin to appear in language and make-believe play, this child may slip even further behind.

THE SELF-ABSORBED PRESCHOOL CHILD

As he gets older, this child's pretend play may lack much spark or creativity. The elaborate dramas that children begin playing as they move through the stages of emotional ideas and emotional thinking don't appear. Instead of plots involving dolls and stuffed animals who chat and squabble, the self-absorbed child's make-believe plots may consist of polite conversation replayed over and over again. Instead of developing a drama in which GI Joes in two armies fight to save a beautiful princess, who is finally rescued by the general of one of the armies, this child may play and replay a thin little scene of a GI Joe doll riding in a car.

More commonly, he may be only manipulating the action figures and touching them. It may not be clear whether there is any theme at all. He continues to play in quiet self-absorption, allowing others to imagine that he is involved in rich, creative fantasy.

It's easy for the parents of such a child to simply let their son retreat into fantasy, assuming that he is simply "doing his own thing." Parents may even take pride in his creativity and skill. But, interestingly, even though these children slip easily into fantasy, their make-believe world is not rich and full. Rather, it has a piecemeal, unfinished quality.

I remember a bright four-and-a-half-year-old who came to see me. He marched into my office for the first time and went straight for the closet full of toys. It was as if he had been in my office a hundred times. By the time I settled down to talk to him, he had organized a scene using four dolls and a house. When I tried to join in, sitting down on the floor next to him and bringing a stuffed bear to the house, he gave me a quick, dismissive glance and kept playing, ignoring my bear. But his fantasy was fragmented; no real plot or theme emerged. The dolls had a quick discussion about where everyone was going to sleep in the house, but then he veered off in another direction. One doll began fighting with another doll, then, abruptly, he brought in a toy tractor that he drove round and round. He talked rapidly, sometimes muttering as he moved the dolls and tractor around the house. I had a hard time following his fantasy.

When I talked to his mother later, she told me that at first she thought her son's immersion in fantasies was wonderfully creative. "It really shows what a great imagination he has," she said with a smile. But after we talked for a while, she acknowledged that she was concerned about him. "I can't seem to reach him," she said. "I can't seem to get him to talk directly or tell me anything."

Whenever she asked him a question, he was silent or replied through his toy Barney. "How about fish sticks for dinner, Barney?" his mother said playfully, leaning down and wiggling Barney's purple tail. Instead of answering, the Barney figure kept jumping up and down on top of a house.

Not all self-absorbed children keep their fantasies simple or confine their play entirely to physical motion. Some are more creative in their fantasies, but they nonetheless share the same basic qualities. They appear bright and verbal: they may even learn to speak easily, and they show a lot of interest in make-believe and play. However, they seem to prefer their imaginary world to reality. They play by themselves for hours on end. When they are a little older, they may become Nintendo or computer game experts and play electronic or computer games endlessly. Communicating with this child about real life—such as what he wants for dinner or how his day at school was—can be challenging.

THE SELF-ABSORBED SCHOOL-AGE CHILD

During "the world is my oyster" phase when children are naturally getting caught up in their fantasy worlds, the self-absorbed child's make-believe has a different flavor. His play may lack assertive or aggressive themes, and still has a self-absorbed quality. He rarely wants others to join in. He may not recruit his parents to play a role, something more outgoing children often demand at this time.

This is the age when children normally begin to flex their muscles and test their relationships—playing one parent off the other, for example. The self-absorbed child may instead stay close to his mother or sometimes to both parents; he may avoid assertive relationships with either parent.

When children begin venturing outside their family and get involved in "playground politics," the self-absorbed child often stays on the periphery. He may prefer to stay home rather than play soccer or visit a friend's house. He often has only one or two friends, who are also quiet and reserved like himself.

When challenged, he may give up easily and retreat to his own world. If a teacher asks him to explain why he thinks the United States should launch a mission to Mars, for example, he may shrug, say, "I don't know," and daydream about having his own rocket ship to take him back home where he can play Nintendo.

The self-absorbed child who is bright and verbal may become quite expert in computer, chess, and video games. A good student, particularly in subjects like math and science, he spends hours in his room doing homework and reading. But he is missing out on the experiences essential to his future emotional development—getting out there and mixing it up with other children. As we have discussed, children hone their capacity for more sophisticated thinking through their relationships with others. The politics of the playground leads them to take their thinking and reasoning to a whole new level of complexity. And it helps them learn to deal with the competitive, assertive side of life.

From about the ages of ten to twelve, when children begin to develop an internal picture of who they are beyond the way their family and friends define them, and when they are thinking about the future ("I want to be a doctor when I grow up, so I need good grades"), the self-absorbed child is still preoccupied with fantasy. He may still worry about "monsters eating me up," usually the concern of a five-, six-, or seven-year-old. His thinking may have a tinge of sophistication, but he seems to focus on issues that are on the periphery of life for most ten- to twelve-year-olds. For example, one eleven-year-old who came to see me spun some interesting theories about various big ideas. He presented me with three different theories about the afterlife, for example. While it was pretty sophisticated stuff, this boy had a hard time talking about the day-to-day events in his life. It was difficult to have a logical dialogue with him about his friends, parents, or teachers.

Over time, this child might develop a negative sense of identity. "I am an unlikable person," he may conclude. "I am easily ignored or avoided. There's no point trying to talk to other people." Or "Nobody cares. I'll just mind my own business."

HOW IT FEELS TO BE A SELF-ABSORBED CHILD

Contrary to how it might appear, the self-absorbed child doesn't prefer his own thoughts and fantasies to the outside world. It's just that, for a variety of physical reasons, it's much easier for him to tune inward. The more a child becomes involved in the "real" world, the more he enjoys it.

Unlike the highly sensitive child, who is easily overwhelmed by *too much* stimuli, this child needs a *lot* of stimuli. He requires a great deal of sound before he takes notice, lots of touch before he feels held, plenty of movement before he feels a thrill.

His hearing is normal but, for some reason (we're not sure why yet) he doesn't seem to respond quickly and easily to sound. Loud noises—the bang of a car door, the roar of a vacuum cleaner, the shriek of an older brother or sister—don't attract his attention as they would other children. As a baby, he doesn't respond to the usual soft coos and smiles of his parents. Instead, they may find that it takes twenty or even forty seconds of talking in an energetic voice ("Hey, Justin! Look at Mommy! Justin!") before he takes notice. He needs to be warmed up with lots of stroking and rubbing before he looks up and smiles at you.

He also may be less sensitive to touch than other children. Instead of reacting with a grin and a wiggle to a soft kiss on the top of the head, a self-absorbed baby may simply continue to gaze around the room as if he felt nothing. As a grade-schooler, he may not react when another kid bumps into him on the playground. He may not be as sensitive to pain as other children: he may not even wince or cry out when he brushes against a hot radiator or cuts himself.

Sometimes a self-absorbed child is less sensitive visually as well. Strong sunlight or a bright light doesn't cause him to squint; he may even like to shine a bright light, such as a flashlight, in his eyes. He needs lots of rich color or bright lights to draw his attention; pale hues don't hold his interest. If he likes to paint, he chooses intense colors all the time.

Much like his craving for bright colors and light, he may also crave a lot of physical stimulation because he is less sensitive to it. He enjoys swings and slides and fast rides at the fair, for example.

Along with being slower to react to stimuli, this child's muscle structure makes it harder for him to tune into the world. That's because his muscle tone may be a bit on the low side. That is, his "flexor" muscles (used to bend the body) are more dominant than his "extensor" muscles (used to stand erect). A baby with low muscle tone has a slumped posture and is slow to sit up. His body feels softer, looser, more "Jello-like" than usual. Relating to the world is more difficult because he has to work harder to hold his head up, turn to look at people, and maintain his focus. His balance and coordination may be poor. As he grows, low muscle tone means he also has to work harder to crawl, push a toy, reach out, jump, and climb. He may also have more difficulty with skills that require sequencing movements (in other words, motor planning). This can include drawing a picture, tying a shoe, climbing a ladder, or moving through a room without knocking anything over.

To imagine how such a child might feel, picture yourself on a hot, lazy summer afternoon. You feel bored, sluggish, not particularly interested in the surrounding world. Your limbs feel heavy. The world seems hazy. You can't quite focus on what people around you are saying; you just want to be left alone. It's an effort to sit up and pay attention to the world.

To further compound matters, the self-absorbed child might also have difficulties understanding what is said to him. This problem often has to do with the processing of auditory information and is sometimes referred to as a "receptive language" difficulty. He has to work very hard to tune into what other people are saying. As a baby, he may have a hard time understanding the rhythm of people's sounds. Whereas most four-month-olds, for example, are able to understand and respond to a complicated vocal rhythm, this child appears confused and looks away. Later, complicated instructions may be difficult to understand. His father may instruct six-year-old Bradley, for example, "Please pick your socks up, put them in the laundry, and then come downstairs to dinner right away." But Bradley, confused, merely stares blankly at daddy. He simply doesn't understand the nature of the command: there are too many words strung together too quickly. So he finds it easier and more relaxing to listen only to himself.

Some self-absorbed children also have trouble with "expressive language," or their ability to put their thoughts into words. They may be slow to talk. When they are older, they find it an ordeal to express themselves. They can't easily find the words to describe what they did, how they felt, or what they want.

Of course, most self-absorbed children don't entirely fit these descriptions. Some children who don't react quickly to many sensations may be overly sensitive to a few other sensations. For example, some children who are underreactive to deep pressure, such as when they are squeezed or massaged, are highly sensitive to certain types of light touches—such as brushing their teeth or combing their hair. Some children who don't respond as well to most sounds may be highly sensitive to a few other sounds, such as a high-pitched yell or a siren. A few are highly aware of their body movements, probably because their low motor tone gives them less control over their bodies. They may be frightened by a slide or a swing. Despite these variations, overall this child is not as easily mobilized as other children by sights, sounds, touches, and other sensations. It takes a lot of energy to get him to focus on other people.

PARENTING PATTERNS TO AVOID WITH A SELF-ABSORBED CHILD

Unfortunately, it's heartbreakingly easy to give up on self-absorbed youngsters without realizing it. Whereas other children "teach" their parents what they need by demanding the right interaction, the self-absorbed child really depends on his parents to lead. He needs energetic wooing in order to be pulled into the world.

Some parents assume that the baby who seems uninterested in relating to them is simply asserting his personality. They have a nagging sense that something isn't quite right, but they tell each other, "I guess he'll grow out of it." They may be naturally low-key themselves and not aware that if they revved themselves up when engaging with their baby, he would liven up himself. Other parents feel drained, with little emotional energy to devote to smiling and cooing at a seemingly uninterested child.

Some parents alternate between leaving the baby to his own devices and then overstimulating him with vigorous rough-housing—poking, tickling, and rolling around with him until he is overwhelmed and irritable. They then may begin blaming themselves, feeling that playing with him only "upsets him." Disappointed, they may revert to leaving him alone before trying to rouse him again a few hours or days later.

Other parents simply find it too painful to keep wooing a child who seems to be rejecting them. "I can't stand it," one mother of a self-absorbed four-month-old told me. "It hurts when I try to play with her. I love her so much, and she hardly even looks at me."

Just as over a period of time the child develops his own self-image, or fantasy, about the world ("I am unlovable" or "Nobody cares"), the parent can also develop his or her own fantasy that interconnects with the child's fantasy. The parent may conclude that "I am a bad parent because my child doesn't love me. I'm a failure as a parent." The parent may have an angry response: "He's not reaching out to me, so I'm not going to reach out to him." Or the parent may create an existential solution: "He needs his space and I need my space, and we are both better off."

A parent's feelings come out in indirect ways. Some, understandably, become critical of their child—yelling at him for ignoring his brother, for example, when actually they are annoyed that he is ignoring them. Or, frustrated by their inability to create the relationship that they had hoped for, they may unintentionally pick at him for relatively minor offenses, such as slumping at the dinner table or leaving a toy on the floor.

For these reasons and others, some parents gradually and often unintentionally allow the child more and more time to retreat into his own world. Because he seems more content on his own, parents may leave him alone for long periods of time in his crib or stroller. At daycare or the babysitter's, busy care providers preoccupied with fussier babies may not give him much attention. Then, after mother and father take him home, they assume he is "tired out" from his long day at daycare and leave him to his own devices while they cook dinner and wind down from their own long day. They may cuddle him, but without connecting emotionally.

It's easy for parents of such a child to remain absorbed in their own activities and work because their child doesn't seem to require much of their attention. He isn't getting into hot water at school (he may even be getting good grades), and he seems quiet and obedient and absorbed in his own activities at home. In addition, the child isn't giving them a lot emotionally. It's important to realize (although we often forget it) that we parents have feelings also. When parents feel repeatedly rejected, they can unintentionally begin looking elsewhere for their satisfaction. The child can isolate himself further and further in his own lonely little world.

HOW PARENTS CAN HELP THE SELF-ABSORBED CHILD

Parents can learn how to pull a self-absorbed child out of his fantasy world and into reality. They can become the bridge between him and the real world until he is able to step out on his own. This involves inserting yourself into his life, ignoring your impulse not to "intrude" too much into his space. In each developmental stage (focusing and engagement, two-way communication, emotional ideas, emotional thinking, the stage of fantasy and grandiosity, the plunge into playground politics, and the development of an inner identity) you need to lend a part of yourself to your child until he is ready to take steps on his own. For example, with a baby, you may make funny noises and faces to draw his attention. The self-absorbed baby takes longer to warm up than most—maybe up to fifteen minutes while another baby might take a few seconds (we'll see how to help an older child warm up to you later in this chapter).

It is important to remember that these children don't want to isolate themselves in their own worlds; it's just easier for them to withdraw than to tune into the real world. The more you can draw your child out, the more you get him involved in the world, the better he will like it (although he may resist at first).

By drawing him out, I really mean gently wooing him. The goal is to make each encounter a pleasurable experience that your child will enjoy. You want to enable your child to get a sense of his own personhood—a sense of himself as an individual in relationship with others. You want him to organize his experiences so he begins to purposefully enter into personal, emotional, and pleasurable relationships with others. The goal is to find opportunities for that visceral sense of pleasure and intimacy that stimulates each one of us to *want* to relate to the human world.

Parents who successfully draw their child out are the ones who generate a lot of emotional energy. They woo him energetically, with a lot of "oomph." There is nothing laid-back about their approach. They crackle with enthusiasm.

That doesn't mean being frenetic or hyperactive. ("Hey, Bobby, look at me! Hey, Bobby! You're not looking at me! Bobby! Turn around! See what I've got! Hey, Bobby! You better look at me or else!") But with your expression, tone of voice, and energy level, you convey the impression of a person with whom it would be pleasant to play or chat or cuddle.

As you are doing this, you want to be mindful of another important goal: fostering the child's own initiative. In one sense, you are inserting yourself into his life. But, at the same time, you are trying to do it in such a way as to inspire him to take charge rather than remain passive. You can't do all of the work for him. Your goal is to motivate him to *want* to join in. For example, with an older child, you can arrange a special activity—a day at a local amusement park—if he will invite another child to bring along. Or you agree to dial the phone if he will ask a friend to come and play. Harness your child's initiative.

Don't hesitate to enter his world. Join him in his computer or Nintendo games, for example. Try to make the competition exciting. If your child is sluggish and not up to the competition, try to even the playing field by giving him certain advantages until he can beat you at least 55 percent of the time. It's best to do this by giving yourself certain handicaps or the child some advantage (such as you can play only with your left hand) so that you can be playing your hardest and keeping the competition exciting though he still has the edge.

You can also use his interest in computer or video games to

motivate him to join in other activities. For example, you might tell him he can play all the Nintendo he wants two nights a week if he will take swimming lessons. If you can create incentives for your child by making activities fun and rewarding, there is a good possibility that he will want to develop his skills and use them in a variety of situations.

At first it may seem like pure torture. After all, you are trying to lure a child from his own cozy world out into the risky open spaces. Don't be intimidated if he gets irritable or even throws temper tantrums. Irritability, tantrums, and the like are, after all, a way of relating to the world. You don't want to provoke your child deliberately into angry outbursts, of course. If they occur, be very soothing and empathetic, help create a calm state again, and accept such ups and downs as part of the process. While most parents naturally prefer to avoid angry feelings, within a certain range a little bit of anger actually helps a child define the boundaries of his own personhood. Many so-called negative feelings—anger, competition, jealousy, and such—have this quality. They tend to generate some energy as well as a clarity of purpose and a sense of definition. A colleague of mine, the psychoanalyst Peter Neubauer, has described in some detail how these seemingly negative emotions sharpen one's self-definition. This is not to say that a lot of rage and competition is helpful; they can overload children. But against a background of warmth, love, empathy, and acceptance, there is nothing like a little bit of anger or jealousy to get the motor going! The self-absorbed child, in particular, has a need to get motivated and get his engine started.

It's as if you are waking someone who doesn't want to get up. He is likely to be a grouch at first. It's easier for him to tune out. But that doesn't mean that he really wants to stay there. With your help, he can gradually join the human race.

Once you get him started, you need to help him *stay* in the game. Two factors can make this difficult: the child's general lethargy and tendency to withdraw and the tendency to avoid certain emotions. You may find that no sooner do you get your child going, then he seems to drift away. You may feel like you are doing too much of the work.

"Getting him to tell me anything about school is like pulling teeth," one tired mother told me. It seems that just as soon as she got her self-absorbed child in a dialogue with her, he "spaces out again." I suggested that she focus less on the *content* of what her child was telling her about school and more on simply whether she was getting him to *talk* to her. That is the critical issue. For example, you may start off talking about what he did in school. Then you may end up moving into a debate about why he should tell you about school, and your right to know— or even about how nosy you are! Just keep the debate, or his critique of you, going. That is just as valuable as his telling you about school. While he is doing this, he is being active, related, and very interactive. In addition, he is showing initiative. If you keep your eye on the process, you will be gratified when your child goes from communicating just two sentences to four sentences and then from four sentences to eight sentences. You won't feel exhausted and depleted because you don't know all about his school day.

You may also notice that your child likes to maintain a fairly low-key emotional state. Any sort of intense feelings are avoided, as are discussions of intense feelings. Your child may, therefore, try to slip out of a discussion about his anger at a teacher or a child who was mean to him or even his gripes at you. Likewise, your child may slip out of discussions about positive, loving feelings or even indications of strong interest in friendship with another child. Intense emotions may make a self-absorbed child feel "It's too hot in here. I'd better cool down. I want my peaceful Nintendo game!" Seeing the feelings that lead your child to want to slip away can help you empathize with how scary, boring, icky, unpleasant, dull, or unimportant he thinks such feelings are. At the same time, your very empathy keeps your child talking about these "icky" feelings he seeks to avoid. Every time you help him stay with these emotions for a few more seconds or another sentence or two, you are gradually expanding his tolerance and reducing his need to run away. Once again, this is a gradual process. But time is on your side if you can be gentle and good-naturedly persistent.

Physical Activity for the Self-Absorbed Child

Different kinds of motions, sounds, touches, and even colors stimulate each child. For example, is your child undersensitive to touch and, therefore, needs a lot of touch to get mobilized? Does he respond to rhythmic movement? Does he react well to bright lights and colors? Once you have an idea of what stimulates him most, you can create the best physical environment to keep him active and mobilized. The child who is not very sensitive to touch may enjoy lots of rough-and-tumble play—rolling on the ground and wrestling with dad and getting piggy-back rides from mom. If he likes a great deal of movement, you can give him lots of time on slides, swings, and the like. You may find that you get your best conversations going while he is on a swing, so you could set up a swing in your yard. If you find that he is undersensitive to sound, you need to talk to him in a loud, booming voice. Music and lots of hustle-and-bustle in the house might enliven him. If he likes a lot of visual stimulation, you could paint his room in lively shades of his favorite color and make sure your house is brightly lit.

At times, you may overdo it. He may get irritated when your rough-housing includes tickles, or you may find he doesn't like high-pitched sounds and prefers low, rumbling noises. But that's OK. At times, it's better to overshoot the mark and learn from your experiences than not try to reach the child.

Physical activity will also help him improve motor tone. Certain exercises can help strengthen those extensor muscles that I mentioned earlier, especially games that call for running and stopping (as in the game "Mother May I"). You could have him lie on his tummy and pretend to be a boat, rocking back and forth. He can also play airplane, putting his legs around your waist while facing the floor and trying to hold himself up horizontally while you spin around. Keep in mind that these activities need to be fun—to feel like play. If they become a chore, they defeat the purpose of helping the child to *want* to interact with you.

With a child as young as four or five, you can start talking to him about his physical characteristics. "Gee," you might observe after your child has squirmed away, "I guess you don't like to be tickled!" You and your child can start figuring out which sensations and activities he likes and which he doesn't. Does he like spinning, jumping, chase games, jumping on daddy's tummy? What's better—jumping on daddy's tummy or having mommy and daddy make him into a "salami sandwich" (the child is "smooshed" between two people)? In this way, the child becomes an active director of his own human gymnasium. Parents may also notice, however, that the child is most alert and vibrant with certain activities that he wouldn't necessarily put at the top of his preference list. Parents want to find ways to make these fun. For example, the child whose motor tone is a little low could probably use lots of boat rocking or "airplaning." He may need a competitive goal ("I'll bet you can't do that for twenty seconds") to make it exciting and fun. Turning physical activities into games, especially the ones the child benefits from, requires ingenuity. But the payoff is big because the child will become motivated to pursue those activities.

As the child lets you know more and more about what he likes, and as you observe the activities that generate enthusiasm, gradually try to let your child take more of the responsibility for initiating them. For example, when dad lies on the floor, making his tummy appealing, it is likely to inspire the child to want to jump on him, as compared to grabbing his hands and saying, "C'mon, we're going down to the trampoline!" The long-term goal is to help your son or daughter enjoy mastering his or her own body. The fundamental principle is to help your child take the initiative and have fun. Critical coaching or constant anger and disappointment from you because he let the soccer ball hit him in the nose or wasn't even watching when someone threw him the ball will only push your child away from the activities that he needs. Empathizing with him about that "nasty ball that surprised you" or how hard it is to watch everything happening on a busy soccer field, coupled with extra practice in kicking and throwing ("Bet you can't hit me in the nose with the Nerf ball!")

can help your child become excited about gaining mastery over his body.

ROBBIE'S STORY

Robbie was four and a half years old when his parents first came to see me. His mother described him as a "mysterious" little boy who didn't seem very well connected to the world. He was gentle and imaginative, but hard to understand. He mumbled much of the time, except when he came out with off-the-wall statements like "I am an egg." He could be warm and affectionate at times, giving his mom and dad big hugs and saying, "I like you," but then at other times he would "shut down," staring into space or at the television or immersing himself in his trucks. "You can't get his attention, let alone get him to talk to you," his mother said. When he tuned out like this, she would make a joke of it by saying, "Earth to Robbie. Earth to Robbie."

He had just started kindergarten (he was young for his class, but his parents had hoped that socialization with other children would bring him out). He tended to be a loner. He was friendly with other children, but had no special friends; he would do things like make funny noises when other children were around, which would sometimes frighten or annoy them. He rarely asked his mother if he could invite a friend over after school to play. When he did, he tended to withdraw and pretend to be an "egg" or a "science book" and refuse to talk to his friend.

His parents, Cindy and George Watson, filled me in on the family background. Robbie was the middle of three. He had a seven-year-old brother and a two-year-old sister. Cindy and George had married right out of high school and were only in their late twenties. Cindy was at home with the children and George worked as a driver for the local mass transit authority. A burly, bearded man with a warm smile, described by his wife as a "big, wonderful bear," he worked hard to provide for his family and was also taking classes at the local community college to earn his undergraduate degree. Cindy, a plumpish, blond woman, described herself as a volatile and emotional person who "lost it" sometimes. But she took her mothering role seriously. She read child development books constantly and took an occasional parenting class through the county. If it weren't for her reading and her classes, "I probably would have just let Robbie kind of do his own thing," she told me at our first meeting.

"I figured at first that Robbie was just really smart," Cindy said. He was already showing lots of interest in science. He could describe how insects digest food and how thunderstorms happened. He loved catching bugs in jars and would peer in through the glass, mesmerized, to watch them scurry about.

Robbie's parents described him as an easy infant, who had slept through the night at six weeks. He was a smiling baby who warmed up to people easily. He slept a lot, so much so that sometimes his mother found she would have to wake him up at 9:00 or 9:30 A.M. By eight months, Robbie was playing peek-a-boo, exchanging balls, and clearly had established two-way communication. But he rarely initiated these types of interactions and often, his mother reported, she would have to work hard to get him "going." For example, he might be holding a toy or a spoon, seeming to study it, and she would have to motion that she was going to take it away to get him to react. Sometimes she could start a peek-a-boo game by taking the spoon and, as he would look up for it, hide it behind her hands along with her face. As he would reach up for it, she would stick the spoon in her mouth and then pull her hands down. Robbie would give a big smile. Cindy reluctantly revealed that often she was unsure whether he delighted more in seeing the spoon or her face. But she also noted that if she played this kind of game with him a lot, he started to seek her out more and she felt that he cared for her. But, she said, "Sometimes I didn't have the energy to keep doing it over and over again."

Robbie loved to cuddle on the living room sofa with his dad when George got home from work and turned on the television. From the way his parents described his play, he could easily get fragmented. He would start banging his hand on the floor when he got frustrated (which didn't seem to cause him any pain).

He was slow developmentally; he didn't crawl until eleven

months and didn't take his first step until fifteen months. "Even then, he seemed pretty clumsy," George reported. "He was always tripping over his feet." Except for an occasional tantrum, Robbie was a fairly affable toddler. He entertained himself for long stretches with trucks and cars, mumbling to himself as he crashed them together. He loved slides and swings and would get very excited about trips to the playground.

His language had come along very slowly and, even now, he was difficult to understand at times. His mother remembered that Robbie didn't seem to communicate very well nonverbally when he was younger. He didn't appear to respond to facial expressions—disapproving looks didn't deter him and encouraging smiles didn't affect him. Now that he was verbal, he didn't seem to understand much of what his parents said to him, and they found themselves yelling at him frequently. When he became overloaded, he flew into tantrums. He was also frequently ill with bronchitis and colds, adding to the stress.

When Robbie turned two, Cindy became pregnant again and frequently felt ill, exhausted, and irritable herself. George was busy with work and school then and said that Cindy's irritability annoyed him. "I yelled at her," he said. "She was acting like one of the kids all the time." George said he always found it frustrating to play with Robbie because his son rarely seemed interested in playing with him. So George mostly just left Robbie alone.

"I try to play with him sometimes," he told me. "You know, just to get him going. We'll wrestle or something like that. He likes it at first, I guess, but he always ends up crying or getting mad. He says things like, 'You hit me, Dad!' or 'My arm hurts!' when I'm trying to be gentle. And then I end up getting really pissed off because here I am trying to play with him. And so I just give up."

Cindy said she, too, found it easier just to leave Robbie alone. "Then he doesn't throw temper tantrums," she explained. As a result, Robbie spent a lot of time in front of the TV set while Cindy busied herself with the other children. "It's easier that way," Cindy admitted.

At the age of three, Robbie had started nursery school at a local church, but he had hated it and refused to go. He also started to get lethargic and tire easily, and his parents took him to an allergist, who found he was allergic to molds, dust, and other substances. Allergy shots had helped. His parents finally took him out of nursery school and kept him home. He had started kindergarten two months ago. Because of his language difficulties, his kindergarten teacher had quickly referred him for speech therapy to help him articulate certain sounds. He was diagnosed as having a word retrieval difficulty as well as difficulty with auditory verbal processing. He got therapy at school for articulation and comprehension.

After a session with Cindy and George, I saw Robbie alone while Cindy stayed in the waiting room. Robbie confidently took my hand in the waiting room, came into my office, and went immediately to the toys. He was a big boy for his age, solidly built, with his father's brown hair and warm eyes. He smiled affably, appearing friendly and engaged, but he avoided eye contact with me. As he made his way over to the collection of Power Ranger action toys on the rug on the other side of my office, I noticed that he stumbled slightly over a few other toys scattered on the floor. He had a curious knock-kneed kind of walk that seemed to send him bumping into things all the time. He brushed by a table piled with books, knocking two of the books to the floor, but didn't seem to notice. He was uncoordinated, moving his arms through the air and pointing at nothing in particular. And, as he played, he seemed to talk to himself under his breath.

Robbie played a bit with the toy house in my office, opening and closing doors and putting small cars and little wooden people inside the house. He played mostly by himself while I watched, although he would always look at me, smile, and make some gestures. If I asked him a specific question, he made an attempt to answer it. I was able to engage him in play when I held a miniature slide upright. He put the little plastic people down the slide and smiled, seeming to enjoy this game. But there was no real story to his play; he didn't add any symbolic content.

Despite his disconnected play and thoughts, Robbie could

sometimes talk in surprisingly complex sentences. "That ball you got," he said at one point, picking up a small, silvery ball that shimmered on my office floor. "It's for magic. I know that 'cause it's so shiny. I saw one in a magic show once. Does the magician use this one for magic?"

My sense was that his mood was even and his attention was focused on what he was doing (in other words, he had mastered the first few steps on the emotional ladder), but he had a lot of difficulty coordinating himself and clearly articulating his needs and wants.

After about fifteen minutes, Robbie looked up. "I want Mommy," he announced. "Where's my mommy?" He wouldn't say why he suddenly wanted her. When Cindy joined us, she sat down with Robbie at the toy house. She seemed relaxed, support-ive, and responsive to his signals. She joined him in his pretend play and, after ten or fifteen minutes of chit-chat with him, the clarity of his language improved. They played out some pretend themes with a whale, the shiny ball, and an octopus going into the house. As they played out the drama, however, I sensed that fragments of a story, rather than a whole story, were emerging. For example, Robbie said that he was scared of the whale and that the whale was hiding in the house. But the outcome of being scared and what happened after the whale hid never became clear; there was no cohesive plot developing between these sub-plots, as you would expect to see with a four-and-a-half-year-old. My sense, in fact, was that he was playing more on the level of a three- or three-and-a-half-year-old. As well, he was rather passive and compliant as he played. "Let's move the octopus outside," his mother said at one point. Silently, Robbie put his octopus out-side and sat waiting for more instructions from his mother.

"Now, let's get the octopus to play with the doll," she sug-gested. Again, Robbie complied, mumbling a bit under his breath as he moved the octopus over to the doll. As he played, he was easily distracted by another toy in the room, getting up as if to explore my collection of trucks. But I was impressed by Cindy's ability to be very patient and engaged with him. "Robbie," she said as he got up. "What about the octopus? Do you think he still wants to play with the whale? The whale looks lonely." She had an unusual ability to be relaxed, tune into him, and create a sense of warm acceptance. Robbie sat back down again and Cindy held out the whale. "I think he needs a hug from his friend the octopus."

But at times, Cindy could also become fragmented, flitting from one subplot to another and not keeping in mind the larger theme. "Why doesn't the octopus ride this truck?" she said at one point. But when Robbie didn't catch up to the new theme immediately, she quickly switched to another subject, asking if the whale had a grandmother. Robbie seemed to tune out again, beginning to mumble distractedly to himself.

In his second session with me, Robbie walked in, again rather clumsily and with a funny expression on his face. But he related well to me, although his engagement ebbed and flowed. He was partially relating but partially self-absorbed. I still found it hard to understand him at times. While he used more complex sentences consistently, some of them seemed to come out of left field.

He saw a picture of a forest in my office. He exclaimed, "That's a piece of clay that's got fire around it!" While examining some of the toys, he pulled the arm off a Power Ranger. He looked at it thoughtfully and then remarked in a garbled way, "The arm is off the Power Ranger. He is from the Power Ranger, but I don't know his name." I wasn't sure what he meant. Sometimes, though, he could take part in short conversations that seemed more based in reality.

"I think you're funny," he said at one point.

"I am?" I said. "What's funny about me?"

"You look funny," he said with a shy grin.

"I wonder why you think I look funny," I said.

"You have a funny pen," he said, pointing to the pen in my hand. It was a bright pink crooked pen—a novelty item that belonged to my daughter. I was using it to take occasional notes as we played.

He could answer some of my questions, such as what his name was, but when we talked about his family, he was confused about the date of his birthday and the age of his brother and what they like to do together.

"Can you count to five, Robbie?" I asked, squatting down next to him as he absorbed himself in the toys.

"One, two, three, four, five," he said rapidly, without looking at me.

"Now, I bet you can do that backwards, too," I suggested.

Still without looking at me, Robbie firmly shook his head. "No."

"I bet you could try," I said.

Robbie remembered the crystal ball from his previous visit. He pointed at it. "It's from long ago," he said.

"What is?" I asked.

"The story," he said.

"What story?"

He pointed to the sparkling ball again. "A witch uses that, I know. The crystal ball tells her what will happen to people."

And then he drifted off again, that funny look returning to his face. "Candy corn made me funny," he said, giving me a bright grin before wandering away to play with another toy. Except for some small islands of realistic conversations, his remarks were fragmented. He tended to withdraw into some private amusement. I sensed that he was a bright youngster who did not have the ability to organize his thoughts or emotions.

At the end of the session, his mother reported that she and Robbie didn't talk in "regular" conversations. Rather, as she explained it, "We talk in his special language." Cindy seemed in some ways proud of the way she had learned to communicate with Robbie but was also anxious about it.

By the end of my initial meetings with Robbie, I summed up for myself his emotional development. My impression was that Robbie could relate well, and he was able to concentrate on what he was doing. But he was unusually uncoordinated in the way he walked and used his hands and he couldn't always make his words clear. He seemed tense when he was by himself and, although he seemed to enjoy his time with his mother, he was passive and compliant, rather than assertive or muscle-flexing in his play, as you would expect of a four-and-a-half-year-old. There were few aggressive themes in his pretend play.

In fact, my feeling was that four-and-a-half-year-old Robbie was functioning much of the time on the emotional level of a two-and-a-half- to three-year-old. I sensed that he had established some idea of shared attention and relatedness, as most children do as infants. He didn't disassociate from the world entirely, unlike some self-absorbed children; he always maintained some connection to the human world. But his relatedness was only partial. He had established some degree of two-way communication—another emotional skill that most children develop as infants—but it was unstable when he was under stress. He would pull away and march to his own drummer in the way he made sounds and facial expressions, the way he used his hands, and the way he used words. Although he seemed able to organize his behavior and even share some ideas logically, there was always the tendency to get disorganized and fragmented and talk more to himself than to others.

It appeared that, like other self-absorbed children, Robbie had difficulties at a number of developmental levels. These difficulties hadn't entirely derailed him, but they had created instability and delay. In many ways, he was a delightful youngster with a lot of creative interests. But he liked to escape into his own world. When he tried to communicate, he sometimes could be logical, but at other times his thoughts would come out in a piecemeal fashion that was hard to follow. It was clear that he hadn't yet mastered the ability to be logical and organize his thoughts as part of his interactions with others.

An evaluation by a physical therapist revealed that Robbie had problems in fine and gross motor skills and in "sensory integration." (He was about six to twelve months behind what we would expect of a four-and-a-half-year-old.) His fine motor difficulties involved what are called "bilateral assistive skills," such as using scissors or buttoning. He also had trouble controlling his posture and processing his movements in space, the therapist said. She also pointed out balance, muscle tone, and motor planning problems. No wonder he was clumsy! Robbie also displayed some sensitivity to certain types of touch and a lot of fidgetiness, and he was easily distracted visually.

On the other hand, Robbie had strong visual motor skills— that is, the ability to see something and then duplicate it (such as copying a design or doing a puzzle), abilities that were appropriate for his age.

My sense was that, in addition to his physical challenges, Robbie's family was also contributing to his difficulties in mastering the basic developmental phases that we expect children to move through. Cindy was a loving but intense woman who could get emotionally fragmented and irritable herself. She had been under a lot of stress herself in Robbie's early years.

Cindy found it hard to help Robbie stay logical when he was getting fragmented. George, who seemed by nature to be calmer, appeared intimidated by Cindy's intensity and stayed out of the picture too much for Robbie's good. He tried to connect with Robbie, but his attempts only overstimulated and overwhelmed Robbie.

It would have been easy for Cindy and George simply to let Robbie drift away. As he grew older, he probably would have gotten more and more absorbed in his fantasy world. To their credit, Cindy and George had recognized the problem and were determined not to let that happen. They loved their son deeply and were motivated to figure out how to help him.

FLOOR TIME: ENGAGING THE SELF-ABSORBED CHILD

Because the self-absorbed child needs lots of practice in relating to other people, generous doses of floor time are especially helpful. But floor time with such a child can be a real challenge. It's tempting to simply take over—to stimulate and let him react ("Here, look at this truck. Push it and see what happens. See it go? Now, push it again and . . ."). On the other hand, it's also too easy to sit back and let the child continue to play in his own world while you watch and let your mind wander.

Instead, you can use floor time to inspire your child to reach out to you, to get more motivated, to get involved in his play.

(Keep in mind that these children usually need a lengthy warm-up period.) Then zero in on his natural interest of the moment and use that as a doorway into his world. Every child has a natural interest; it may be simply wandering from room to room, it may be just staring into space or at the television set or the video game, or it may be examining a particular object or toy. You can seize on those interests and build on them. Say your two-year-old is staring blankly into space and absently running his fingers along a toy car. You could sit down next to him and, after a few moments, reach out for the car. "I'm going to steal that little car right away from you," you could say in a bright, teasing tone. "Here comes my hand!" Your hand slowly snakes over to his toy car (if you grab it away too quickly, he might just let you take it and continue to stare into space). Maybe he responds by pulling his car away. Victory! By building on his natural interest of the moment (staring into space and stroking his car) you have spurred a response.

Consider a three-year-old who is simply staring out the window and who doesn't turn as you talk to her. Let's say the window is on the first floor. So you sneak outside, gently open the window, look in at her with a funny smile, and say, "Why are you looking at me?" This is guaranteed to get either a delighted smile back or a turning away and walking to the other side of the room. In either case, you have kindled the beginning of an interaction pattern.

Keep in mind that when a child is tuning you out, he is almost always tuning *into* something else. Aimless walking, staring into space, playing computer games—all represent interests. Some are more obvious to identify, such as the toy car. Others, like aimless wandering or staring, are harder for us to acknowledge as interests. But they are. In other words, whatever the child is doing represents his *interest of the moment*. You have two choices. You can build on those preoccupations by, for example, talking about whatever your child's interest of the moment is—whether it is what is out the window he is looking through or the video game he is staring at. Your second choice is to get *playfully* between the child and his object of interest. When mommy puts her

head in the window, she is getting between the child and whatever the child was looking at. When daddy teasingly takes the toy
car away, he, too, is getting between the child and his interest.
With an older child absorbed in video games, you can first try
talking about the video game—seeing if you can play or if your
child will at least instruct you on how to play. As a last resort,
getting your hand "caught" in the control switches is guaranteed
to generate some emotion and interaction!

I worked with Cindy and George so that each of them
would engage in at least a half-hour of floor time every day. Once
they were following Robbie's lead, which is the basis of floor time,
they needed to try to maintain two-way communication with
him. Robbie's communication skills—so essential to children's
emotional development—were not well developed, so his parents
had to work on becoming collaborators, or even fantasy figures,
in the drama under construction.

It was hard at first for Cindy and George simply to find a
half-hour a day for floor time. In fact, George responded with
exasperation at first. "I thought bringing him here would kind of
fix things," he said. "Look, can't just Cindy do this floor time?"
Then he added a remark I have heard before from fathers: "She's
better at this stuff than me."

It was clear that we were going to have to find a way for
George to make his relationship with Robbie so satisfying that he
would *want* to spend time with him.

"I wonder why spending time with Robbie isn't more pleasurable," I said.

George grimaced and thought. "I guess it's because he's so
damned tough to talk to." Of course, George was right. Robbie
was hard to talk to. But it also turned out that George simply
didn't have to communicate with his children. Cindy responded
to all their questions and concerns. Robbie seemed quite self-
sufficient, drifting off quickly into his own world, turning his back
on George, and muttering to himself as he moved his trucks
around.

"What do I do?" asked George. "Just sit there for a half-
hour while he does his own thing?"

"Well, it sounds like you're not able to connect with him quite yet on the verbal level—on the emotional level of using words," I said. "So try going to a developmentally earlier level. And, if *that* doesn't work, move back one level even earlier. And so on."

George shook his head. "You lost me."

"Well, think of that ladder of emotional development we talked about," I said. "As a child grows, he moves from somebody who engages emotionally with people, with smiles and hugs and just a sense of pleasure, to a child who uses gestures, like pointing and grabbing your hand, in order to let you know what he wants. After he learns to use his behaviors and gestures to let you know what he wants, he starts using ideas. That is, he uses words to tell you he likes the juice, but not the milk. Or that he likes to play with this toy but not that toy. So the child and the parent go from just being together to using his behaviors and gestures to using words. So, if you can't use *words* to communicate with him, try gestures and behaviors. And if gestures and behaviors don't work, try simply to connect by getting him to look at you or smile at you."

The idea was not to permit Robbie to "space out," but to connect at one level or another.

"Then," I said, "once you have that emotional connection, you can work back up the ladder of emotional stages—from merely getting a sense of connectedness to communicating with gestures and behaviors and then communicating with words."

George looked doubtful, saying with his eyes that it looked too complicated. But he gave it a try.

The next time he sat down to play with Robbie, who was rolling cars, and Robbie turned his back to his father, George rolled his own car next to Robbie without saying anything. He made his car go faster than Robbie's, glancing at his son and smiling as he did. Robbie frowned and speeded up his car. George speeded up his car. Robbie speeded up his car, a smile twitching at his mouth. George made his car go faster, and Robbie made his car go even faster. Pretty soon, the two were racing cars across the living room on all fours before collapsing and chuckling at the other end of the room.

George had found an activity that he enjoyed and could share with his son. I realized that, given George's reluctance to do floor time, it was important to help George see that he could build floor time around his own interests as well as Robbie's interests. George was very interested in sports. "Do you think you could find a way to get Robbie involved in your interest in sports?" I asked.

Once again, George looked doubtful. "OK, but he's going to make it tough."

George hit upon the idea of buying a few baseball cards. Even though Robbie couldn't read, he could look at the pictures. They could look at the pictures together, and George could tell Robbie about the players while Robbie fingered the cards. Then Robbie could tell George about the players he had seen on TV. The challenge was how to join this interest of George's to one of Robbie's interests. The opening came when Robbie was watching the local baseball team on television. George said, "I bet you don't know who that is up at bat." And, as Robbie tuned George out, George flipped the card for that player in front of Robbie's eyes and said, "It's Brady Anderson." Robbie was fascinated with the card, grabbed it, and immediately started studying it.

But George, like many parents in floor time, had to be careful about sailing off on his own tangents. When Robbie set up a nice pretend game with his teddy bear, who "grabbed" all the baseball cards, George wanted to respond with "Hey, don't be so greedy!" Instead, I suggested he say something like "Boy, that bear wants all the cards!" That way, George was gently inserting himself into the action instead of turning the game into a lecture on manners.

With Cindy, we first worked on getting her more animated when communicating with Robbie. Cindy tended to be fairly soft-spoken and rather poker-faced. I helped Cindy pretend she was a mime with very exaggerated facial expressions. We also talked about her expectation that Robbie wouldn't respond, and the hopeless, almost depressive tone of voice that she used with him. To help Cindy become more outgoing and enthusiastic with Robbie, we also explored her own background and how she had herself learned to feel hopeless much of the time. Through this recognition and the chance to practice becoming more enthusiastic and energetic, she was able to start being more animated with Robbie.

"Sometimes he seems so *into* his playing that I don't like to interrupt him," Cindy told me.

"You're not so much interrupting him as just trying to become part of the drama he is creating," I told her.

"What do I do when he tells me to go away?" she asked.

"Congratulate yourself!" I said. "You've succeeded in engaging him, even though he doesn't want you involved.

"You see," I explained, "keep in mind that there are two 'dramas' going on here: the solitary fantasy drama your child is playing and the drama between you and your child over his desire not to have you play with him. In this drama, you aren't concerned with what you say or what your child says. You are only concerned with the *process* going on between the two of you. How many times are you looking, frowning or smiling, pointing or grimacing, or exchanging words with each other? The more interactions there are, the more success you are having. In fact, the play with toys or the story you are developing is only an excuse for this interactive process. So feel successful when you are discussing for ten minutes with your child *why* he doesn't want to play with you or why you are so boring."

One day during floor time, Robbie absorbed himself in playing with his GI Joe dolls and trucks, ignoring Cindy. He was sometimes babbling and sometimes talking to himself. Cindy couldn't quite figure out what was going on. Robbie's "drama" seemed a little disjointed: a fight had broken out, a truck was going somewhere, and one of the GI Joes seemed to be in danger. So Cindy picked out one element of the drama and asked permission to join in.

"Which side can I be on?" she said, sitting down next to him on the floor.

Robbie ignored her at first, finally saying, "Go away."

This time, Cindy wasn't deterred. At least Robbie was responding to her presence, she thought. "Why should I go away?" she asked.

" 'Cause the bad guys don't like you," he said.

"Why don't the bad guys like me?" she asked.

"Because, that's why. Now go away."

Cindy felt pleased. At least she had gotten a dialogue going with her son—a logical, give-and-take dialogue, however abrupt.

Another time, Robbie was playing with his little sister's dollhouse. He put one of the dolls in and out a window and remarked, "The doll is jumping out of the moon." This time, Cindy joined him in the fantasy. "OK, where's the moon going to be?" Robbie gave her a funny look, as though she were a little peculiar for jumping into his illogical fragment of thought. But by entering Robbie's world, however silly the content, Cindy was helping him become more reality-based by showing him how to take into account another person and that person's intentions.

"How can I help the doll jump out of the moon?" Cindy asked. "Is the window going to be the moon?"

Gradually, through exchanges like this with Cindy and George, Robbie began assigning them roles.

"Put your finger here," he ordered Cindy, showing where to hold the doll in the window. "Hold still. The rocket wants to fly to the moon and rescue the astronaut."

Another time, he simply smiled and said, "It's not the moon. It's a *window*."

The idea of using pretend play to draw someone into the real world may appear paradoxical. But remember, what draws a child into the real world is logical give-and-take with another person—not the *content* of what he is saying. The more give-and-take, the more logical the child is becoming.

Gradually, by opening and closing more circles of communication with behaviors and with words, Cindy and George were pulling Robbie into the real world. As they worked with him, he made slow and steady progress. He gestured more and communicated verbally as well. He was still hard to understand, but he used difficult words in a more organized way. He loved to look at books about dinosaurs and practiced pronouncing their names. "That's a pterodactyl," he would say slowly, pointing out the beast in the book to his dad.

His play began to be more organized also. He liked to play with a toy castle he had at home. One time he sat down with George and pulled out some of the toy warriors. "This is Grayskull and this is Space Mountain. These are going to be the good guys and these are the bad guys. They are going to fight." George asked him why. Robbie looked at George as if he had asked a silly question. "Because one is good and one is bad." By this time, Robbie had progressed to the point where he no longer resisted Cindy or George joining in his play by ignoring them. He didn't attempt to pull them in, but he readily accepted their overtures with much less resistance than before. He wouldn't explain what the bad guys had done and what the good guys had done; he just wanted to bang the bad guys into the good guys. He had begun to arrive at the early stages of emotional ideas and emotional thinking—he could make connections between different categories of ideas and feelings. George and Cindy noticed that the theme of good guys and bad guys fighting for dominance continued: Robbie began to devise elaborate strategies for the good guys in their attack on the bad guys. One time in a session in my office, I commented to Robbie that he seemed very interested in understanding how the good and bad guys were going to attack each other.

"I bet there are some good and bad guys at home," I said.

Robbie nodded and thought for a moment as he fiddled with the warriors he had been playing with. He then noted that he was "really mad" at his sister.

"I wonder why," I said.

"She wrecks my things," he said. "And I get real mad."

He let me know that he was always "mad at some people" and that he hated it when people wrecked his things. A theme emerged in which people who overwhelmed him were viewed as "wrecking things." It was his main complaint and could happen at school or at home, in particular with his younger sister but less so with his older sibling.

PROBLEM-SOLVING TIME: ENGAGING WITH REALITY

In addition to the half-hour of floor time a day, George and Cindy soon began problem-solving time. Because the self-absorbed child can easily try to escape from reality, problem-solving time is an especially valuable opportunity to engage the child in confronting actual challenges. Fifteen or twenty minutes a day or more, separate from floor time, are needed to establish some logical give-and-take between parent and child. With Robbie, our goal was even more ambitious—to get some reality-based, logical conversations going as many times a day as possible.

This is where the concept of opening and closing circles of communication becomes important. The only way a child can learn to communicate—to open and close circles of communication—is through practice. Because the self-absorbed child is used to simply ignoring your overtures or retreating into fantasy, getting a two-sided conversation going takes a lot of patience.

As Cindy and George began practicing with Robbie, they learned to be happy at first with only one or two direct responses from him. With a child who has difficulty communicating, the first few responses are the hardest.

"Look at that rabbit out there!" Cindy said one day, pointing to a bunny hopping around the backyard. Robbie looked at her for a second and then went back to playing with a truck. He hadn't closed the circle of communication. Cindy tried again. "Take a look at the bunny. He's got big, floppy ears!"

Still nothing. Cindy made another attempt, keeping her tone of voice light and animated. She'd learned that Robbie wasn't simply being stubborn or difficult. This was hard work for him. "He's eating some dandelions!"

"He better not eat the flowers I planted," Robbie replied.

Victory! His response wasn't gracious or enthusiastic, but that is not the goal. The goal is simply to elicit a response and build on it.

With an older child who has just come home from school, you could ask, "How was your day?" He may ignore your query and turn on the television.

"Hey, I guess your ears are full of that hamburger they served at lunch," you could say playfully. "How was school?"

"What's for dinner?" he may reply. No good. You haven't gotten a response to your communication because your child wasn't logically responding to your query. If the child doesn't build on your comments or questions, then the circle of communication isn't closed and any exchange of ideas that's occurring will, at best, be fragmented or piecemeal.

When children aren't able to close circles of communication, it is due to the collaboration of their parents or parent. Parents often unwittingly fail to give the child practice in this type of communication: they may not spend much time actually conversing with their child or they may not encourage a response. With a self-absorbed child, it is difficult. Children like Robbie require an active, participatory parent to teach them how to be communicative and logical.

With a child who won't respond and instead changes the subject, you can begin by simply empathizing with his desire to watch TV or whatever and point out (gently!) that the two of you haven't finished your conversation.

"While you were at school, I was cooking the most wonderful dinner," you might say. "I can't wait to eat it."

If you're a good cook, you may now have your child's attention.

"I'll make a deal with you," you continue. "If you tell me what you did in school today, I'll tell you what's for dinner." Don't hesitate to be funny or amusing, but try to avoid getting angry, sarcastic, or impatient. To escape feelings of impatience, anger, helplessness, and incompetence, many parents retreat into a pattern of minimal conversation with their child.

The idea is to bring your child back to the theme of the conversation while empathizing with his desire to talk about something else. It's also useful to inquire periodically why he doesn't like what you say or why he won't answer your questions.

It's a time-consuming process, but it helps children to experience a two-way conversation and its rewards.

"I don't want to talk about it," he says in exasperation.

"Why not?" you may ask curiously.

Once you get into a discussion about why he doesn't want to answer your question and why you want him to answer the question, you may be closing three or four circles of communication on that subject without necessarily getting back to your original question about his day. That's fine. As you get rolling, eventually you can talk about friends, school, and many other subjects. But the first goal is to get that dialogue going.

That doesn't mean you have to turn every conversation into an ordeal. At first, Cindy and George tried to work on opening and closing circles of communication with Robbie at least once a day for fifteen or twenty minutes (although that sometimes slipped away in their busy schedules) and then at shorter intervals—three, four, or five minutes at a time—whenever there was opportunity for easy practice.

When Cindy or George asked Robbie how kindergarten had gone that day, he often looked at them blankly or said something apparently irrelevant like "The chimney has water in it." Cindy and George learned to use these unrelated responses as a transition to a more realistic response.

"Did something happen to the chimney at school or with water?" Cindy asked with a gentle smile. "Or are you just kind of saying something to say something?"

Sometimes Cindy or George would discover that Robbie had done something that made his response appear more logical. At other times, he would smile and say, "We didn't do much today."

Often, Cindy and George would try to "cue him up." A child like Robbie with a word retrieval problem may *want* to talk about what's on his mind, but has a hard time figuring out how. He may, for example, have difficulty describing the game or recalling the names of the children he played with, even though he knows what happened.

"Sometimes it's hard to remember the stuff that goes on at

school," Cindy said one day after Robbie had told her they had done "nothing" at school. Robbie nodded. Cindy was pleased. At least she had gotten a logical, if nonverbal, response to her question.

She persisted: "Well, in the nothing that you did, did you do it in story time? Usually on Wednesday you have story time with Mrs. Beattie."

Robbie got that familiar goofy expression on his face. "The owl was in the green boat."

Cindy suppressed her impatience. "Did you read a book about an owl?" she asked.

"The cat ate all the honey," he replied.

Cindy tried again. "And was there a cat in the story, too?"

Unexpectedly, Robbie replied, "Yes."

"What did the cat do in the story?" Cindy asked.

"She sat in a boat."

It was beginning to dawn on Cindy. "Robbie, did you read 'The Owl and the Pussycat' in story time today?"

Robbie gazed off into space for a moment. And then he said, "I think so."

Sure enough, that was the book they had read.

Problem-solving time can also be used to help an older child understand how his physical makeup affects his personality. During the early school years, a child can begin to understand the physical basis for some of his feelings. For example, the two of you can play a game where you figure out which touches, sounds, sights, and so on he likes and dislikes. You can brush a child's hair gently and then vigorously, asking her what feels good. Similarly, you can talk to your child about whether he finds it easier to listen to your ideas or his own ideas and whether it takes more work to listen to you than to tune into himself.

As your child begins to get a picture of his tendencies, you and the child can team up to begin mastering those that present problems. For example, you can talk about how hard it is to listen to other children's words and to consider their feelings because it takes so much work. It's easier to tune into your own ideas.

At the same time, always try to balance any focus on his

difficulties with attention to strengths. The child who has trouble making friends may draw well. Parents will notice that a self-absorbed child's attention and responsiveness will be much better in his area of strength. When children can recognize both their strengths and their areas of vulnerability, they can sometimes use their strengths to help out. For example, one child who fit our description of a self-absorbed child was an unusually gifted poet for a ten-year-old. His parents were encouraged to use this interest to assist him to get dressed in the morning. He composed a jolly poem that contained his whole morning ritual: putting on his socks, brushing his teeth, buttoning his shirt, and so forth. By reciting the poem, he enhanced his usually forgetful motor performance.

Too often, parents and educators sell a child short by assuming his problem with putting on socks or finishing homework assignments is a general cognitive or attention difficulty rather than one related to a specific challenge, such as motor planning.

Children also have a tendency to globalize their difficulties. "I'm all bad" or "I'm always scared," they may assume. What is often missing from children's discussion of their problems is any "gray area" thinking, such as "I'm a little good at this and a little better at that." Talking with children about their views of themselves, and using yourself as an example of a person who has strengths and weaknesses, helps children make these distinctions. Also, as youngsters learn that all children's bodies work a little differently—some are fast on foot and some are fast with words, some are great magicians, some are the world's experts at finding ways to avoid hard work—it helps them put their physical vulnerabilities and their talents into perspective.

Problem-solving time is also an ideal opportunity to get some insight into how you are feeling and how your child is feeling. If he looks forlorn or self-absorbed, you might ask him directly how he is feeling or wonder out loud, "It looks like you're giving up or don't think it's worthwhile to talk. I wonder if you think that nobody wants to listen." You're not trying to read your child's mind or even guess correctly what he is feeling. In fact, you may not get a direct response (after all, how realistic is it to expect a child to say, "Gee, Mom, you're right. I feel lousy. Thanks for helping me see that"?). Your child may disagree with you. And that's fine. A disagreement or a "Leave me alone!" is a genuine response, for a start. Then try to read his expression and see if you can find an empathetic comment to make.

Many parents don't want to hear a son or daughter talk about "bad" feelings about themselves. That's only natural because we love our children so much. Parents often fear that if children talk about these feelings, they will believe them even more. But the fact is that if these beliefs remain private, the child holds onto them more tenaciously. When the child reveals them, however, they become part of the relationship between parent and child, subject to new impressions, to insight, and perhaps to change.

This same effect holds true for you as a parent. If you feel angry because your child is "unlovable," or you fear that you are a "bad" parent, you need to figure out what brings out such emotions. Was there something in your upbringing that caused you to feel this way when someone didn't relate to you? Your spouse might be able to help you, or you may need to seek professional help. Avoiding your child or becoming angry at your child will only make matters worse. We all have Achilles' heels—emotional patterns based on our upbringing that make certain feelings or behaviors hard for us to deal with. The more we know about our own patterns, the more flexible we can be with our children.

EMPATHIZING WITH THE SELF-ABSORBED CHILD'S PERSPECTIVE

It was difficult for Cindy and George to empathize with Robbie at first until I explained to them that empathy doesn't mean *agreeing* with the child's point of view. Your verbal agreement is less important to the child than your interest in how he is feeling.

Whatever a child's coping strategy, no matter how inappropriate, it's important for parents to look at it first from the child's perspective. A child's behavior has a reason. How are certain actions benefiting the child? How do they minimize some pain of the moment?

Parents may be all too aware that the child is digging himself into a deeper and deeper hole by running away from a particular feeling. *They* may realize that he is only causing himself greater pain. But the *child* doesn't see that yet, and if he doesn't sense that his parents empathize with his present situation, he won't collaborate with his parents on solutions.

Cindy and George began to attempt to figure out why Robbie tried to shut them out with his nonsensical responses or by ignoring them. They noticed that whenever he was worried about something or nervous, or unsure of himself, he became more self-absorbed and "spacey." Whether he was trying to deal with competitive feelings about his siblings or other children or the stress of feeling unhappy about something, his way of coping was to retreat into his own world.

Noticing this, Cindy and George gently brought it to his attention.

"You know, I can tell that it's sometimes more fun to play with your truck than talk to us," Cindy said. "You must have a good reason for this."

As they drew Robbie's attention to his tendency to withdraw into himself, he reacted unhappily.

"Go 'way," he muttered.

But Cindy and George stuck with it. When he withdrew, they would say things like, "We've lost Robbie! Where's Robbie?" Sometimes, with sympathetic voices, they would say, "I know Robbie doesn't think it will be fun to talk to us. But maybe he could try."

After weeks of this, Robbie finally burst out with "I'm mad. Now go 'way." Now that Robbie had mentioned his anger and was more assertive about his feelings, we had already achieved a great deal of success.

Intuitively, children know it's better to face their feelings, but they often don't want to. But once they *tell* you to go away, rather than simply withdrawing into silence, they are, in fact, beginning to confront their feelings. And once children talk about the fact that they don't want to face their feelings and nothing terrible happens—they don't disappear, you don't disappear, and the world doesn't disappear—they are encouraged to do it a little more and a little more and a little more.

BREAKING THE CHALLENGE INTO SMALL STEPS: SMALL CIRCLES OF COMMUNICATION

You'll recall that we broke down into smaller segments Robbie's challenge to learn to be more realistic and logical by teaching him to open and close small circles of communication. Cindy and George had started by talking about things in the here and now, such as the toy Robbie was playing with or the TV show he was watching. Then they moved on to asking him about things that had happened in the immediate past, such as at school that day. Then they began talking to him about his feelings. Finally, they had asked him to examine his own coping strategy, which was his desire to escape into fantasy and his assumption that he shouldn't have to face anything that was difficult. Keep in mind that, even within those areas, we were constantly breaking the challenge down into smaller pieces. One or two small exchanges, bits of dialogue, were all we tried for at first.

Why is engaging in a two-way logical conversation so difficult for some children? It's not because they are stubborn, willful, or stupid. Many of them, like Robbie, have word retrieval difficulties; that is, it is difficult for them to recall the words they need in order to express what they want to say.

SETTING LIMITS: STICK TO WHAT IS IMPORTANT

Despite Robbie's progress, he was still throwing temper tantrums, collapsing on the floor to kick or scream or flail around wildly if he couldn't get what he wanted. In the past, Cindy or George had either ignored him or tried to figure out what to do in order to give him what he wanted. We worked together on other approaches. The first was to help Robbie to calm and soothe *himself*. There would be no yelling and screaming when

Robbie was out of control. George and Cindy tried a soothing tone of voice, coupled with certain physical actions—such as firm pressure on his back, rhythmic rocking, and sometimes interactive activities, where Robbie could use his large muscle groups. For example, George would hold him, rhythmically rocking him. Then, still holding Robbie tightly, he stood up with him and wondered out loud whether Robbie could see if he could touch the ceiling. As Robbie became focused in reaching for the ceiling, he sometimes wanted to climb on his daddy's shoulders. Through focusing on his body and reaching, he was often able to get over his tantrum.

Crying was not a punishable offense. However, it was off limits for Robbie to hit or scratch his sister. During earlier problem-solving discussions, Cindy and George discussed with Robbie losing TV time and the use of certain toys if he crossed a certain line—hitting or biting or hurting—even when he was upset and in a rage. In discussing the different punishments that would be used, Robbie was invited to negotiate and suggest other sanctions if he felt that the ones his parents suggested were unfair. While respecting Robbie's opinions, his parents nonetheless had the final authority to set up the code of behavior and the sanctions. I suggested that they try not to limit too many behaviors at the same time. When Robbie did cross the line, his parents let him know, then comforted him and helped him calm down. Once he was calm, the agreed-upon "penalty" would take place. As Robbie was paying the penalty, his parents would talk to him about how he could avoid getting into trouble the next day. And in addition, as must always happen when you begin setting limits, Cindy and George increased the amount of floor time with Robbie so that they could maintain the warm rapport that they had so carefully built with their son.

5

THE DEFIANT CHILD

S TUBBORN, NEGATIVE, CONTROLLING—THE DEFIANT child somehow manages to turn even the simplest activity into a trial. His first reaction to virtually anything is negative: "I don't want to!" "I don't care!" "No!" "Do I have to?" He deals with his world in a very bossy way. In the 1940s, René Spitz, a pioneering observer of young children, suggested that a child's first "no" is an attempt to define himself—a way of establishing a boundary between himself and the rest of the world. Most children eventually move on to a more collaborative way of relating. But the defiant child seems to get stuck in the "no" stage. He

124

seeks to define himself through what he *won't* do rather than what he *will* do.

"My child's first word was 'no,' " one exasperated mother of a defiant seven-year-old told me, "and that's all he's been saying ever since."

Parents most frequently notice this defiance and negativism around transitions. This child has enormous difficulty going from Point A to Point B. Getting out of bed in the morning, going to school, sitting down at the dinner table—all can become long, drawn-out battles. Even activities that the child likes—going to the swimming pool or to a birthday party, going out for ice cream, visiting a friend's house—can bring on the same dig-in-the-heels stubbornness. "Why do I have to?" the child may ask over and over again, even if he really wants to go. "I don't want to."

Alongside stubbornness and negativism, the defiant child has enormous energy and persistence. Many defiant children are also unusually clever, figuring out ways to defeat your most sophisticated arguments. They can also be extraordinarily well organized and methodical, as well as deliberate and purposeful. As such a child gets older, he may also be a "big-picture" person, able to see the forest and not just the trees, and to delve into realms of abstract thinking that can surprise parents, friends, and educators alike. The key challenge for parents and teachers is helping the defiant youngster use these various assets in a constructive way so that, as he gets older, he can use his talents for such pursuits as science, mathematics, philosophy, law, or any other field where persistence and organization are an asset.

THE DEFIANT BABY AND TODDLER

A defiant child's behavior can appear as early as the first year, often as soon as the child begins to learn intentional communication. He may whine, pout, and cry much of the time and reject any attempts by his parents to comfort him. Offered toys, food, or cuddling, he may squirm away or shake his head. "Nothing I do pleases him," parents of a defiant child often complain. As a toddler, this child takes the natural negativism that goes with this age to new heights. He will often seem to deliberately choose the activity that is opposite of what the parents want. For example, a mother tells eighteen-month-old Brittany, "It's dinnertime," and reaches down to pick her up. But, even though she is hungry, the toddler scrambles out of mother's reach. "No!" she shouts, grabbing her toy. "Look," says mother, holding out a carrot stick. "Mmm, your favorite!" But Brittany shakes her head. "No!" she says again.

Of course, every toddler is going to say his share of "No!" But most toddlers are often pleasant, joyful, and cooperative, while the defiant child seems to be *mostly* negative:

PARENT: Do you want to go outside?
CHILD: No!
PARENT: What if we played with your trucks?
CHILD: Don't want to!
PARENT: I know! Let's watch your *Barney* video.
CHILD: No! No stupid Barney!

Keep in mind that the negative patterns I am describing can appear at *any* age. Your child may not necessarily start out with these patterns. You may find that your child is cooperative in the first or second or even third year but then begins to display these negative characteristics in later years.

This negative attitude can extend into all areas of life. The child may be a very picky eater, for example, refusing anything but peanut butter sandwiches and macaroni.

THE DEFIANT PRESCHOOL CHILD

Between the ages of two and four, when children begin using words and pretend play with emotional ideas and emotional thinking, the defiant child's play seems rigid and inflexible instead of rich and creative. Instead of a drama in which a mommy bear takes care of her baby bear during a fierce storm, for example, this child may just line up his teddy bears and move them one by one into a dollhouse. If a parent tries to join in ("Michael, what if some of the teddy bears stayed outside to play. Here, I'll help—"), he may protest furiously, screaming, "No! No! Leave 'em alone. They're mine!"

He may play with only a few toys or games over and over again. He may prefer things to people because he can control objects and bring order to them. He may not want other children in his room or his house for fear they will take his toys or mess up his room. He may not like going to other children's houses because they don't have his favorite toys.

The defiant child will probably be very controlling—insisting that he is right all the time and wanting his own way about everything—bedtime, the clothes he wears, the food he eats, even the people he meets. To the embarrassment of his parents, for example, he may refuse to talk to certain people. "Say hello to Grandma," a parent may say. "No!" replies this child, running from the room.

That bossy, controling outlook also extends to friendships. He may try to insist that other children always play the games he chooses and then gets upset if they won't. Or he changes the rules of games so that he always wins. "No," he may insist during a game of Chutes and Ladders. "The rules say I can climb up the chutes, but you can't. I know it!" Some defiant children are very shy. Others are very verbal—arguing for their point of view all the time.

THE DEFIANT SCHOOL-AGE CHILD

In the early grade-school years, during "the world is my oyster" phase, with its expansive fantasies of heroes and heroines, a defiant child's rigidity may hold him back. Instead of pretending to be an astronaut or a powerful GI Joe, for example, the defiant child's fantasies might be more structured and guarded. He often plays out scenes of control, games in which he is guarding a "castle" from attack, with all kinds of secret weapons. For example, one six-year-old boy I worked with built an imaginary fort in my office. As he explained it to me, his fort came equipped with metal shields to protect it from rocket attacks.

This is the age when children are full of wonder—asking lots of big questions about how the world works. But the defiant child seems more concrete, focused on mastering a small piece of his world rather than embracing the sheer wonder of it all. He might ask the same question over and over. In school, he may be a good student—bright and hardworking—a good reader and good with numbers. In fact, he may be a real perfectionist.

Because he has such a need to feel organized and in control, he prefers to focus with intensity on one task. On the playing field, for example, he may decide that the only position he can play in soccer is goalie; he refuses even to try any other position. In school, he may like to focus on one subject exclusively and dislike skipping from subject to subject. Difficulties arise, for example, with transitions from subject to subject during a typical school day. Later in life, perhaps, he may demonstrate this preference by choosing his concentration in college (chemistry, for example) right away, rather than experimenting with different classes. (He may even date only one type of person.)

In the "playground politics" phase of development, when children normally are exploring the complexities of their peer group, defiant kids often have only a couple of friends whom they seek to control. A little boy may befriend only children who are passive and who will do everything he wants them to do. If he can't find such children, he will complain—loudly—that "the other kids won't do what I want to do." He may come home complaining, for example, that "Maurice wouldn't play with me."

"Not at all?" the father may ask.

"Well, he wanted me to kick the soccer ball with him. But I don't want to play soccer. I wanted him to play baseball and he wouldn't."

He may isolate himself from the group with more solitary pursuits—Nintendo, for example, or a hobby, such as stamp or coin collecting.

In the phase of "the world inside me," when children begin to work out internal identities for themselves, the defiant child defines himself and the world in a perfectionistic way. He may have very high expectations for himself, all As in school, for example. If he gets even one B, he will feel badly about himself and attack himself ("I'm so stupid. I'm the stupidest person in the world!"). And he could have a very moralistic stance toward other children, becoming very critical of them if he feels that they are "selfish," for example.

A defiant child is generally not flexible in his emotions. He tends not to move from the "all-or-nothing" thinking that pervades earlier ages to viewing the world in relative terms, understanding that life often operates in shades of gray. He may find it difficult, for example, to compete with someone and still be his friend, to be rivals on the baseball diamond but then invite the friend over to his house for ice cream afterward.

Because of his strong visual-spatial abilities, the defiant child, as I have said, is usually more of a "big picture" sort of person and less oriented to the details of life. While he seems to obsess about certain details, such as how to get the checker pieces into a certain pattern on the checkerboard, or how to get his stamps lined up in a certain way, his focus on these details is in a narrow range. He does not pick up on the details of other people's emotions, or how they are dressed or what they are talking about. If he is sensitive and worried about being criticized, he may become acutely aware of any sign of disrespect that he senses toward himself. But here, too, he is not sensitive to the wide range of nuances that go on in our interactions between people. He sees patterns in the areas that interest him, so he may grasp concepts in math or in a science project but not patterns in terms of relationships among people. He applies his good abstract thinking skills to areas that he is interested in. The challenge is to broaden these areas of interest and to help him see the subtle nuances, particularly the emotional ones, that characterize day-to-day life.

HOW IT FEELS TO BE A DEFIANT CHILD

Physically, the defiant child resembles the overly sensitive child in many ways. His protection from the world feels thin: sights, sounds, smells, and touches that are pleasant to other people may be downright irritating or overwhelming to this child. He feels invaded by the world. But instead of reacting by becoming fussy and finicky like the highly sensitive child, the defiant child copes by trying to control his world as tightly as possible. Unlike the highly sensitive child, the defiant child has some physical characteristics that make a more aggressive approach possible. First, he tends to have relatively better visual-spatial abilities. That is, he can organize into patterns what he observes better than many other children. He uses this strong ability to help keep himself from getting overwhelmed by what he is experiencing.

In terms of auditory verbal processing abilities, he may have relatively more difficulty with detecting and processing everything that is going on around him than a highly sensitive child. Therefore, in terms of what he hears, he may not pick up on subtle emotion or double meanings in the way that the highly sensitive child can. While some defiant children have excellent vocabularies and excellent command of language, in general, they find it easier to create their own "language" and use their own ideas than to pick up all the messages coming from others.

Like the overly sensitive child, the defiant child may have some motor-planning difficulties (such as putting on socks or copying a series of complex shapes). However, the defiant child also tends to have a little better postural control than the overly sensitive child. He probably has enough motor-planning capacities to use them to remain organized and to avoid situations or challenges that could overwhelm him. In contrast, the highly sensitive child is more apt to let himself get overloaded and frazzled. For example, a defiant child might draw very neat stick people in one corner of his paper—methodically crafting each line—when asked by a teacher to draw a picture of the story she had told. A highly sensitive child might scribble circles, squares, and lines on the whole page, using lots of colors but constructing what could be described as a "mishmash." The meaning of the defiant child's stick figures might be quite clear, while the sensitive child might be the only one able to decipher his creations, explaining that the red blotch was the sun, the green line was the tree leaning toward the sun, and so on.

Our defiant child may be easily overloaded like our sensitive child, but uses his physical characteristics to contain, organize, and avoid. In essence, the defiant child makes a trade-off: because he is so sensitive physically and so easily overwhelmed, he must tightly restrict his experiences in order to stay organized and in control. He is careful not to bite off more than he can chew. He uses his relatively strong visual-spatial abilities to organize those experiences that he does venture into. His "bossiness," controlling behavior, and resistance to new situations, experiences, and people all come about because he has to work so hard to stay organized and in control. No wonder he says "No" a lot! He copes with his tendency to be overwhelmed by restricting sensory and emotional input and avoiding challenging new experiences.

PARENTING PATTERNS TO AVOID WITH DEFIANT CHILDREN

Parents can inadvertently contribute to a child's defiance and negativity by being too intrusive and by constantly imposing their own agenda. With a baby, for example, parents may over-stimulate him by talking too loudly, tickling too many times, and bouncing him around too much. In attempting to cope with all that stimulation, the baby protests with fussing or crying.

With a toddler, a parent who doesn't read the child's cues and constantly insists that the child do things the parent's way can contribute to a defiant child's rigidity. For example, an eighteen-month-old who is playing with a Jack-in-the-box and focused on figuring out how to open the latch to get Jack to pop out of the box is suddenly interrupted by his father. Dad, thinking the child can't do it, tries to move his son's hand forward on the latch. The child defiantly shoves dad's hands away. Hurt, the father inadvertently intrudes on his son by putting an alphabet book on top of the Jack-in-the-box, muttering, "Let's do something else." The toddler, trapped with both hands under the Jack-in-the-box and the book, tumbles everything over and begins a tantrum, banging his head on the floor. His world has been invaded by his father. A power struggle develops, as the toddler digs in his heels even further the more his father takes over.

With a school-age child, parents may unknowingly intrude and overload him by the way they boss him around—even when doing something potentially enjoyable together. An eager father may try to coach his daughter in soccer. Rather than letting her experiment with different ways to kick the soccer ball and perhaps setting up ingenious games, father insists on instructing, ordering, and demanding too much. He gets impatient and angry when the child doesn't want to do it daddy's way. The whole enterprise disintegrates into a struggle between an irritable dad and an ever more defiant child.

Parents sometimes contribute to a defiant child's rebellion by getting the child involved in too many activities. Actually, the number of activities is less important than the way in which parents get involved. If the activities are fun and spontaneous and the child is learning through discovery, parents find that their child has lots of energy. On the other hand, if the child is feeling bossed around and controlled, it can dampen even the most energetic child's enthusiasm. (If you have had a controlling, intrusive boss at work, then you know how such an attitude can rob you of your motivation and desire to participate and excel.)

In general, parents who are very rules-oriented or rigid are more apt to set up monumental power struggles with the defiant child. When they also often take the child's behavior personally, seeing his negativity as aimed directly at them instead of as an attempt to organize his world, the situation is compounded. "He's just doing that to make me angry," such parents tell me. There is nothing wrong with having rules and standards of conduct for your child, of course, but too many arbitrary rules and regulations can drive a defiant child into doing precisely the opposite of what you are demanding of him.

These struggles, I have found, are often played out around certain recurrent issues. The parent insists that homework be done at a certain time or in certain ways. "You have to do your homework before dinner, in your room, at your desk with the radio off and the door closed!" Such rigid rules almost inevitably set up a nightly struggle that exhausts everyone. Another incendiary issue is clothes. The child may want to wear an old cotton shirt and comfortable, worn jeans to school while the parent insists on a newer, stiffer shirt and pants. "You're not going to leave *my* house looking like *that*," parents will say. The child's response, of course, is "I won't wear that junky stuff you want me to wear!" And another battle is under way.

Even more important for the child's response than parents wanting their way is the style by which they try to get their way. When it comes to homework, cleaning up toys, or respecting other people, parents can persuade, negotiate, and set limits in a calm, empathetic, and supportive way. In contrast, an "in your face," domineering attitude is sure to set up or intensify the child's defiance.

When these struggles become entrenched and parents come to me for help, I see several different types of responses. I see parents (often, but not always, a mother) who feel defeated, frustrated, angry, and depressed by the running battles. They feel guilty and are embarrassed by their child's behavior—what they see as his horrible manners, his rudeness, his sloppiness. Feeling helpless and angry, they rage at the child, throwing temper tantrums themselves.

Another reaction I see from parents (often fathers) is a punitive, "You-won't-get-away-with-this" stance. This father is a law-and-order kind of guy who expects to be obeyed. He may punish the child frequently, often physically, hoping to force or scare him into better behavior.

"If you don't sit straight at this table, you're going to your room for an hour," he may roar at the dinner table each night at his slumping child, who merely stares back in defiant silence. "All right, that's it! Go to your room, and I don't want to see your face until seven o'clock!" As this scene is repeated over and over again about major and minor issues, a fierce duel between parent and child develops. The parent tries to intimidate or scare the child into backing down. While this approach may frighten some children into obedience (although the parent will have sacrificed the child's goodwill and respect in the process), the defiant child only digs in deeper. Open negativism turns into stony passive resistance. His grades suffer. He may get headaches and stomach aches. He may use more primitive mechanisms to battle back. At the extreme, he might even begin wetting or defecating in bed. But often he will still refuse to give in. As the battles between parent and child rage on, the whole family begins to suffer. By the time such a parent reaches my office, he is often so enraged that he is willing to sacrifice anything not to lose face. Mortified at the prospect of appearing weak and impotent, he forgets that his adversary is just a child. "I don't care what happens," I hear from such parents frequently, "he will not be a spoiled brat!"

There is yet another worrisome parental pattern that I sometimes see among parents of defiant children. They become so drained of energy in the power struggles, and so angry at their child that, without meaning to, they inadvertently become less nurturing and empathetic. There is less love and understanding in the family as a whole, and sometimes between the parents as well. Parents tell me, "I love Joey deeply. Because I love him so much, I get frustrated and withdraw like that." Unfortunately, children pick up on this response. One eight-year-old child told me, "I know my parents love me, but they hate everything I do." As the special nurturing care in the family erodes, not infrequently children will tell me, "I wish I were never born" or "Sometimes I think it's better not to be alive." Or the child may simply wall himself off more and more in a defiant corner, refusing to be a part of the family. A parent's lack of nurturing, added to overintrusiveness, is a double whammy that very few children, especially those with a defiant nature, can deal with. Most often this double whammy intensifies the child's difficulties.

HOW PARENTS CAN HELP THE DEFIANT CHILD

The most important way to help your defiant child is to become aware of his underlying insecurities and vulnerabilities and be as soothing as possible. Underneath the child's defiance is his inability to let you know directly how much he needs you and how much he depends on you for comfort and security. The only response he knows is to act defiantly (hardly a way to win friends!). Therefore, you want to first gain your child's trust and confidence and somehow slip under his defiance so that you can offer him what he needs.

Establishing Trust and Security

Establishing trust and security is not easy, of course. For example, when you ask your eight-year-old how school went and he replies, "Don't ask all the time! Why do you care?" it's hard to see his underlying vulnerabilities. It is easier to be soothing with a highly sensitive child who is clingy and frightened than with a defiant child. The defiant child, with his constant need to be the boss and his ongoing power struggles with you, makes life more difficult. Yet it is crucial to remember that this child is just as prone to being overwhelmed and overloaded as the highly sensitive child. The defiant child uses bossiness and defiance in an attempt to feel secure. To protect himself, he shuts out part of the world—including his parents at times. Your goal is to provide tender, loving care in spite of his negativity and defiance.

At first such a child may not trust you completely. He is not sure whether your attempts to soothe will be comforting or upsetting. He is so accustomed to taking charge, and so fearful of intrusions, that he feels he can trust only himself. You have to convince him that *you* can be comforting. Review in your mind the kinds of experiences that tend to be soothing for him. Which kinds of sounds help him relax and which are upsetting? Does he like light or firm touch? Does he prefer soft music boxes or rhythmic beats? Is he sensitive on certain parts of his body—his feet, perhaps, or his head, or his mouth? If he is a baby, what kinds of rocking motions does he like? Fast? Slow? In an older child, does he like to run fast or just putter along? Does he like you to be laid-back with him or very focused on him and very enthusiastic? Over time, by watching and playing with your child, you can build a profile of his likes and dislikes. Then you can use that profile to adapt your approach in trying to calm and comfort him.

Start slowly and gradually. With a sixteen-month-old, for example, who pushes your hand away or turns his back when you try to play with him, sit just outside his "boundary," so you don't intrude. Find some way to relate to him—working down the ladder of development if need be. That is, if you can't get him to brighten up by talking to him, try using gestures—point at the block tower he is building and put one of your blocks right at his "boundary." Maybe he will reach out and take it. But if he still responds with irritation—pushing your block away, for example—back off and go down one developmental level. Try just exchanging some attention: see if you can exchange a smile and a flirtatious glance with him. See if he'll respond with a little grin. As you do this day in and day out, you should start seeing him loosening his "boundary" and begin relating to you in more complex ways. From exchanging glances, you can move up to exchanging gestures (you hand him a block, he accepts it and adds it to his tower while you clap softly and smile), and then to exchanging words (you say, "That's a great tower!" he says, "Want more blocks!"). Soon, he will learn to be more flexible and will be relating to you at whatever developmental level he has reached.

You can follow the same strategy with a preschooler. If your child is lining cars up in a row, come in as close as you sense he will let you. Offer to help him make his line of cars longer. Keep your motions slow and relaxed. Try to remember to use voice tones that he is comfortable with. If he is sensitive to touch, be respectful of that. You probably don't want to muss his hair or pinch his cheek, for example, if he doesn't like being touched on the head or around the face. Be especially cautious about trying to control his body with grabs or unwelcome hugs. It's better to let him know you are available through a warm look and outstretched arms, gesturing your interest in hugging him and seeing if he'll meet you halfway. Wherever possible, let *him* be the boss.

With an older child, the same principles apply. Approach him slowly. Make sure your movements and voice tone are as relaxing to him as possible. For example, your eight-year-old is sorting through his baseball collection and reciting batting averages. "Cal Ripkin batted .280 last year," he says as you enter his room. You sit down on the edge of his bed, respectful of his "boundary" and say quietly, "Oh, I didn't know that." Your goal is to establish a calm relationship on his terms. Let him boss you around. If your child is playing Nintendo ask if you might play together and let him assign you to your role.

Even more than with most children, the general goal with the defiant child is to be warm, soothing, and respectful as much as possible. Meet his inflexibility with flexibility. For example, you're helping tie his shoes. He pulls his foot away—"Not so tight, stupid. It hurts my foot!" Instead of saying, "Don't talk to me that way!" you could take a deep breath and say, "I guess your foot is a bit sensitive," as you tie his shoe one more time. "Is this way better?"

At another point (when he isn't feeling so finicky) you can raise the more general issue of why he gets so mad at you and calls you "stupid" whenever you're not "perfect." Here, you can help him reflect on the fact that maybe he is being extra hard on you. As you help him see this pattern and encourage him to become more flexible, remember that he is probably being harder on himself, calling himself "stupid" or worse. For this reason, a defensive strategy ("You can't talk to me like that!") and then blowing up with anger over his "spoiled, insensitive" behavior (understandable though that response may be) not only doesn't work but strengthens the child's defiance. Whatever your child is doing to you, he is probably doing worse to himself. When you come down on him too hard, you may only intensify his own self-criticism and probably even self-hatred. Empathy and flexibility, coupled with quiet explanations help him see that he is being hard on both you and himself.

Setting Limits

Firm limits also need to be implemented. Being empathetic doesn't mean always giving the child what he wants. But when he is being refused another helping of ice cream or punished for kicking his sister or trying to scratch his mother, the limit setting needs to be done in a firm but very gentle (and I stress "gentle") manner. Gentle limits coupled with empathy and flexibility will gradually help your child be less critical of you and himself.

Expand the child's dialogue about what comforts and what bothers him. For example, say he doesn't like the way you put his shirt on. So you try again, only this time asking him to help direct you so that you are exchanging lots of words and gestures and, at the same time, following his general guidelines. This tends to ease the tension. Trying too hard to get it "right" or putting the shirt on him in a rough or annoyed fashion will start a battle. As you build his trust and confidence in you, he begins to see you as a colleague who can help him, rather than as an adversary out to get him.

In response to such advice, parents tell me they fear they will "spoil" or overindulge their child and worsen his angry, demanding behavior by being so understanding. I tell them that parents can't spoil a child by helping him to feel more secure. They spoil him by not setting limits. Underneath a spoiled child is a child who thinks, "I can't get the boundaries I need. I have to push more and more and more because nothing works." But you need to set limits on his aggression, not on his need for comfort and security. You don't set limits and soothe at the same time. And you need infinite patience—not an easy thing to accomplish.

In setting limits, take advantage of your child's debating skills to hash out rules, rewards, and punishments in advance together. Try to avoid surprises and avoid throwing a tantrum yourself.

Also, it is best to try to avoid situations where a family becomes so stressed and exhausted that the parents stop nurturing each other and a great deal of anger develops in the family. Under those circumstances, one parent commonly tries to overprotect the child in an anxious, hovering way, unsettling the child with his or her needy intrusiveness. And the other parent, feeling deprived and jealous, often becomes overly punitive with the child. It's only when parents have their own needs met that they can be truly gentle and collaborative in setting the required limits.

Encouraging Self-Awareness

As your child gets older, help him to become aware of his own sensitivities and tolerance level. Help him to see what he does and what he doesn't do when he gets overloaded. Urge him to verbalize his feelings and develop a reflective attitude toward his sensitivities. That way, he eventually learns to prepare himself for challenging situations. Because this child is so sensitive to feelings of embarrassment and humiliation, his needs must be respected. But, at the same time, see if you can build in some humor as well. Shared jokes about his perfectionism and critical attitude, if done in a warm and accepting manner, allow him to become aware of his sensitivities. Help him acknowledge some of his tyrantlike and greedy tendencies. "I guess more is always better," you may tease gently. Or you could jokingly ask him how he thinks you should be tortured for being so imperfect!

While empathizing with such a child is difficult, it can be made even harder by his aversion to being patronized. You may find, for example, that comments like "I know it must be hard" when said in an exhausted tone of voice will not have the desired effect. On the other hand, using both empathy and humor to help your child verbalize his anger and outrage may prove especially helpful. For example, if he is glaring at you and muttering under his breath, complaining that the soup is still too cold or too hot, a remark like, "Gee, I guess you're ready to fire me" or "I guess you think I'd better practice my cooking a little bit more" will respect your child as an intelligent, though outraged, individual and is more effective than a patronizing "I know how sensitive your little tongue is."

Parents benefit from self-awareness as well. Sometimes parents feel some embarrassment and guilt toward defiant or stubborn aspects of themselves. Without being aware of it, they may see pieces of themselves in their child and, if they hate that part of themselves, they will often take that hatred out on the child, rather than be aware of its origins. All of us have negative characteristics that we aren't proud of. These hidden "truths" often resonate with characteristics in our children that we don't like. It's as if all the "bad elements" in the collective family psyche hang out together. Being aware of these patterns allows us to take a more supportive and empathetic posture with our children, rather than an overly critical one.

A defiant child can also learn to choose certain physical

activities to decrease his oversensitivity and overload. Many of the same physical exercises I describe for the highly sensitive child are also helpful for the defiant child: jumping with joint compression, large muscle movements, and rhythmic actions in space (such as swings or spinning games). Be sensitive to the particular patterns of sensations that comfort your child. Again, the most important thing to remember as you develop a program of physical activity is that the defiant child needs to be the boss. Let him direct how fast mommy is swinging the "airplane" or how many times in a row he wants to jump on daddy's tummy.

KYLE'S STORY

"Kyle Lehman, what are you doing?"

Katherine Lehman stopped at the door of the family room and stared at the scene in front of her. Toys blanketed the floor. Trucks were overturned, blocks spilled out of containers, board game pieces were tossed on chairs, and Kyle's collection of Power Rangers was scattered everywhere.

"This place is a mess," Katherine said, trying to keep her tone of voice light as she surveyed the chaos and her six-and-a-half-year-old son planted in the middle of it, his face slowly hardening into a scowl.

"I'm playing wars."

"Well, I think you can play wars in a neater room, don't you?"

Kyle shook his head. "No."

"Kyle," Katherine began, "I'm just asking you to pick up a few things—"

Kyle shook his head again and folded his arms. "*You* clean it up! I'm busy!"

"Kyle. . . . " Katherine could feel her face tightening and her voice rising despite her best efforts. "Mommy says you need to clean up a little bit." She so much wanted to avoid another pitched battle with her son. It would be the fourth one today. But she could sense it coming.

"It's not my job," Kyle's voice was rising and he kicked a pile of trucks at his feet. "That's *your* job."

"Kyle. . . . " Katherine stepped forward.

"You're stupid. A stupid, stupid mommy!" Kyle shouted and kicked at another pile of trucks. "You're a poop head, too. I'm playing wars!"

"What's going on?" thundered Gary Lehman, appearing at the door, annoyed at the commotion.

Katherine felt tears in her eyes. Nothing was simple with her son.

"I just wanted him to put away a few toys," she said, "and—"

Kyle collapsed on the floor kicking and screaming. "I hate you. I *hate* you!" he howled as he rolled through the mess. Katherine threw herself against Gary and dissolved into tears.

By the time Katherine and Gary came to see me, they were at the end of their rope. Scenes like the clean-up fiasco in the family room were erupting several times a day, and they were exhausted.

"Sometimes I think I am the worst mother in the world," Katherine wept in my office while Gary sat rigidly, an angry look set on his face.

"She's a tremendous mother," Gary told me. "But Kyle is just unbelievably impossible. We can't do anything with him. There are days when I think we made a mistake."

Gary and Katherine, who were in their mid-forties, had adopted Kyle from Korea at the age of three months after years of struggling with infertility.

Kyle had seemed like a dream come true when he first arrived, with his dark eyes, pudgy face, and silky black hair. In fact, so delighted had they been with Kyle that they had started proceedings to adopt a second child. Rebecca arrived two years later from Korea when she was four months old. She was now four. The two children had completed the family that Gary and Katherine had dreamed of since they got married twenty years ago. But Kyle's behavior was turning that dream into a nightmare.

"He never quits," Gary told me, striving to keep his anger in check. "He's always pushing us. He'll never do as we say—even the simplest thing. He's an absolute tyrant in the family."

Kyle would come downstairs in the morning and order his parents to serve him breakfast. He insisted on having everything a certain way—throwing a temper tantrum, for example, if his mother or father was sitting in "his" seat at the breakfast table.

"It's impossible, just impossible, to get him ready for school," said Katherine. Kyle refused to get dressed, and his parents had resorted to stationing him in front of the TV, turned up loud, while they hastily stuck a shirt and pants on him. Katherine, a schoolteacher, left early for work while Gary struggled to get a recalcitrant Kyle to the bus stop and Rebecca dropped off at the babysitter's.

At school, Kyle was a little more cooperative. He was a good student, his teachers reported, though he grew extremely frustrated if he made the slightest mistake. Writing in his "journal" each morning, he angrily crossed out entire pages if one of his letters didn't come out "right." In class, his teachers said he had trouble moving from subject to subject and would act up, throwing pencils and rough-housing with the other boys, when the class was asked to put away their pencils and gather for another activity.

He had few friends, mostly because he insisted on bossing other children around.

"That's a stupid game, I'm not gonna play," he would announce at recess if a child tried to play with him. He had one friend, Adam, whom he idealized. When Adam was away, Kyle missed him a great deal.

In the afternoon, when Katherine picked him up from school, there were more struggles over changing clothes and moving to the next activity. Katherine had enrolled Kyle in several after-school programs, including soccer, T-ball, and basketball, depending on the season, as well as a karate class, which Kyle adored.

But it was in the evenings that the worst fights broke out. Kyle pulled out all his toys and refused to clean up before going to bed. "You can't make me!" he would shout. Bedtime was an epic battle. After years of trying to enforce a regular bedtime, Katherine and Gary had just given up. They usually just waited until Kyle collapsed on the floor in front of the TV and then carried him to bed and cleaned up themselves. At night, Kyle usually awakened at least once, demanding juice before he would go back to sleep.

Katherine and Gary finished telling me about their son and looked at each other. "Of course, we love him very much, but sometimes . . ." Gary's voice trailed off.

Gary was an electrical engineer for a defense contractor in the Washington area. He clearly was uncomfortable being in a psychiatrist's office and kept glancing nervously around my toy-strewn office. A tall man with thick brown hair and rugged good looks, Gary grew up in an Army family that had moved around a great deal. He was a very involved father, coaching Kyle's sports team and helping him ("When he lets me") with schoolwork. He and Kyle loved to rough-house together, rolling and wrestling on the ground. But Gary liked an orderly life and believed that children should obey their parents. He was constantly setting out rules for Kyle, only to see Kyle ignore or defy them. If Gary forbade toys in the living room, for example, he would come home from work to find Lego parts scattered all over the living room floor. If Gary tried to limit TV to a half-hour a day, Kyle would insist on watching shows his parents knew he wasn't even interested in. Gary would end up shouting at Kyle, who often responded by shouting back or turning his back and ignoring his father, further angering Gary.

Katherine also liked order and structure in her life. She was feeling defeated with and angry at her son.

"I'm a teacher," she said. "I should know how to handle children like this." Embarrassed by her son's behavior, Katherine assumed that there was something wrong with her mothering.

After this introduction, it was time to meet Kyle. He turned out to be a slight boy with dark, wary eyes and black hair cut short. He came in to my office willingly, looking around my office.

"What toys do you have?" he asked. He turned his back and seemed only to want to use me for help in finding an extra toy or action figure to manipulate in his drama. He set up two rows—the good guys and the bad guys—and took meticulous care in making sure there was a clear line separating them. When I asked what they were doing or why they were lining up in two groups or what made some of them good and some of them bad, he peered at me with an annoyed look as though he was a father figure telling his kid to be quiet and not interfere. As Kyle was setting out figures for play, I eventually got the idea that the setting up of the figures was, in fact, probably going to be the whole drama. As such, the plot never developed emotional depth or richness and, instead, continued to focus on themes of how these action figures were going to be organized and deployed. The good guys had all kinds of secret shields that could protect them from the bad guys as well as weapons that could dissolve the bad guys' rockets. Kyle described this in terms of the good guys never getting hurt and being able to hit the bad guys' rockets with their special zappers. But he never quite let me be a part of his drama.

When Kyle finished playing, we began talking about his daily life. First we talked about his friends. "My best friend is moving, but he'll live close so my mom can drive me to see him," he told me. He said his friend only had Nintendo to play with because "all his other toys are all packed up." Kyle struck me as very logical and thoughtful in his descriptions, although he seemed eager to skirt the emotional aspects of his friend moving.

Kyle said his parents weren't always "nice" but then, when I inquired what was "not nice" about them, he ignored me and began to line up his action figures again. Repeatedly, he would escape into his pretend play or just flat out ignore what I had asked. When I pressed at one point, saying that it seemed that he didn't want to tell me about his parents, he said testily: "I told you. They're not always nice." He talked a little about his sister. "She has an ear infection," he told me. "She's nice but she can also be a pain. She breaks my stuff but then if I push her, I get in trouble."

He drew some pictures for me, holding the marker awkwardly. Although he didn't have very good control, he seemed to have a good concept of what he wanted to draw on the page. He attempted to craft his shapes slowly and methodically and tended to make small shapes that fit into one corner of the page. "I'll make a bird," he said, but couldn't quite execute the drawing.

During this first session, I summed up Kyle's developmental abilities for myself, as I do with all the children I see. I observed that Kyle's development was appropriate for his age. He could tell the difference between reality and fantasy. Language, understanding, and logic were well developed. However, he was somewhat constricted in emotional range. Themes of control or avoidance dominated, and other emotional themes, such as anger, assertiveness, showing off, sexual curiosity, neediness, and dependency, didn't emerge either directly or indirectly.

When Kyle came in for a second session, I was impressed by his great expressive and receptive language ability. He understood and clearly answered all my why, how, and what questions.

He started telling me about school, and I asked him what he liked about it.

He thought for a moment. "Recess," he said. "And playing with the trucks during play time."

As our session progressed, he took out the pieces of a toy farm and played out a scene with a cow who got onto a farm truck with other animals.

He seemed to want to assign roles to each of the animals. "See, this one is fixing the motor," he said, pointing to a toy pig. "And this one is driving, and that one is going to be the passenger." I was struck by his great attention to detail and how systematically he assigned roles. While he was willing to inform me about what he was doing, whenever I tried to talk to him as a passenger or a farm animal, he gave me a disapproving look and turned slightly away from me.

Then I asked him whether he wanted me to talk or not and how he felt about my talking. He said, "Animals can't talk." I was very impressed with his clever retort. I expected to see a sly grin and a twinkle in his eye but, instead, he looked serious, and he continued manipulating the farm animals. When one of the farm animals accidentally fell off the truck I asked him, "How does that animal feel?" I tried to get him to elaborate on different feelings—either through the animals or with regard to himself. We talked first about scary feelings. He told me he was "scared of the dark, especially when it gets dark at night."

A little later in the session, I turned to the subject of anger. He said: "Sometimes I cry if my mom takes away TV when I hit my sister." He paused, fingering the toy cow, looking at it as he talked. "They take her side." I asked him how that made him feel, and he said, "I cry." He also said suddenly, "I won't kiss my mother." And, a minute later, he said, "I won't clean up my toys." He poked hard at the toy cow. I followed up by asking him how he felt when he cried or wouldn't pick up his toys.

"I don't know." He looked annoyed and a little sad. Still later, I asked him if he knew what got his parents upset sometimes. He had another quick comeback. "Ask them," he said, still looking serious.

Subsequently, when we explored his happy feelings, he looked at a particularly interesting Transformer that was lying there and said, "I'll be happy if I can take that home." He also volunteered that "sometimes my mom gives me good stuff to eat, like hot dogs and pizza."

Near the end of the session, I did some brief listening and visual exercises with Kyle, seeing if he could remember numbers backward and forward and copy certain shapes. He had a little bit of difficulty with reproducing the shapes. His diamond looked more like a square. But he worked very hard at it, holding the pencil tightly. He knew all the shapes he was supposed to copy, and he described them and laid them out in the same sequence as the form that he was copying. He could recall six numbers forward, but when I asked him if he could give me the numbers backward, he couldn't quite get the concept. He couldn't repeat two numbers backward. Many children his age can do two numbers backward, and some can do three.

At the end of this session, I was again impressed by Kyle's ability to organize thoughts, negotiate between fantasy and reality, control impulses and mood, and keep his behavior organized and consistent with the implicit rules of the playroom. However, I was also impressed with the fact that he was constricted in his ability to elaborate a range of feelings in make-believe play, this time keeping it more contained around the farm animals rather than the action figures. He also showed in a more specific manner that he did not yet have the ability to elaborate on his different feelings. When anger was discussed, for example, he could describe some of his behavior, such as crying and refusing to do required chores, rather than elaborate with words or pretend play on his angry feelings (such as sharing a wish to retaliate toward his sister or get even with his mother or father or create a fantasy where aggression was a theme). Also, I noted, he tended to deny anger and jealousy toward his sister.

In a separate session, Kyle's parents filled me in on his development. When he had arrived at their home at the age of three months, he was fairly finicky and demanding, his mother recalled. "But we just assumed that it was because of the big change in his life," she said. Kyle cried quite a bit, and they learned that stimulating environments—such as a crowded, noisy room or too many distractions—would cause him to cry even louder. He was a very alert baby.

By four months, he was responsive and smiled engagingly. He enjoyed being talked to and loved funny faces. If Gary gently tossed him in the air, however, or talked to him playfully in a low, gruff voice, Kyle had wailed. And when he cried, it was very hard for him to stop. Katherine recalled that while Kyle was often delightful, he seemed to demand that his parents cater to him in a certain way.

"We wound up taking him for long rides in the car to settle him down. Whenever we tried to cut the ride short, he seemed to rev up again," she said.

"After all those years of trying to have a baby, I guess we had expected the perfect child," said Katherine. The adoption agency had told them to expect a letdown like that, she said. "I just assumed for a long time that Kyle was difficult to deal with because I had this dream child still in my mind."

Kyle was apparently slightly delayed in his motor skills; he didn't walk until he was eighteen months old. His mother re-called, however, that he had been very expressive with gestures and facial expressions as a toddler. Whenever he wanted some-thing, he tended to sit in one spot and make nasty sounds and grimaces, pointing in its general direction but, it seemed, refusing to crawl over to get it for himself. This, plus his charm, usually worked. If not, he would cry loudly as his parents continued their frantic search for what he was pointing at.

"We felt silly treating him like an emperor," Katherine re-called. "But he was our first and, at that point, our only child, and we had waited fifteen years. I guess he knew he had us. . . . " She smiled slightly. "We probably spoiled him."

To reassure Katherine and also because it was partially true, I told her at this point that the extra flexibility and soothing and nurturing she gave him were most likely a big help, given his nature. However, I acknowledged, even with a child who has a lot of sensitivities, we need to help him collaborate more and learn to be a more assertive partner in getting his needs met. If children like Kyle expect the world to produce whatever they want without their lifting a finger, they will become increasingly stubborn and defiant. Kyle's slow motor development, coupled with his strong sense of what he wanted, made it natural for him to try to get his parents to bend to his will and do most of the "dirty work."

We could see how Kyle, as he was learning to attend, en-gage, and interact purposefully, was also gradually forming an expectant and defiant attitude toward his world.

When Kyle was between eighteen and twenty-four months old, he began talking in two- and three-word phrases ("Want juice!" and "Give me dat!"). Gary and Katherine also recalled that he had not engaged in pretend play with them. They didn't remember ever getting down on the floor and playing make-believe. "Perhaps we were so busy trying to keep him from being mad at us that we never realized we weren't working on his imag-ination," said Katherine. Sometimes it is hard for parents to see, particularly with a demanding, stubborn child, that pretend play and imagination can give their stubborn child increased flexibil-ity. He can satisfy himself and explore different options in fantasy, thus reducing his need to control the real world quite so much. But as a mother of another defiant child said to me, "Who feels like playing house with a crying brat?" Katherine mused, "Besides, he was running the show. So if he wanted to do pretend, I guess he would have done it."

Kyle's bossiness began to emerge late in his second year, as his language improved. "Want dat!" was his oft-repeated phrase. He also couldn't be budged from certain routines. His parents said he insisted on sitting at a particular seat at mealtime and using a certain fork and knife his grandparents had given him. He wanted to watch back-to-back episodes of *Barney* and would scream furiously if either parent tried to flip the channel even briefly to catch a glimpse of the news. He became a very picky eater—eating only frozen waffles and peanut butter sandwiches "for days at a time," Katherine said. If his parents insisted that he try something different, he would simply refuse to eat at all, sparking a big battle with Gary, who tried to insist that he stay at the dinner table until the meal was over. Kyle would knock over his juice or milk while his parents weren't looking.

He was an extraordinarily verbal child by this point and, by the age of four, could engage in long arguments with his father. "I am not going to wear a turtleneck today," he would rage. "It's not that cold anyway. The weatherman said it's going to be warm today. I *heard* him say that." Katherine and Gary said that another reason that they had rarely played pretend or fantasy games with him was because it was difficult to spend one-on-one time with Kyle without getting into an argument.

Kyle's parents struck me as committed, caring parents who longed for some organization and structure in their lives. They had had a fairly set routine before the children arrived. They liked order.

"I'm a very neat person," Katherine said. "I don't like clutter or messes. They really upset me." She recalled that in her childhood she had engaged in many compulsive rituals, such as washing her hands many times each day and making sure that her bedroom was in "perfect condition" before she left for school in the morning.

Gary was the oldest in his family. He had a younger brother with a language delay who got a lot of attention. Gary, at first, said, "I didn't care. I was the oldest." But it soon became clear, as he talked about his brother and anyone who was weak or vulnerable, that he was very intolerant of other people's vulnerabilities. He saw his son's demanding behavior and crying as a sign that "something must be wrong with him." He said, "And I won't let him get away with it. Even if I have to hold his hand, we'll pick up every toy together, and we'll make sure that each is in the proper basket." While he claimed to admire his wife's overall competence, I noticed that he glared at her whenever she defended Kyle's behavior. It also became clear that he viewed her protectiveness as a weakness. Except when, he grinned shyly, she was protective toward him.

I summarized for Katherine and Gary my sense of where Kyle stood at this stage. He had some mild tactile and auditory sensitivities, I told them, meaning that he was overly sensitive to some sensations and sounds that ordinarily don't bother people. He had some delays in fine motor skills and motor planning, meaning some movements that were easy for other people were difficult for Kyle. He also was a very purposeful child with a clear sense of what he wanted and expected. And he didn't like being out of control. The result was that he had resorted to bossiness and defiance as a way to keep control of his often overwhelming world and his slightly out-of-control body.

His parents were engaged and involved. They had helped Kyle share the center of attention, engage warmly with the world, and establish two-way communication. However, they had done little to develop emotional ideas and emotional thinking, to help Kyle put his feelings into words. They were rarely involved in his make-believe world and provided few ways for Kyle to elaborate his feelings and behavior. Their need for structure and order and their constant imposition of sometimes arbitrary rules only increased Kyle's defiance.

Katherine's anxiety and intermittent overprotectiveness, coupled with Gary's anger and intrusiveness, intensified Kyle's need to be stubborn and defiant as a way to maintain his self-definition. Kyle had a passive approach to conflict—stubbornness and a negative attitude—and difficulty with taking initiative and expressing his feelings.

Our first step with Kyle, as with other children facing the same issues, was to work to improve his most important relationships and, within the framework of these relationships, help him renegotiate (or negotiate for the first time) the stages of development that he had not fully mastered. Even as I was still learning about Kyle and his parents, we focused on the five-step process so that Katherine and Gary could learn about their child, and I could learn as they learned.

Parents often tell me that they already know their child. After all, they spend many hours with him! But there is always something more that parents can learn about their child, and the better a parent knows the child, the easier it becomes to see him in a new light.

PROBLEM-SOLVING TIME: UNDERSTANDING WHAT DEFIANT BEHAVIOR MEANS

With most challenging children, I advocate that parents think about floor time—creating empathy and relatedness—as the first objective. But a stubborn, argumentative child may try to draw you into too many debates as you try to establish a connection. For this type of child, then, I'm going to talk about problem-solving time first, since you may find yourself doing that anyway.

During problem-solving time, you are trying to have a logical dialogue with your child in which you not only review his day, but also anticipate his most important challenges. For many parents of defiant children, the biggest initial challenge is understanding what the child's negative reactions actually mean. Parents often get drawn inadvertently into feeling either guilty or outraged because of their child's long list of criticisms.

The defiant child, seemingly out of left field, will bring up something that happened long ago, when his feelings were deeply hurt. Defiant children are intense and have tremendous determination. As a result, they can have great memories and can come up with a list of your wrongdoings a mile long! The defiant child may forget how to tie his shoes, but he can remember the time two years ago when you were fifteen minutes late in picking him up at school. This is consistent with "big picture" thinking; these children are not distracted by irrelevant detail, they remember the essential things that fit in with their emotional needs. That means they can pull events out of the past that, to anyone else, might seem trivial. It's easy for a parent either to dismiss these or to think "Oh my God, the time I was late picking him up must have been terribly traumatic if he remembers it two years later!" But the fact that the child remembers it doesn't mean that the event in itself was that important. The child is simply searching his psyche to find some past event to get his point across. If he is angry and his point is "You're a lousy mother," the fact that you overcooked his scrambled eggs this morning may not, in his mind, make his point strongly enough. But his psyche reminds him about the time you made him wait at school fifteen minutes all by himself two years ago. He is finding the image—or metaphor—to dramatize his emotion of the moment.

The parent should not get lost in the two-year-old experience (unless it was indeed truly traumatic) but should understand the child's intent. He is trying to tell you about his emotions. Show him you understand the feeling. For example: "You mean you feel sad and like I don't care when I don't cook your eggs properly?" The child may agree, "Yes, exactly." You may feel that it's silly that he should have such strong feelings about scrambled eggs, but that is the reality for him. Over time (through problem-solving discussions), he may learn to have some perspective on the intensity of his feelings. But the starting point for that process is having a common understanding and a common ground. You establish that common ground by staying with his emotion and not worrying too much about the criticism, event, or past injustices that he uses to convey that emotion.

Once you understand what your child means, you are in a position to have longer logical conversations about a range of subjects. Katherine needed to learn not to overreact to Kyle's accusations, which were often embedded in many descriptions of his day ("My teacher was mean to me today—just like when you forgot to get me a present on Thanksgiving"). Instead, she simply empathized with the anger that Kyle was communicating. After a while, she found Kyle was able to talk more easily about a range of subjects. This allowed Katherine and Gary to not only talk to him about his day but also help him anticipate challenging situations.

The challenge they elected to work on first was Kyle's tantrums. Their first attempt didn't go well. In trying to talk to Kyle about his feelings surrounding his tantrums, Gary ended up sounding like a movie parody of a psychiatrist. "So how do you really feel when you are screaming at us?" he asked Kyle earnestly. Often, in parents' first attempts at problem solving, they sound rather wooden. As your child gets older and smarter, he may look at you as if you are joking. If he's younger, he may say, "I'm not going to talk about feelings!" A more natural way, particularly with the resistant, stubborn child, is to start talking about the difficult moment that you're helping the child anticipate. For example, the new children in your child's class are threatening to him. He threw a temper tantrum at school when two of the newcomers took his soccer ball.

You could say, "Let's picture what you are going to do tomorrow if they take your soccer ball again." A more natural way, perhaps, would be, "I wonder if those kids are going to be mean or nice tomorrow. What do you think?" Or, with a somewhat older child, you could introduce the subject, "I bet you hope Jason and Bobbie stay home tomorrow." Or at home, after a day when Jason and Bobbie were particularly mean to your child, if your child seems preoccupied with a toy that has lots of shields and weapons, you might say empathetically, "You know, it would probably be great to have something like that in school to use if Jason bugs you again." In all of these examples, you are making a comment, much like you might to a friend, that introduces the situation the child is going to confront. You are finding a way to do this in a natural, not contrived, manner.

Once you have established this dialogue, it is also helpful to try to find a phrase or shorthand way of summarizing your child's pattern. For example, Kyle had tantrums when he didn't get his way and would trash his room. But he was able to join with his parents in picturing situations where he got frustrated, such as when they pulled him away from the TV set before he was finished with his program. He learned to picture what he felt ("very mad") and what he usually did ("not talk to anybody, run up to my room and throw things around"). He could even talk a little bit about punishing a bean bag chair instead of throwing things.

However, while the intensity of his throwing and the fury of his screams diminished a bit after these discussions, Katherine felt that any time she went in to get Kyle away from the TV set for bedtime, it was still like pressing a button that brings on a hurricane.

Let's focus on how you might use the general principle of anticipation to help a child get some perspective.

When your words are likely to push his buttons, use anticipation. As you are about to move into a discussion with him about turning off the TV, try to anticipate with him what you are going to say before you say it in order to ease the tension and help him on the spot. For example, your child trashed his room yesterday and today he is glued to the TV set again, way past his bedtime. You find yourself getting nervous because you know that as soon as you open your mouth, you could be in for another tantrum and room trashing. As you find yourself tensing up, you are aware that your voice is going to be particularly intrusive since you are already angry and nervous. But you are also probably saying to yourself, "I won't be intimidated by him!" Instead, however, you could say to him, "You know, in just about a minute I'm going to need to tell you it's time to go to sleep. And when I do that, is that going to put you into your 'I-wanna-trash-my-room' mood?" By doing this, you give him and yourself a warning and soften the upcoming blow. Your voice is likely to be calmer because nothing has happened yet. His response will probably be less chaotic and furious because you haven't yet insisted he leave the TV set. If he ignores you, or says, "I gotta watch this part!" you might say again, "I know. But what do you think is going to happen when I have to tell you in a minute that it's bedtime? Are you going to get so mad that you get into your 'trash-the-room' mood?"

This mini-conversation might then lead to some negotiation. He might say, "Give me five minutes and I'll go up nice." Or "Just to the next commercial and I'll go upstairs and be good." And since you believe in helping your child meet new challenges in small steps, you are willing to negotiate. You hadn't expected to get him upstairs much before the next commercial anyway because his storming and yelling would take at least five minutes. Often, with negotiation and by anticipating with your child what you were going to ask of him, you can help your child make a smoother transition so that his "trash-the-room" mood never emerges. The reason it *does* emerge is because a lot of your child's rage springs from a sense of shock and surprise that only compounds his frustration. Introducing the inevitable through an anticipatory discussion takes the shock out of it, allows your child to see things in perspective, and helps him be more cooperative. Even if he does lose his temper the first five or six times you try this, there is a strong likelihood that, slowly but surely, your respect and gentleness in the anticipatory discussions will help him learn to see the pattern and be more flexible.

This approach reached a certain epitome with one eight-year-old child I knew who gave her parents the following "rules." Rule 1 was "You have to tell me what we're going to talk about before we talk about it so I can decide if I want to. If you want to change what we're talking about, you also have to ask me first if I want to. If you want to talk about feelings, you have to first tell me what feeling it is, and then I'll tell you whether I want to talk about it today." The child was very deliberate in her approach to relationships. While it's humorous in one sense, it's actually not dissimilar to great nations coming together to negotiate and spending the first two weeks discussing the size of the table and who sits where and the rules by which they will talk to each other before they ever get down to the talking. With this child, and with children like her, it is often helpful to take their suggestions literally. For example, one child who threw a tantrum every time his parents suggested it was time to shut off the TV and go to sleep was helped considerably when his parents first said, "In a minute, I'm going to want to talk to you about bedtime." At this point, the child was alerted to a conversation to come, rather than being pulled abruptly from his semitrance in front of the TV.

Problem-solving time with the defiant child (particularly an older child) also presents a good opportunity to help him become aware of his particular sensitivities. You can help him recognize what he likes and doesn't like and what he does and doesn't do when he gets overloaded. It's also a good time to encourage him to verbalize feelings and develop a reflective attitude toward his sensitivities. That way, he can eventually learn to prepare himself for difficult or challenging situations. Because this child is so sensitive to feelings of embarrassment and humiliation, you can't press him before he is ready. At the same time, see if you can build in some humor as well. Gentle kidding about his perfectionism may help him become aware of his hypercritical reactions.

FLOOR TIME: FINDING A SECURE BASE

Now that Katherine and Gary understood Kyle's physical sensitivities, they could use floor time to show Kyle that he could be soothed and comforted by their presence. I encouraged them to set aside at least a half-hour a day for floor time.

Parents often approach floor time with a verbal child at the level of words and pretend play, trying to join the child in a discussion or make-believe. But with the defiant child, as we have seen, this routine overture may be met with objections (perhaps with a dirty look and "Leave me alone!"). With a child like Kyle, the best approach is slow and gradual. Sometimes even a slow and gradual approach may still get you a "no" or a turned back, leaving you feeling much like a rejected friend. In that case, the strategy of moving up and down the ladder of development to find the right rung on which to get the interaction cooking and to foster engagement can be useful. If Kyle wouldn't talk or play make-believe with his parents, they stepped down to the preverbal, presymbolic level and tried simple behavioral and gestural interactions.

For example, one time he was busy lining up a series of toy trains from smallest to biggest and didn't seem to want any interference. So Gary began doing the same thing in front of Kyle using toy cars, but occasionally motioning to Kyle for some help in reaching the car he needed next in the sequence because the cars were closer to Kyle (Gary deliberately sat where he would need Kyle's assistance). He set up some of the cars out of the proper sequence and looked at Kyle, gesturing questioningly with his hands, as if to say, "OK?" Kyle, not known for his tolerance of mistakes and imperfections, changed Gary's cars around. Sometimes, when Gary was feeling very brave, he slowly and cautiously tried to shift one of Kyle's trains to a different position. Needless to say, Kyle would push his hand away or quickly grab the train back and put it back where it belonged. In either instance, some interaction was beginning to occur with behavioral and gestural exchanges. When Kyle was reluctant to engage even at this level of interaction and ignored his father, Gary simply sat with an admiring and respectful look on his face. As Kyle looked pleased with a particular configuration of cars, Gary would smile approvingly, hoping to make eye contact and share some pleasure. Since Kyle enjoyed sharing some of his proud moments, Gary could almost always engage Kyle at this level if he was patient.

With a child who won't engage even at this level, we might do something to involve one of the child's senses, such as touch, more directly. With one little boy who was extremely defiant and stubborn, refusing even to look, interact, or talk with me, I very gently and slowly put a toy elephant on his leg, which was sticking out in front of me, and asked, "Could my elephant rest over there for a minute?" This child gave me a scowl and shook the elephant off, but I asked again if "my elephant couldn't rest for just a few seconds." This time, the child moved his leg even before the elephant touched it, showing that he was at least reacting to my presence. It wasn't much, but it was a start.

The first goal of floor time with the defiant child, as with any child, is to establish some sense of pleasurable relatedness at the highest level (hopefully words and make-believe) the child will allow. When you go down the developmental levels to make contact, you can go back up as soon as you establish some warm rapport at that level. For example, when Kyle showed his father how to line up the toy cars properly, there would be a sense of shared pleasure in this endeavor. After a while, it was easy for Gary to start talking about "which way would be better to take a trip to California? With the cars or the trains?" As they got into a discussion about the advantages of cars or trains in going up the mountain passes into California, Gary even asked a doll what she preferred. Kyle giggled.

As you are going up and down the "ladder" to establish communication and relatedness, be mindful of how easily a defiant child can be overloaded. He has elected to soothe himself by shutting out interactions that he feels are too much. This often comes across as stubbornness and defiance. As we gradually show him that we can be comforting in our tones of voice, in the subdued way we approach him, in the way we look for shared pleasure in behavioral, emotional, and verbal interactions and in the way we always try to build on *his* natural interests, he has the chance to learn that another person can soothe him. He doesn't have to shut things out or control everything in order to be comfortable and relaxed.

With older children, the same principles apply. Approach them slowly. Make sure your movements and voice tone are as relaxing and soothing as possible. For example, your eight-year-old is sorting through his baseball collection and reciting batting averages. You sit down on the edge of his bed, respectful of his "boundary."

"What did Brady Anderson hit last year?" you ask.

He eyes you suspiciously before going back to sorting cards. Again, move down the ladder of development. You pick up a card and carefully move it over to a pile. Then you pick up another card and move it onto the same pile.

"What are you doing?" your child asks.

"Picking out the players whose batting averages I don't know," you answer.

"Oh," he says. "Well, Anderson batted .310 last year."

As you expand the dialogue, without being intrusive, you

begin to build his confidence in you. He begins to see you as someone who can help him rather than as an adversary.

When I suggest this gradual approach, parents inevitably worry about spoiling. As I noted earlier, a child is spoiled when limits are not being set and the child is hitting, biting, taking other children's toys, or demanding and getting six extra toys. Spoiled behavior often persists when the child feels insecure: if there is not enough nurturing, the child becomes demanding and greedy, inconsiderate and aggressive because he is hungry for more. If you give more nurturing and firm limits and sprinkle in a little extra work on fostering independence, you will often help a child overcome any tendency to be spoiled.

Gary had more difficulty than Katherine with floor time. It wasn't easy for him to let his son make the rules. Gary was used to trying to make the rules and then engaging in endless power struggles over them with his son. At first, Gary said, he felt as if he was "giving up" something every time he let his son set the agenda during floor time. But as Gary grew used to the process, he gained some insight into his own pattern of subtle and not-so-subtle domination of his son. In the past, whenever Kyle had tried to get the upper hand or be the dominant one, Gary had switched the theme of the game or the game itself so that *he* was the one in control. But Gary became aware that this subtle form of competition was undermining his son's ability to feel competitive and assertive in the world and to experiment with aggression in ways other than defiance.

Gary noticed that the emerging themes in Kyle's play revolved around Kyle being the good guy who was protecting the other good guys from the bad guys. Kyle enjoyed showing lots of anger through his toys, which fought and knocked things down. Earlier, Gary had liked to change the game so his bad guys beat Kyle's good guys. Or he tried to get Kyle to switch from the pretend play, where Kyle could be the boss, to a real game where Gary would have to explain the rules and thereby get the upper hand. Gary found pretend play "one of the hardest things I've ever done" because "I never let people dominate me." Having his son jump on his stomach and having his son's action figures beat up on him was a whole new experience for him. As he later said, "It's doubly hard, because Kyle is bossing me around in real life. Now I can't even enjoy teaching him how to play checkers. I have to let him tell me what to do every step of the way."

I explained to Gary that if he could enjoy Kyle's creative imagination in pretend play and permit Kyle to be the "director and screenwriter" perhaps Kyle wouldn't need to be quite so bossy in everyday life. Perhaps he would even let Gary teach him a few things.

"I'll believe it when I see it," Gary said wryly. Eventually, Kyle did become more flexible, letting his father sometimes make up the rules for games and letting his father's action figures beat his action figures.

In Kyle's floor time with Katherine, he told her he liked to pretend he was "baby Kyle." Also, he told her he liked to "help people who are sad." He made up a song, "Don't leave me, Mommy."

Katherine came to recognize that while she loved her son very much, she tended to treat him like a baby and not let him be independent. She was controling and anxious about him, and liked to keep everything very organized, controled, and neat. We talked about what would worry her if she didn't treat Kyle like a baby and encouraged him to be big and strong. Katherine immediately thought about Kyle getting out of control. She pictured him as being very aggressive. Eventually she was able to relate this back to her aggressive brother and to her father, who often lost his temper violently. She had always been a tidy person who tried to keep everything "just so" in her own family. She was frightened of Kyle's ability to "defeat" her.

As floor time progressed, Kyle's parents felt he was growing by "leaps and bounds" in the words of his father, in terms of his fantasy life. He had action figures involved in long conversations with one another and playing out themes of protection and fighting. As he played out both sides of dramas, his parents were impressed with both the detail and the elaboration of these dramas. Sometimes he even made a little doll into his sister and pretended to shoot or hit her or blow her up. He was able to talk about having mixed feelings toward his sister, being mad at her some of the time. At other times, he said he enjoyed his sister and found her "cute."

EMPATHIZING WITH THE DEFIANT CHILD

Empathizing with a child who is often angry and defiant is not easy, but it is essential. This child feels continually overwhelmed by his world and has difficulty trusting anyone to soothe or calm him.

Once Gary and Katherine had built a physical profile of their son's sensitivities and were mindful of his underlying vulnerabilities, they could empathize more easily.

"It's hard to put shoes on when they hurt your feet," they would observe when he had difficulty getting dressed in the morning. They realized that there were many things in everyday life that Kyle found hard—switching from watching TV to going to sleep, for instance. By anticipating that they were going to ask him shortly to shut off the TV and go to sleep, they were being respectful and acknowledging how hard this transition was for him. They tried introducing new experiences with little comments, such as "Do you think it would be too hard to try on a new pair of pants? Could you think about it?" Kyle often said, "Let me think about it." To his parents' surprise, often five minutes later, he would say, "Let me try them on in a little bit." With one new pair of pants, he tried on only one leg and said it felt too stiff. But this was a big advance over his refusal to wear anything but sweatpants!

Thanks to empathy from his parents, Kyle was eventually able to identify his assumptions about the world—for instance, that people were out to "bother me." Needless to say, once he recognized that feeling, he was able to talk about people bothering him rather than becoming stubborn and shutting them out.

BREAKING THE CHALLENGE INTO MANAGEABLE STEPS

A key goal is to make sure that the child's tasks are divided up into small enough steps so that mastering each step generates some success and enthusiasm. That supplies the encouragement the child needs to continue. If he is experiencing too many challenges at one step, then break that step into even smaller ones. However slow a child's progress seems at first, remember that *any* change is a momentous accomplishment. If a child's progress seems agonizingly slow at first, take heart. Remember that progress will speed up as he masters the first few steps of a particular challenge and gains some confidence.

For example, Katherine was particularly frustrated over Kyle's refusal to eat anything but a few foods. To introduce a greater variety into Kyle's meals gradually, his parents took his favorite fare, peanut butter, and a speck of apple and mixed them. They hoped he would get used to the texture, smell, and taste of the apple. Then they added two bigger pieces, and then three, and so on. They did it with other foods too, putting a tiny amount of hamburger in his macaroni and cheese and building that up.

In order to help him become more comfortable with kids his own age, his mother arranged lots of play dates. Kyle had play dates four or five times a week, but he often ended up playing alone. To let him master this challenge, she would observe what he was doing with a friend. Not infrequently, when he turned his back and played with some of his new toys, having given the friend some old toys to play with, Katherine came in. For just a few minutes, she tried to get some interaction going between Kyle and his friend. She would usually build on something Kyle was interested in and create a connection around that. One time, Kyle was neatly putting his Power Rangers into different trucks, and Katherine skillfully found a big truck that she knew Kyle would like and gave it to the other child. She then sat behind Kyle and said, "Peter has a great truck. Maybe if you ask him for it nicely, he will let you have it." With a reluctant sigh, Kyle said, "I need that truck." Peter, a sweet and pleasant youngster, happily brought the truck over. Katherine then engineered them into putting Power Rangers in the truck together. After a few minutes, Kyle turned his back and returned to his more self-absorbed, controled style of play.

During each play date, Gary and Katherine tried to extend by a few minutes the amount of time they drew Kyle into interactive play with another child. Every minute adds up, and six months later Kyle was playing together for over an hour with some regular playmates. Gary and Katherine came in to help out periodically, but that was becoming less necessary. The more practice Kyle got, the more he seemed to enjoy it. It might have seemed that Kyle simply wasn't interested in other children, but as with most children, that simply wasn't so. Rather, children who feel unsure of themselves often cope with that feeling by playing it safe and keeping their anxiety to themselves. Slowly but surely, we can help them reach out and start enjoying the pleasures of playing with a friend.

NEGOTIATING LIMITS

As much as Kyle was supported in floor time, as intrigued as he was by solutions he found in problem-solving time, and as proud as he was of the successes he gradually achieved, he still lapsed into his pattern of defiance and aggression.

Gary, Katherine, and I discussed setting limits and agreeing on a sanction every time Kyle expressed his dislike or anger through physical force. We wanted to encourage him to put feelings into words.

First, Gary, Katherine, and Kyle sat down together in my office. Katherine and Gary took advantage of Kyle's debating skills to hash out the rules. They eventually agreed that if Kyle hit, then his parents were to forbid TV watching for two nights. Katherine and Gary's mutual agreement on a punishment and simply discussing it with Kyle was helpful in itself. But Kyle was much too smart to let it be easy! He would frequently hit his sister or his parents and claim it was "just a strong touch." Katherine or Gary would say that it was a "strong hit." Kyle responded, "I should know. I did it." Katherine wanted to give Kyle the benefit of the doubt, but Gary didn't. Was it going to be this easy to defeat the limit-setting structure they had set up?

As they began bickering about how to interpret his behavior,

I tried to empathize with their own differing emotional reactions and the fact that they were falling into their own traps again. After they explored their personal reasons for being so susceptible to reassuming their old habits, I tried to explain that it wasn't terribly important where they drew the line. The key was having a line, which Kyle would most certainly test, and then being supportive of each other in providing limit-setting consequences. After some discussion, we established that if Kyle used an open hand or his fingers, in what he called "touch" and what they thought was a gentle "push," they could give Kyle the benefit of the doubt. But they should acknowledge that he was getting "awful close to the line" with a grin. If he used a closed fist, even if he didn't hit very hard, he had definitely crossed the line. Whichever parent witnessed the scene automatically became the referee. The other parent wasn't allowed to question the call. If both parents witnessed the act and had different opinions, they simply alternated being the referee. The idea was to find a way around their tendencies, based on their character structures, to get in the way of setting effective limits for Kyle. To be sure, Katherine and Gary needed to work on their underlying tendencies to bicker with each other, but sometimes it takes a while for parents to come to grips with these patterns. In the meantime, they can sidestep some of the patterns by creating routines for themselves that serve the more important, general goal of providing their child with firm, but gentle, boundaries somewhere.

As always, Katherine and Gary increased floor time with Kyle, as a way of increasing intimacy and their availability, at the same time that they stepped up limit setting. That way, they could keep the emotional closeness that Kyle needed and, at the same time, provide him with firmness and structure. After a time, it began to work. Kyle seemed better able to set up internal limits for himself.

6

THE INATTENTIVE CHILD

THE INATTENTIVE CHILD SEEMS TO FLIT THROUGH life, never landing in one place for long. Her parents complain that she is "spacey." She forgets to tie her shoes, bring home her homework, pick up her toys. Her teachers say she doesn't pay attention in school. They point out that she can't follow instructions or concentrate. She may make one or two scribbles on her schoolwork and then giggle and whisper with other children. At home, she wanders around, perpetually touching and picking up things. At the dinner table, she can't sit still—she bangs her knife against her plate, eats one bite, and is off. She is constantly on the go, running around, pushing other kids, throwing toys. She may be absent-minded; you ask her why she forgot to bring her home-work home for the fifth day in a row, and she says, "I was going to. I had the book in my hand. But I put it down to look at this cool game that Amy brought in and . . ."

An inattentive child may have trouble finding the words to describe things. Asked about her day, she shrugs. "It was fine, I guess," she says finally. She constantly changes the subject when she talks. It's difficult to have a conversation with her because she skips from one topic to another.

Parents of school-age children worry, and rightly so, that children who are unable to pay attention for even short periods will suffer in school. But attentional problems aren't confined to school-age children. They are very common among children of all ages. In fact, we can now even observe these problems among infants and preschoolers. Babies may be unable to focus in on their father's face or on one toy; their attention shifts rapidly. Some toddlers are unable to focus on what someone is saying to them or follow simple directions.

The term "attentional problems" is being used more and more frequently in schools. Many children who are having diffi-culty in school are labeled as having Attention Deficit Disorder (ADD). In some cases, children believed to suffer ADD are being medicated without adequate medical, developmental, and mental health evaluations to determine whether they actually have an attentional difficulty or some other challenges and whether medi-cation is needed.

A NEW WAY OF THINKING ABOUT INATTENTIVE CHILDREN

Developmental observations of a large number of infants and young children growing into childhood and beyond have led us to identify processes involved in paying attention and different problems associated with each. For example, some children have difficulties with attention because of how they sequence actions and *move* or use their bodies (they get distracted while tying shoes or writing a word, for example). Other children have attentional challenges because of the way that they process what they see or hear. Still other children may have attentional difficulties because of the way their bodies *react* to the world (some are easily distracted when there are too many noises or too many people around, for instance). There are various "kinds" of attention and types of difficulty with attention: for example, motor pattern types of attention and auditory processing or visual processing types. We can also think about attention in relation to reacting to sensations—visual, auditory, tactile, and smell.

Children with attentional problems in one area may have no problem concentrating when they are working in other areas. For example, a child could have difficulties carrying out acts that require many movements in a row or connecting a series of movements to something she sees or hears (motor-planning skills). Say a child is asked to copy some sentences off the blackboard; she may have great difficulty concentrating. After two minutes she starts fooling around. Or her teacher may look up and see her staring at the ceiling. "What in the world are you doing?" he may ask.

"I don't know," she shrugs.

On the other hand, if this same child is strong in picturing things in her mind, the visual-spatial capacities help her comprehend mathematical concepts concerned with quantity. When given a complicated math problem, she may work diligently and quietly for fifteen or twenty minutes, experiencing only slight challenges in making sure all her numbers are lined up properly. In one area, her attention is fleeting. In the other, her ability to focus and pay attention is very strong. If the room is quiet and she doesn't have to "do" anything, this same child may also be quite gifted in her ability to figure out what another person is saying and to think creatively about it.

I have seen many children who are described as severely deficient in attention capacities and as having Attention Deficit Disorder. I often find that such a child is able to talk to me for a half-hour or longer on a variety of subjects—her personal interests, her family, feelings, peer relationships, and attitude toward schoolwork—and not only maintain her focus but discuss all this quite intelligently and even analytically. Then I watch the child attempt to draw a picture and copy letters and shapes. All of a sudden, I see a girl who is fidgeting, looking out the window, wanting to know when she can see her mother, getting up and wandering aimlessly around the room, and, occasionally, causing me to duck because she has lofted a block or ball at my head. In conversations with her teacher and her parents, as well as my own observations, I hear detailed descriptions of and see this behavior, which is invariably related to schoolwork involving writing, copying, or other aspects of motor performance. When I ask how she is when a parent or teacher simply talks to her one-on-one in a quiet setting, I often hear "Oh, she's a bright child who can talk quite well. She has a pretty good vocabulary. But she has all these troubles with her schoolwork."

Lost in such descriptions is the fact that this child excels in one type of attention—involving verbal performance in a quiet, supportive, one-on-one setting. Parents and educators generally emphasize the severe challenges in maintaining her attention when it comes to motor performance. On standardized IQ tests, such a child scores in the superior range in word definition, analogies, and short-term auditory memory but is average to low average in tasks involving motor performance—particularly those that involve motor planning and are timed. Such children vary in some visual-spatial skills. If we are preoccupied with the child's difficulties and ignore her strengths, we can easily assume that she has a generalized attentional problem, rather than one related to specific skill areas. So much of schoolwork in the early grades involves the motor system that it is easy to overlook other areas of competence.

An experiment we once tried was revealing in that respect. Whenever teachers or parents found a particular child in a highly distracted, provocative, aimless mode while trying to accomplish a motor task, they converted the motor task to a combined verbal and motor task. They would, for example, begin talking to her—interrupting her chaotic behavior—with a question: "Can you tell me what it is we are trying to do here?" They would then help the child describe how she had to copy those "stupid letters" or make "these dumb shapes." They were careful to be empathctic about her annoyance at having to do things that obviously made her feel stupid and dumb.

"Let's see," the teacher said, "what is this dumb thing we are asking you to do? You mean we are asking you to make this letter [a *B*] by drawing these two dumb-looking hills attached to a line?" The teacher then asked, "Can you make up a rhyme that describes these two hills?" The child replied, "Hills on a line are fine." She repeated that to herself until she, with her teacher's support, copied the letter *B*. We developed a method whereby this girl could use her strong verbal skills to talk herself through a complex motor task. Slowly but surely, her motor attention improved.

We see differences in attention in many areas. Some children are able to focus very well on music—they can practice the piano or another instrument for a half-hour or an hour at a time. But give them a math problem, and they wander around the room, daydream, or fidget. They're not deliberately trying to get out of doing their math homework. It's just that when using that aspect of their nervous system, it is difficult for them to concentrate.

These individual challenges are often combined. In fact, most children with significant attentional problems tend to have more than one area of their nervous system or functional abilities less developed than the rest of their system. For example, some children who are weak in visual-spatial processing—that is, perceiving objects in space—also have a difficulty with motor planning. In addition, I frequently see children with poor auditory processing skills who are also underreactive to sound. Some very verbal children may be overreactive to noise and certain types of touch and visual input. This makes paying attention to a task in a busy schoolroom very difficult.

Parents may wonder whether these distinctions are really very significant. "I just want my child to pay attention better," parents complain. "Are the underlying reasons really that important?" They *are* important. Only by understanding the specific nature of an attention problem can anyone—parent or teacher—help a child to overcome, or compensate for, it. For example, a child who has difficulties processing what she sees can learn to process more information through what she hears, while she is strengthening her ability to figure out what she sees. Or a child who gets easily distracted during motor tasks, such as tying her shoes, can, as described earlier, learn to use verbal skills, for example, to talk herself through the task. ("Now I make a rabbit ear with this shoelace and twist the other shoelace around the rabbit ear. . . .")

THE PROCESS OF PAYING ATTENTION

Some people think of paying attention as a passive process, in which a child just opens her ears and eyes and lets the adult (or television, toy, or tape) inundate her with sensations to which she is open and receptive. That child, it is believed, is "paying attention" to the adult or television, toy, or tape. But "paying attention" is actually a more active, dynamic process. Concentrating on someone or something usually involves some kind of interaction with that person or object—whether it's playing with a toy, talking to mom or dad, or listening to a teacher. With a toy, for example, the child plays with it, taking in information from it, such as its color, how it feels, what sounds it makes. She develops a picture of how it works. She bangs it a certain way to see if it makes a certain sound or turns a dial to see what happens. It's that active give-and-take between what she is taking in (what she sees and hears) and her own manipulation of the toy that constitutes her focus and attentiveness.

If the child has difficulty manipulating the toy and/or taking in information about the toy—what it looks like or how it sounds—then she is less likely to spend much time paying attention to it. These difficulties will affect the quality of her attention. Since attention is part of the active process of *doing* something, anything that interferes with that "doing" will interfere with the attention. In addition, a child's frustration and (very human) desire to avoid things that are difficult lead her to try to "escape" the situation. The more she does this, the more easily distracted she is.

Try, for example, throwing a ball into a basket with your

right hand (if you are right-handed) and then with your left hand. With the right hand, there is not only the fun of mastery, there is also the intrinsic pleasure of muscles working in a smooth and coordinated manner. Anyone who is good at a sport like basketball or skiing knows that feeling of both competency and mastery and of pleasure in the *doing*. Gifted athletes have described these feelings: When they are in the middle of a game, they say, their bodies are moving effortlessly and automatically into the right positions while they are excitedly planning the next step in their strategy. Tasks at which we are skilled "feel good." They are pleasant at the level of our motor system, and mastery makes them satisfying in a most basic bodily way.

But when a right-handed person throws a ball in the basket with her left hand, none of that pleasure is there. And, of course, left-handed people find the same thing in reverse.

To help you better understand this process, let me suggest a simple exercise. Imagine that you've been handed a piece of paper with a simple maze on it. Your job is to get from the beginning to the end of the maze without lifting your pencil from the paper. It probably won't be too difficult. Within a few seconds, the point of your pencil will emerge from the maze. But imagine that you have to get through the maze while looking through a mirror, which reverses the image. Now try to make a line through the maze without touching the boundaries of the maze. The whole experience changes. Your progress is slow and tortuous. Your mind will ache, and you will want to give up. That's because the feedback you're getting from your muscles or motor system doesn't feel good.

Children with difficulties in one area or another are asked all the time to do things that their bodies rebel against. They don't get the natural feedback that makes them want to continue. If a child is gifted in copying shapes, writing, reading, or math, she gets good internal feedback from her own body in those areas. Writing, reading, or working on a math problem feels natural—effortless at times. But a child who has difficulty with motor sequencing or with processing quantitative information is having to go against what feels "natural" when she writes, reads, or works on a math problem. Her natural tendency will be to avoid that area or be inattentive to it.

For many people, attention is quite automatic. They have no need to put much effort into it because the sensations they are looking at, hearing, or feeling are compelling and draw their attention. But if those sights, sounds, or movement patterns are difficult to engage in or comprehend, focusing and concentrating can become a minute-by-minute struggle.

I'm reminded of the difference between my wife and me when it comes to reading. My wife has always been a good reader; she enjoys nothing more than getting comfortable with a good spy or mystery novel. The words, she says, just "lift off the page" into her mind as effortlessly as if she were watching a movie. Her energy is not involved in the act of reading but in engaging with the excitement of the story. Therefore she can sustain her attention on the book easily for a couple of hours. In contrast, I have never found it easy to read. I have always had to work at it. I never read for fun. If I try to read a novel, even an exciting one, I find myself wondering after each paragraph how much longer I have to go on. The words don't lift off the page; each word, each sentence, each paragraph is a conscious, planned effort. I can read short newspaper stories or scientific articles or book chapters related to my professional work. Occasionally, I study a whole book, but it requires enormous effort and energy—hardly the effortless, pleasurable activity my wife describes.

Obviously, there is a vast difference between the easy, almost automatic attention that my wife can expend in two or three hours of reading versus my minute-by-minute effort. Each time I struggle to move from one sentence to another, one paragraph to another, there is an opportunity for my attention to wander, my concentration to flee. That is how inattentive children feel. As they move their eyes across a page, their bodies across a room, as they are surrounded by bright, noisy sights and sounds, endless opportunities arise for them to focus their attention on something else. We tend to focus on feedback from the outside, which, as I will discuss later, can be used to overcome some of the challenges we have been exploring.

We have tended to ignore the critical challenge of lack of feedback from the *inside*—feedback that can sustain your attention if the activity itself feels pleasant, such as throwing a ball with your right hand if you're right-handed. When this is not present (such as trying to throw with your left hand if you're right-handed), the activity may provide negative internal feedback; it feels so uncomfortable that it is unpleasant and can undermine your attention because you want to avoid the activity. In working with children with attention problems, according to parents and teachers, we have found that many had specific difficulties in one or more of the areas outlined in the next section.

ATTENTION PROBLEMS

Difficulties with planning sequences of behavior, comprehending verbal or visual information, or reacting to sensations all influence our attention. Each child may have a different reason or reasons for having a hard time paying attention. Clinically, my sense is that the difficulty in planning or sequencing actions or behavior is the most common contributor to attentional difficulties. A child with this difficulty cannot do things on "automatic pilot" as other children may. Obvious behaviors such as checking your bookbag to see if you have your homework books require conscious effort and therefore can be forgotten.

Motor planning or sequencing difficulties will be discussed later in this chapter. We will discuss each general area that can influence attention, beginning with comprehending sensations.

Information-Processing Difficulties

As I explained earlier, some children have difficulty paying attention because of the way they take in and interpret what they hear or see. They are easily distracted because sights or sounds (words) haven't sufficient saliency and meaning to hold their attention.

Problems in processing information that a child *hears* is known as an *auditory-verbal processing difficulty*. It is hard for such a child to hold a sequence of sounds or words in her mind. As a baby, she may not respond as pleasurably as other babies to complex rhythms. For example, she may only brighten up and look interested with simple rhythms, such as "BUM bum, BUM bum." If you hum the rhythm "BUM bum-bum-bum-bum BUM BUM" ("Shave and a haircut . . . two bits") she may turn away. She can't decode or comprehend the pattern, and she loses interest. (It's like playing classical music to someone who is unfamiliar with it. Because he doesn't comprehend the pattern in the music, he doesn't find it interesting and begins daydreaming rather than listening.) A toddler with auditory processing difficulty has trouble following simple instructions because it's hard for her to hold sounds in her mind. For example, she reacts with puzzlement to the instruction, "Come here!" But if you point to the child and then point to yourself, saying "Here, here," she sees and responds to your gesture. By the age of two to two and a half, when most children can comprehend a couple of instructions in a row, such as "Please pick up your plate and give it to Mommy," this child may obediently pick up her plate, but then stop, staring at you in puzzlement. You may then have to repeat, "Give it to Mommy."

As a preschooler, she may have problems opening and closing what we have described as circles of communication. For example, when you are playing with her and you wonder aloud why one doll is beating up another doll, she may look confused and simply repeat what she has just said.

As a school-age child, she encounters difficulties comprehending instructions. When the teacher says, "Get a piece of paper and a pencil out of your desk and write down these words," she may be confused because there are too many commands at once. Distracted, she tunes out, daydreaming until the teacher asks her why she hasn't taken out her pencil and paper. Remembering school lessons or phone numbers poses a problem, and reading skills may come slowly because she has difficulty connecting sounds to letters.

As she gets older, she may have difficulty comprehending abstract concepts that are communicated through what she hears.

She may have a hard time with words that portray abstract concepts and may reason more in terms of *action patterns* and *spatial concepts*. For example, when most of us as children heard a new word, we thought about other words in association with that new word in order to figure out its meaning. (A child might, for example, hear the word "objectionable" for the first time. When a parent explains it in terms of a series of simpler, more familiar words, such as "not nice," she must hold in her mind the series of simpler words and the new word and understand the connection between them—quite a challenge for someone who has trouble holding in mind verbal patterns.) Similarly, trying to figure out the meaning of a story involves understanding the author's use of metaphor or other descriptive techniques, a hard chore if verbal patterns are not easily understandable.

Many children with verbal processing difficulty go on to become gifted interpreters of literature or become erudite in philosophy or social sciences. What many such individuals have done is to use their superior spatial abilities to buttress their weaker verbal pattern comprehension abilities. In other words, they may take a little more time to study a passage, visualize it, and then dissect it with almost mathematical precision and logic.

Often, a child with weak auditory processing skills may have excellent analytic or "big picture" thinking abilities. She is less oriented toward detail and more toward how the parts fit together. Academically, she struggles with the rote, memory-based skills that characterize the early school years but has an easier time in high school, college, and graduate school when concepts and analytic reasoning skills become more central.

Sometimes a child with auditory processing difficulties faces problems finding the right words to express herself—a word retrieval difficulty. She may have trouble describing her day or answering teachers' questions. She tunes out and daydreams while talking, causing endless annoyance to parents and teachers. "You're not answering my question!" they say in exasperation over and over. Two-way conversations are hard for a child who has word retrieval difficulties. Sometimes she knows the answers but can't find the words to express them. This difficulty with word retrieval may be part of a problem with the motor system (which will be discussed shortly) or it may exist on its own.

Another processing problem is *visual-spatial difficulty*, in which a child has trouble comprehending what she *sees*. A baby with such a challenge may be able to look at you more easily when you simply smile at her than when you smile *and* wiggle your hands at her, for example. A toddler may tune out and get distracted when pictures in a book become too intricate. She is better able to focus on simpler pictures. A preschooler might get confused by such games as sorting blocks by shape. A school-age child would probably have difficulty in such subjects as math and geography because they involve picturing objects in space. She will have more trouble solving a maze or finding her way around unfamiliar places, such as a new neighborhood or new school.

Sometimes the child who is relatively weaker in visual-spatial abilities may be stronger in the auditory-verbal processing area. Thus she may be more sensitive to nuance, subtlety, and detail and have a harder time with the big picture—she has more difficulty in understanding how the pieces fit together. For example, she tends to learn math in a rote way—memorizing addition and subtraction rather than picturing the concepts in her mind. She hasn't a feel for quantity. She will, for instance, simply memorize that $8 - 2 = 6$, rather than visualizing, say, eight apples and then imagining two taken away to leave six.

This child is likely to have difficulty with abstractions that are communicated through what she sees, such as mathematical and scientific concepts. Understanding the concept of velocity or acceleration in physics, for example, involves picturing different types of movement patterns and requires visual imagery rather than just memorization of a formula.

Most children tend to have a mixture of strengths and weaknesses. Children who are weak in visual-spatial skills tend to have strong auditory-verbal skills, for example. So the child who may not be able to find her way around a new neighborhood or school easily, for example, because of weak visual-spatial skills, will probably pay more attention to what people say. Since she is sensitive to subtlety and nuance, she may turn out to have strong writing or critical skills. Conversely, the child who is strong in visual-spatial skills may lean toward science or mathematics or architecture or enjoy working in hands-on situations, in mechanics or with computers.

An interesting point worth remembering is that our schools, in the early years, tend to be biased toward children who are strong auditory-verbal learners. Verbal systems are highly valued as children learn to talk, read, and write. Even if they have trouble picturing math concepts, they can master them in these early years because the simple concepts can easily be memorized. Because the verbal system is so overvalued in those early years, visual-spatial learners, who can understand math concepts but may not be able to memorize multiplication tables and have more difficulty with reading and writing, are thought to be slower in learning. Verbal children are more apt to be labeled "gifted" in those early years. Later, in high school and beyond, when science and math become more challenging and when even subjects like English and history are more analytical than factual and descriptive, visual-spatial learners (who are very analytical) may begin doing better. Some of the gifted auditory-verbal learners who depended too much on their outstanding memories and never grasped the concepts or principles behind what they were learning may begin to struggle.

Instead of assigning equal value to strengths in different areas in the early grades, we tend to try to explain away this bias. The child who struggled in earlier grades but now performs well is called an "overachiever," while the "gifted" student who is now struggling is "lazy" and not trying an "underachiever." These labels may not fit at all. Nor have the "less smart" kids suddenly become smart while the "smart" kids have suddenly become average. Rather, the criteria for success has changed. Ideally, we should value different types of skills even in the early school years so that children would get a sense of their relative strengths no matter what they were. The child who can find his way to grandma's house, even after going there only once, should feel just as smart as the child who can read directions about how to go to grandmother's house. Also, if we value different types of abilities in the early school years, we can be more tolerant of children's relative weaknesses. Children who fit a certain mold will not get a false sense of "I'm good at everything," leaving them unnecessarily depressed when they discover in college that certain areas are very hard for them. Instead, they would have had the opportunity to work on their more vulnerable areas as they were growing up.

Related to auditory-verbal reasoning and visual-spatial reasoning are other unique abilities that children possess. The ability to see beauty in nature and re-create it in art certainly is enhanced by strong visual-spatial perception, but it involves much more, such as motor performance, which will be discussed later. Creative writing ability, as opposed to simple verbal fluency and competence, is certainly related to the auditory-verbal system, but the creative aspect cannot be reduced to one skill. Musical ability does involve aspects of auditory perception, but characterizing it in that way alone would be simplistic. The ability to perceive subtlety and nuance in musical sounds, while more prevalent in people who have sensitive auditory perception, has many other aspects that stand on their own. Children's talents are best described in their own unique terms. While for discussion purposes I have to simplify the world into broad areas, such as auditory-verbal, visual-spatial, motor, and so on, we shouldn't lose sight of the fact that many of our unique human talents involve combinations of these skills and have their own, often indescribable characteristics.

Attention Problems and the Motor System

A child's motor system also influences the way she pays attention. Unlike information processing, which is how the child *takes in* data, the motor system is the "outflow" system—how the child communicates to the world her feelings, thoughts, and ideas. The motor system contributes to how she organizes her behavior in terms of sequences or patterns of movements, so if it is difficult for the child to organize her body and movement patterns, it will be hard for her to pay attention. The very act of looking or listening involves organized, purposeful movement patterns. If something is hard for us, such as sequencing three or four motor acts together, we tend to get distracted more easily.

A child's difficulties with her motor system tend to fall into certain categories. She may have problems with *motor tone, motor planning,* or *perceptual motor tasks* (in such tasks as copying shapes). *Motor tone* depends on balance between the "flexor" muscles (used to bend knees, bend at the waist, and so on) and the "extensor" muscles (used to help us stand erect). A child with "tight" (or high) motor tone probably has greater extensor tone than flexor tone. She may appear stiff and perhaps awkward. Low motor tone involves greater flexor tendencies. A child with low motor tone will appear loose, even floppy. As a baby, she may have had a hard time holding her head up, for example. As an older child, she may be extremely flexible, but also have to put so much effort into routine activities, like walking and sitting erect, that she tires easily.

Motor planning is the ability to carry out a series of physical activities—such as crawling, sitting, skipping, buttoning, tying shoes, or writing—in short, anything that involves sequencing a series of actions into a pattern. Motor planning also involves behavioral sequences, such as greetings (saying hello and waving your hand), waving good-bye, and other social sequences that we often take for granted. These social behaviors also involve creating a sequence pattern—one behavior after another. A child with motor-planning difficulties, however, may have to think through behaviors that for others are automatic. Figuring out how to start a conversation, or choosing the appropriate distance between yourself and another person to avoid invading the other's space, or knowing where assertiveness ends and aggressiveness begins can also involve motor planning.

Perceptual motor ability has to do with taking in information, comprehending that information, and then translating it into a motor action. For example, when a child has to copy a triangle, she has to absorb the visual image of the triangle, comprehend that image, then carry out a physical task based on that image. A perceptual motor problem refers to a glitch anywhere along that pathway—taking in the image, comprehending the image, and going from comprehending the image to a plan for a motor pattern. Or there may be a problem in actually carrying out the motor pattern (that is, getting the hand to do what you want). "My hands won't do what my eyes see" is how some children have described their difficulty.

Since perceptual motor skills involve motor planning, some professionals lump all of these steps under the category of "motor planning." You need to be aware that these terms are sometimes used differently. But no matter what you call it—a motor-planning problem or a perceptual motor problem—parents will find it helpful to figure out whether their child is having a problem in taking in information, comprehending the information, or planning or implementing her motor response. If the challenge is in implementing, parents will also find it helpful to note whether the problems are more with gross motor skills (running, jumping, climbing, kicking) or fine motor skills (writing and drawing).

At first, it may not be obvious why a child's "outflow"—how she sequences her behavior—contributes to attentional difficulties. But keep in mind that "paying attention," as I have said, is not a passive process. It is an active, dynamic process, usually involving some kind of interaction with a person or object. Consider a child who wants to take a toy car and move it from her house to your house as part of pretend play. She then plans to pick up "passengers" at your house and take them to the doctor, where she will be the nurse and the doctor and give them all kinds of interesting injections. But because of motor-planning problems, her hands aren't easily able to implement this well-constructed drama. As she is trying to get the car out of the garage, the simple motor act of putting up the door on the toy garage and slipping the car out before the door comes down is too great a challenge for her limited sequencing abilities. How can she go on a trip if she can't get the car out of the garage?

There are two consequences here. The first is that the motor pattern, which has many elements to it, gets cut short. The attention associated with this potential pattern also gets cut short. What started out as nice make-believe now looks like a very fragmented sequence as the little girl simply bangs the garage door. When a child can't easily carry out what her mind wants her hands to do, frustration is likely to set in, and that often breeds chaotic, seemingly aimless behavior. Some children with this motor-planning problem may gradually give up their active, organized imagination. It's a bit like a writer who has no access to pencil, typewriter, computer, or paper and no one even to talk to about her great plot ideas. Through simple disuse and lack of feedback, she may stop conjuring up stories. The old saying about adults' mental skills—"Use it or lose it"—is often true for people at all stages of the life cycle. Some children are fortunate in that their parents or teachers provide an excited audience for their ideas and plot lines. Even though they can't perform the drama, they can describe what they want to do and receive appropriate feedback. But before learning to talk fluently, or if she is in a family or educational system where paying attention to a child's creative thoughts or play is not a priority, the child may give up her ability, especially when she can't perform the motor acts that bring to her creative planning a sense of mastery.

In a number of instances, I have seen a child with motor-planning trouble, whose teachers and parents believed that she had a paucity of ideas, blossom into a rich, creative thinker overnight when she is given a tape recorder. Her "outflow" track has been made easier. That is, rather than having to craft each letter painfully and arduously, the child now simply speaks into a machine. The child who also has word retrieval problems can be assisted by a parent or teacher who helps her find a word to express herself when she hits a stumbling block.

Motor planning, as you can see, is a key component of attention. It can even affect one's thinking ability. The longer and more complicated the motor pattern the child can navigate, the more attentive she appears. The shorter the child's sequence of expressive behavior, independent of the creativity of the thoughts underneath stirring her desire to act, the shorter the attention span. There are many children who, as our earlier example suggested, literally can't get the "horse out of the barn."

Let's illustrate that once again with shooting a basketball.

An experienced basketball player with good motor sequencing skills will dribble the ball up to the net, and then shoot the ball into the hoop. The different steps involved in dribbling the ball, planting the heels and pulling up, rising in the air, bringing the ball up, rolling it onto the fingertips of one hand, sliding the other hand down to the side of the ball, and then shooting it toward the basket are all part of a smooth pattern. Each element of the sequence is no longer separate but a step in one apparently seamless movement. Once the player starts this movement pattern, it's easy for her to continue in an organized, focused, and attentive way because the elements are part of a larger pattern. She doesn't separate out the components in her mind. But when this player was just starting to learn to play, her coach probably broke the sequence into separate parts—dribbling the ball, picking it up with one hand, raising her arms, balancing it on her fingertips, and pushing it up and toward the basket. As a beginner, she needed quite a bit of concentration to sustain that five or ten seconds of attention to produce one smooth movement. If each separate element, which took only a split second, was hard to master, the basketball player could easily lose her concentration. The more conscious effort it takes to sustain the sequence of motor movements, the more opportunity there is to lose one's attention between two movements.

The same is true with a child with a motor-planning difficulty who is writing the word "store." Her motor system can't organize itself in terms of a long pattern. So each component— putting the pencil down to the paper, making the curved line for the letter *s*, lifting the pencil back up, putting it back down to make the vertical line for the *t*, and so on involves separate motor acts by the child—each one providing an opportunity for a loss of attention. On the other hand, a child who can effortlessly put together the whole pattern can start the word without even thinking about finishing it. The whole word flows as one—it is taken for granted. She doesn't have to stop and think, "Now I am making the *s* and now I am making the *t*," unless she is just beginning to learn to write the word. If this motor action flows effortlessly, one's attention is sustained easily and effortlessly. But if one sees a series of separate motor acts, like the novice basketball player or the struggling young writer, these separate components remain isolated—each one with its own task of attention. And it's easy to see how stringing together ten separate units of attention is a lot harder than having one ten-second pattern of attention.

Children who have difficulties with *perceptual motor skills*—perceiving and then translating what they perceive into activity, such as copying a teacher's sentence off the blackboard—have the same troubles. A child with good perceptual motor skills will effortlessly copy the sentence on the blackboard onto the paper at her desk. Those letters and words are part of one large perceptual motor pattern; the child does it almost without thinking. But a child with poor perceptual motor skills has to separate out each step in her mind. The child pictures the word "cat," trying to hold in mind the word and print letters that look like the word "cat." But it's no longer a smooth, automatic motor pattern. As she writes, the *c* starts to look like a *d*, the *a* looks like a *v*, and the *t* looks like an *l*. The child looks at her work. It doesn't look like the word the teacher wrote on the blackboard. Her work was a series of separate efforts—picturing each letter, trying to copy them, getting dissatisfied. At each juncture, there is a breakdown in attention because the work requires sustained conscious effort.

When you have smooth, automatic patterns of motor planning or perceptual motor behavior, you have a large "unit" of attention. It's easy, then, to string these large units of attention together into minutes and hours. On the other hand, when you must undertake a separate, planned, conscious action every few seconds, there is room for lots of interruptions in the breaks between each action.

With a series of smaller attention units, there is also more room for frustration and avoidance. This, of course, compounds the opportunity for inattention because anytime a child (or adult) feels uneasy or unsure of herself, she is going to be more easily distracted and more willing to "escape" (either physically or through such tactics as daydreaming).

The challenge is a little different for a child with low or high motor tone. But the result is the same—a child who has trouble performing certain tasks will find more opportunities for inter-ruption and more chances to become frustrated and inattentive. A child with low muscle tone may have trouble holding her head up to watch the teacher move back and forth in front of the blackboard. A child with high muscle tone may have difficulty controlling her pencil enough to make the subtle movements that are necessary to copy a letter. Normally, the balance between ex-tensor and flexor muscles carries one along, whether the activity is walking, writing, or riding a bicycle. One's muscles work auto-matically. But when the extensor and flexor muscles aren't work-ing together easily, a child has to put more of a conscious effort into activities that, for the rest of us, are easy and effortless. Imag-ine, for example, taking a stroll through a garden with a friend. You walk along, lost in conversation. It's effortless and relaxing. But picture yourself on ice skates for the first time. You have to think about every little muscle movement. You are exhausted af-ter ten minutes because you are thinking so hard and because you are training your muscles to do something new. A child with low motor tone has much the same challenges as you would as you struggle on ice skates. For her, every new skill—whether it is writing a word or holding her head up—is like learning to ice-skate. Each of these motor acts must be conscious rather than automatic. And each time the child has to make a new conscious effort like that, there is an opportunity to lose concentration.

Reactivity Problems

Attention also lags because of the way the child reacts to sensations. Children who *underreact* or *overreact* to sensations may find it difficult to tune in and concentrate.

A child who underreacts, as you may recall from chapter 4 on the self-absorbed child, needs a lot of input. If she underreacts to *sound*, it means that it takes a lot of noise before she responds. You need to speak to her in a persistent and energetic way and with a compelling voice tone. If she doesn't get that energetic input, her attention will wander. When she was a baby or a tod-dler, her parents may have needed to speak loudly and persis-tently in order to get her attention. If their voices became too soothing or quiet, she lost interest and looked away. As a preschooler, she probably preferred tuning into her own world in pretend play—not because she wasn't interested in the words of her parents but because she couldn't pay attention to them unless their voices were clear and insistent. As a school-age child, she seems to be preoccupied with her own daydreams and inner thoughts, staring out the window during class. But if the teacher comes over to her and says in a commanding voice, "Jennifer, did you hear me? I said, 'Please turn to page 53 in your history book,'" she will turn, surprised, as if she hadn't realized until then that she was being spoken to.

In fact, it's easy to assume that such a child, with her dreaminess and inattentiveness, is deliberately not paying attention, that she doesn't want to listen. Others may find themselves repeatedly saying "Please listen to me" or "You're not listening to me!" What they often don't realize is that this child simply requires a more commanding, persistent sound before she can pay attention, and that it takes her a little while to turn from her own inner thoughts to tuning in to those who are talking to her.

Children who underreact *visually* need vivid, compelling imagery to command their attention or else they also will stay tuned into their own thoughts. As babies, they don't necessarily respond quickly to a mother's smiling face or a father's big grin. They need parents to be persistent with animated faces and big smiles before they can really tune in. As preschoolers and school-age children, they need brighter colors, more vivid designs to help them pay attention to what is before them. Otherwise, their attention wanders. Teachers sometimes wonder why these children are riveted to Nintendo games or action movies but unable to concentrate while writing on the classroom blackboard. That is because the fast-moving images and the bright colors of the games or movies hold their attention, while the static, black-and-white images of the blackboard do not.

On the opposite side of the scale are children who have difficulty paying attention because they are *too* sensitive to such sensations as touch, sound, movements, sights. As was explained in chapter 3 on the highly sensitive child, we used to think that everyone's senses operated similarly—that we were all tuned to the same frequency. But we now understand that everyone has a unique level of response to sights, sounds, smells, touch. Many highly sensitive children are too "tuned in." Their senses lack an adequate filter: sights, noises, odors, and touch that bring other people pleasure can be overwhelming, irritating, and sometimes downright painful to them.

Such oversensitive children may have attention problems. A baby may have trouble focusing on her parent's faces because she is so distracted by other sights, sounds, and smells surrounding her. A toddler distracted by every new sight and sound darts around to look at this or that rather than focusing on one person or one toy for a time. A preschooler involved in pretend play with her dolls and toys turns from one toy to another because each one grabs her attention, and she can't decide which one to play with. A school-age child has trouble concentrating in the classroom because she is overwhelmed by the hustle and bustle. She may sit at her desk and hear not only her teacher's voice, but also the giggling and whispering of the children two rows back, a horn honking in the school parking lot, footsteps in the hall, and the paper being crumpled by the child seated next to her. Even her own thoughts are hard to ignore. No wonder it is hard to concentrate! If she is sensitive to touch, she may not be able to sit and listen to the gym teacher's instructions in gym class or focus on the principal's words during assembly because of the children pressed up against her on the gymnasium floor.

It's not that the sensitive child is stubbornly refusing to stick to one thing. Her sensitivity to every type of sensation in the world around her pulls her in many directions at once.

Not all overly sensitive children have attentional problems. This would depend on just how sensitive the child is and how her nervous system compensates for her sensitivity. As we will see, the type of parenting she receives can make a difference. If teachers and parents can help her focus (in spite of being pulled in every direction), she will have less difficulty.

EMOTIONS AND ATTENTION

As we discuss the different ways in which children process information and react to sensations, we also need to be aware of the way emotion, or "affect" (a technical term to describe specific types of emotions), influences attention. We tend to think of a highly emotional child as being inattentive, driven by her emotional needs of the moment. But consider for a moment how all of us decide what to pay attention to and how vigilantly to attend to something. Some desire—that is, emotion—of the moment actually directs our attention. We are interested in a picture, we find that car exciting, we enjoy certain music. We are enthralled by a story, fascinated by a TV show, or bored to tears by a dull teacher. However, if we desperately want to get an A, we virtually will ourselves to pay attention. In all of these circumstances, including situations in which we force ourselves to pay attention, there is a desire or some feeling guiding the attention. In fact, we can think of attention in part as the persistence of a state of *focused motivation* or desire or emotion.

When there is persistence of an emotional interest, be it focused on a toy, a computer game, or a math problem, there is persistence of attention. Therefore, emotion, which can interfere with attention when it is extreme, is nevertheless the cornerstone of attention. This fact has a number of immediate implications. For example, when helping children achieve longer and longer states of attention, we have frequently found the most success by discovering areas of very high motivation (states of mind charged with feeling) in the child and working with these to expand attention. One child who flitted around the room, spending only a couple of seconds with each toy, decided he wanted to climb out the window. Here was a chance, I thought, to sustain his attention through his emotional interest. His parents got in front of the ground-floor window and, with my encouragement, started talking to him about what would be great about climbing outside and what he would do there and why climbing over the windowsill was more exciting than going through the door. To be sure, the child whined and pushed at his dad, but it was the only time during the session that he talked directly to his father. He stayed focused for a full seven minutes. This child, who had been diagnosed as having a severe attentional problem, was previously thought to be incapable of spending more than a few seconds on anything, let alone seven minutes involved not only in focused attention but also in a logical, purposeful interaction.

Sometimes what appears to be distractibility is actually the child's passionate, often stubborn, interest in something else. I remember one mother who was trying to engage her five-year-old child in a back-and-forth sing-along game. The child seemingly kept getting distracted by a little blue toy car he was fingering. "See?" said his mother to me. "I can't keep him on anything. He is so distractible." I wondered out loud if in this particular instance his stubborn refusal to engage in the sing-along game wasn't part of his keen interest in that blue car. We tried an experiment. His mother joined him in playing with the blue car and made the car begin to speed away from the boy, who diligently chased and caught it. After recapturing the car for a moment and quickly hiding it in her pocketbook, the mother had the car sing clues to its whereabouts to the boy. With a big smile, the eager boy found the car and then wanted to hide it for his mother. A focused game around the car evolved and went on for at least five minutes before we stopped it. In this instance, the child's lack of attention on one thing was actually his greater *emotional* interest and attention to something else. His emotional interest was guiding his attention. For this reason, as I suggested earlier, we could define attention in part as *the persistence of an emotional interest*. This does not mean that some individuals do not find it easy to pay attention even when they lack motivation or emotional interest— a type of dutiful attending. It does mean, however, that emotions are a very important component of attention. Looking at the persistence of emotional interest may open up new understanding of how we pay attention.

ATTENTION AND LEARNING DIFFICULTIES

While some children are very attentive despite having a learning difficulty in a particular area, such as reading or math, most children with learning difficulties tend to get easily distracted, especially in the areas where they are having difficulties. Traditionally, we have thought about learning difficulties (or learning challenges, as I like to call them) in terms of particular subjects: Jennifer is having trouble with penmanship, Matthew is struggling with reading, while Rena wrestles with math. It seems useful to relate these learning challenges in certain subjects to difficulties in the three areas we discussed earlier (as many educators are doing): *processing information, motor problems,* or *under-* or *overreactivity* to the world. Many "learning disabilities" can in part be related to these challenges. For example, difficulties with certain kinds of math problems are often related to visual-spatial processing. Difficulty with writing and penmanship is often a result of motor-planning trouble or perceptual motor challenges. Difficulties with following spoken directions or remembering a story are often related to auditory processing. Each type of difficulty can be broken down into more details or parts, and we are constantly learning new ways to conceptualize and remediate the processes associated with such basics as math, reading, spelling, and writing.

What are sometimes referred to as organizational learning problems (including remembering to get homework assignments, bring home the right books, even hand in completed assignments, or many other details that are associated with being "responsible") are often related to motor-planning or sequencing problems and, not infrequently, to auditory or visual-spatial challenges as well. There is difficulty either in carrying out a sequence of behaviors, such as writing down assignments or selecting the books (motor planning) or remembering the assignments (auditory processing).

PARENTING PATTERNS TO AVOID WITH AN INATTENTIVE CHILD

Many parents (and educators) focus so hard on problems of attention that they ignore or downplay the child's many assets. By stressing her weaknesses, they undermine the very abilities that may help her compensate for her challenges. Imagine if you had to spend 80 percent of your adult life doing tasks that were extremely difficult for you. For instance, think of being a poorly coordinated person spending the day shooting baskets, or a right-handed person spending all day writing left-handed. Needless to say, it would be hard to concentrate. You would probably day-dream or even want to run away.

That's how a child with these challenges can feel. For example, the parents of a child who is good in math but a slow reader may work with her exclusively on her reading. At school, her teacher gives her extra reading assignments so that she can practice. No wonder this child has trouble concentrating on the assignments. She ends up looking inattentive because she is spending most of her time practicing a skill that is hard for her. It's easy to see how she could mistakenly be labeled as having a general attention problem when, in fact, her attention problem may be specific only to the areas that are hard for her.

When parents or educators aren't balanced in their appreciation of the child's strengths and vulnerabilities, they may not only overemphasize the child's vulnerabilities but also use the vulnerable area as a mode of general communication, further compromising the child's ability to attend and comprehend. For instance, a child who has an auditory processing difficulty may find it hard to attend to sounds and words, but she could be quite gifted in attending to visual input and to interactive opportunities as well as hands-on doing. A constant stream of spoken advice and directions that this child is less able to comprehend will thereby exaggerate her difficulty.

Another hazard in dealing with inattentive children is treating them in a mechanical and inflexible manner. Since such children are not viewed as being very reflective or motivated, they are simply told what to do. Rather than helping the child develop motivation and a reflective attitude about her behavior, parents tend to deal with the child in lots of "do's and don't's" and avoid debates. They don't help the child ponder her behavior so she can figure out better strategies. Rather than supporting the child's particular interests and encouraging her problem-solving ability, they stress rote approaches and fixed, repetitive behaviors.

With a child who is struggling yet apparently not paying attention, it is all too easy to humiliate or frustrate her with unrealistic demands rather than realizing that the child wants to understand but needs to develop her own unique pathway to concentrated attention. There is a tendency to want a child to learn like other children. The demand for immediate conformity also may push the child into more rote, mechanical ways of doing things, rather than developing and using particular strengths to bypass the processing or motor challenges.

HOW PARENTS CAN HELP AN INATTENTIVE CHILD

Children with attention and learning difficulties require more practice and work to master basic emotional milestones and skills than other children. Like teaching a right-handed person to throw a curve ball with her left hand, it can be done, but only with patience and practice. Such a child also needs help in learning to use her strengths as an ally in overcoming her vulnerabilities or weaknesses. She needs to be able to reflect on her own behavior, feelings, and tendencies more than the average child. If she knows what her challenge is, she is more likely to be able to observe herself and develop compensatory strengths. She also needs to be able to collaborate constructively with parents and teachers rather than escaping or withdrawing her attention. The inattentive child requires a greater degree of self-acceptance and patience with herself than most children because of the frustrations she and her parents often encounter.

Building on Strengths

The principal task for parents of an inattentive child is to develop a sense of mastery around her natural strengths. Rather than spending all their time trying to correct her weaknesses, they need to spend at least 50 percent of their time on her strengths. A child has to *want* to learn; it has to be fun and pleasant.

Even during early infancy, we can begin to note attentional challenges and work with the child's abilities. In the first stage of development—that of being able to focus in on the world and stay calm while looking and listening—the parents may notice that certain types of sensations tend to distract their child. Talking or singing rapidly to a child with auditory processing difficulties, for example, may cause her to tune out. Communicating more slowly and calmly and in shorter segments may help her to focus better. With a baby, you might hum and sing in simple rhythms to get and hold her attention rather than in more complicated patterns. With a toddler, you would keep your questions and instructions simple at first: "Please pick up your truck" instead of "Please pick up your truck and ball and put them in your toy chest." With a preschooler, you would focus on simple questions (such as "What do you want to eat?" or "What do you want to do next?") before asking more complex why, how, and what questions (such as "Why would you want to do that?").

Many children with auditory processing difficulties are strong visually. If so, you may want to relate to this child both visually and verbally. With a baby you would use animated facial features. With a toddler, you could gesture to your toddler a lot (instead of asking your child if she wants "juice in your favorite big orange cup," for example, you might pick up the cup, point to it, and then point at the juice container, while asking "Juice?"). While playing with a preschooler you might communicate visually. For example, if your doll is going to drive her car, in addition to saying, "I'm going to take the car for a ride," you could have the doll point at the car and make driving-type gestures as she enters it. In this way, your toddler sees and hears the key elements of the drama and can respond, perhaps by having her lion chase and eat up the doll and the car! An older child may benefit from having pictorial instructions as well as verbal ones or from having some schoolwork, such as math problems, presented both verbally and with visual symbols.

With a child who is the reverse—strong in auditory-verbal skills and weaker visually—you would focus more on talking and less on showing. With a baby, use lots of babbling, singing, and chattering. You would use more complicated sentences with a toddler ("Would you like your juice in your favorite big orange cup?"). And with a preschooler or a school-age child, you could expect longer and longer dialogues.

If you ask this child to draw a map of how to get to the playground, or to build an intricate structure, you might suddenly see a very inattentive child. When this happens, a useful tactic can be to have your child talk her way through the task. In other words, because the child may not see it or picture it easily, she may be better able to find her way to the park through a series of verbal statements than to picture it graphically. If you then help your child practice going from the verbal to the visual, she can strengthen her spatial reasoning abilities. For example, a child who knows all her math facts but doesn't have a good internal spatial sense of quantity may say quickly, "two plus three equals five" because she has memorized it. Then you could say, "Show me with your hands how much two apples would be if you put them side by side. And now show me what three would be. And now show me what five would be." Then you could add, "And now can you close your eyes and actually picture five apples end-to-end? Then can you put two away and picture three?"

Such an exercise will help a verbal child become more attentive to her visual-spatial world. Without such an ability, she most likely will become more inattentive as she gets into higher-level math where picturing a problem is essential to a solution.

With a child who has vulnerabilities with motor skills—motor planning or perceptual motor skills, for example—the same principles apply. Look for an area of strength (if your child is weak in motor skills, she may be strong in either auditory or visual skills) and use that strength to help her over developmental hurdles. This strategy helps avoid endless frustration to both child and parent. A child who has trouble getting dressed or tying her shoes or copying a sentence off the blackboard can easily get frustrated and give up. Power struggles ensue between the understandably frustrated parent or teacher and the increasingly recalcitrant child:

> PARENT: Come on! I've shown you how to tie those shoes a thousand times.
> CHILD: I can't! I get all messed up. These are stupid shoes anyway. I hate them!
> PARENT: I paid good money for those shoes. Don't throw them like that!
> CHILD: I won't wear them. They're ugly!

Instead of such an impasse, I've seen one such child who has strong verbal skills learn to talk herself through tying her shoes after her father described it to her beforehand. "Now I grab the right lace with my right hand and the left lace with my left hand," she would mutter as she bent over her shoes. "Then I cross the right lace over the left lace and tuck it under . . ." and so on. With a child who is strong visually, you could diagram the process for her. She then follows the diagram until she feels comfortable tying her shoes without it.

As you can see, this approach is based on the idea that many children do not have a problem with paying attention in *all* areas. Rather, they are relatively more attentive or less attentive depending on their ability to *process information* in a certain area. With flexibility on the part of the parents, children can usually compensate for some of their areas of vulnerability. Remember, in an area where a child has a processing difficulty, always use infinite patience (as hard as it may be!) and practice. Power struggles over the child's vulnerability will only make the challenge greater. Children can handle pressure in areas where they are, relatively speaking, strong. Vulnerabilities, however, require "P & P"—Patience and Practice.

As I discussed earlier, in addition to the processing of information, children can also be inattentive because they are either over- or underreactive to information presented to them through one or another of their senses. In this case, parents can adjust the type and level of sensory information they provide. If the child is underreactive, the parent attempts to energize the mode of communication and make the information richer and more salient, as if to say "Hey, pay attention!" For the overreactive child, the parent may lower the level of stimulation. Words may be spoken more softly and slowly. Less color, brightness, and texture may help with visual information. One-on-one teaching or small groups may be preferable to a noisy classroom all the time.

Sometimes, as a usually attentive child enters preschool, she is suddenly labeled inattentive. The child hasn't changed, but, instead of dealing with one-on-one relationships or just two neighborhood friends, she is now coping with ten to twenty children in a busy, noisy classroom. If she is sensitive to touch and sound, being jostled by other kids coupled with their loud chatter is enough to make her easily distracted. Even during an activity that seems to be very structured, like circle time, the mere physical proximity of the other children may be enough to overly stimulate the highly sensitive child. Simply creating a smaller group within the larger group (one to three children in a corner of the room) settles some children down and helps them be attentive. This child may also be helped by rhythmic motion (swinging) or steady, firm touching, such as a back rub.

Harnessing Emotions

The most important helpers a parent can have with an inattentive son or daughter are the child's own emotions and desires. This is often overlooked. Simply talking to a child or presenting certain tasks without harnessing the child's natural desires and emotions can be a dead end.

For children (both young and older) who have difficulties maintaining their attention because of motor planning, auditory processing difficulties, or any other reasons, it's worthwhile to try to maintain their attention through behavioral and emotional interactions, allowing the more difficult, symbolic verbal, visual, or motor acts to "tag along."

You have probably noticed that if you try to just talk to a child, she may fidget, daydream, look out the window, or ignore you and start playing. Similarly, if you ask her to draw a picture of her family and she is not very gifted in motor sequencing or picking up visual details, she may also tune out. But if you start playing with her, stealing her favorite Barbie and hiding her under the rug, the formerly verbally inattentive child becomes verbally attentive and interactive: "Give her back to me! I want her now! She's mine!" Sometimes a lively tea party or a great car race provide the subtext for what I would call higher-level symbolic dialogues. Combining behavioral interactions with higher-level symbolic activity works well to harness attention because, as I said earlier, emotion or desire plays a critical role in focusing. When you talk to a child and she seems to tune you out, talking instead about what's for dinner, or going back to events of three days ago, or interrupting you with "Where's Aunt Anne?" it is easy to assume that her attention is wandering. In fact, what's happening is that she is attending to ideas other than the ones you are presenting to her. She is attending to what happened three days ago, her own hunger, or her aunt's visit. Her desire is not with you, but with these other interests. Focused attention, as I said, is in part the *persistence of desire or affect.* If we want our child to pay attention to what we are saying to her or doing with her, we must then help her become emotionally involved with us. Nothing does that better than creating a state of behavioral and emotional interaction. The more we are "doing" with another person, the more involved we become. Stories, pictures, and games capture a child's undivided attention. I often see a child who completely tunes out math but, in negotiating how many more minutes she can stay up to watch her favorite TV show, appears to be a master mathematician. "No, No, NO, five minutes isn't enough. I need at least twice that much because the commercial takes three minutes, and the show has at least twice that many minutes to go!"

While the child who finds it easy to pay attention is often thought of as having a "better" attention span, it may be that she really has a much greater desire to please or a much greater sense of satisfaction from listening and responding verbally so that there is more *emotion* generated in routine situations to harness her attention. Our seemingly more inattentive child may get turned on by something other than conversations with her parents. They will need to be especially mindful of her motivations and create situations that are charged enough to capture her attention. Students who learn best by doing hands-on work or through active debate, rather than by listening or reading, are examples of the need for this flexible approach.

Encouraging Attention at Each Stage of Development
Parents can encourage their child's ability to attend during all the stages of childhood. For each emotional milestone, they can reinforce her strengths and slowly present her with bite-size

pieces of information in her most vulnerable area. Don't be tempted to skip a challenge just because it seems too hard for your child. For example, if a baby tends to be more of a listener and finds it difficult to concentrate visually, parents might be inclined to assume that the baby likes to listen and doesn't like to look. They may decide not to spend that extra ten minutes talking while making animated facial expressions. But, in fact, the baby who doesn't find it easy to look may just need some extra practice in order to feel more comfortable maintaining a visual focus.

In the early stage of two-way communication, when gestures become more important, extra practice with children who find it difficult can make all the difference. For example, a toddler who is having a hard time with motor planning may not take mommy by the hand, walk to the bookshelf, rustle through the books, and point to a favorite picture book because stringing together that many actions may be difficult. Instead, the toddler may simply look around and get irritable, and appear more and more scattered. But the mother can encourage practice by breaking down this sequence of motor movements into simpler pieces. Along the way, she provides cues and signals to help the child with the next step. In a sense, she is helping her child practice being more attentive because, in fact, a child who is purposeful is by definition attentive. Here's how it would work: when the child looks across the room at the bookshelf, for example, mother could play dumb, saying "What?" and pointing to the shelf also.

"Want something?" she may say with a quizzical look and an inquiring shrug of her shoulders. "Show me."

Thus encouraged, the little girl gets up and starts walking toward the books. She stops, then, looking confused.

Mother helps her out. "Over there?" she says, pointing to the couch.

The toddler picks up on that cue, shakes her head, and points at the bookshelf. Mother walks over, but the toddler simply stares at the shelves. Mother helps her out again, pointing at a book she knows the toddler doesn't want. "The moon book?" she asks, pointing. This will help the toddler get the idea that she needs to point to something if she is going to get what she wants. The little girl points to her treasured favorite.

In this manner, the mother has helped her child piece together a fairly complex (for a child with motor-planning and motor-attentional difficulties) pattern of actions. Each step along the way, she provides a gesture or word of her own and offers inspiration and guidance for the next step, without doing the work for her (in other words, she doesn't immediately rush over and pull out the right book). In this way, the mother gives her child valuable practice in learning to put together some motor actions. After helping her out several times, the mother may cue her child for, say, every fifth step, letting the child carry out more and more actions on her own. Thus, bit by bit, the child learns to string together more complicated sequences.

The stage of emotional ideas, when make-believe becomes important to a child's development, is not always easy for a child with attention problems. Such youngsters often find it hard to contemplate what they want to do long enough to create the idea or the visual image, say, of building a castle or a bridge on which to stage a fight. Instead, they simply quickly put their impulses into action or become self-absorbed. When we look for the basis for attentional difficulties at this stage, in many instances, we find auditory or visual-spatial processing problems. In other words, they can't organize the words they hear or the images they see into a series of workable ideas. Therefore it is hard for such children to move from simply acting out what's on their minds (hitting, for example) to putting it into ideas (saying, "I'm mad!" or illustrating it through pretend play).

A child with auditory-verbal processing difficulties, for example, may not be able to talk for her dolls. She may find it easier just to bang the dolls together. Similarly, a child with a visual-spatial difficulty may not easily notice how different building materials or action figures fit together. For instance, it would be hard for such a child to construct a drama where she has two castles, with the good guys sneaking after the bad guys through a tunnel that runs between the two buildings. When you think about it, you realize that such a drama involves some rather complicated spatial concepts—different three-dimensional structures connected by an underground passage.

Parents can encourage both spatial and verbal concepts in play and thus increase their particular child's ability to pay attention. For example, a parent can encourage a child who doesn't easily understand words or can't communicate easily with her own words to practice with games that involve verbal communication. The parent's panda could talk to the child's bear first with simple words: "Tea?" the panda could suggest. "Cup, please!" "Enough tea? More? Less?" By constantly using words as part of your interaction and as part of your "character," you encourage your child to use words too or, at least, to process your words. As you open and close circles of communication with words, responding to your child's words and, in turn, helping your child build on your words, you create longer and longer sequences and, hence, help your child pay attention for greater periods of time.

With a child who is relatively weaker visually, you can emphasize play that builds these skills. For example, in a fight between the Power Rangers and the bad guy Putties, the parent could wonder, "Where are the Putties going to hide?" "How will the Power Rangers get back to their school?" and so forth.

Emotional thinking, the next step in emotional development, and attention also go hand in hand. In order to think emotionally, a child must remember and connect a number of logical units of ideas. For example, a child who is arguing for a later bedtime points out, "But I'm not tired! And so since I'll just lie awake in bed, I might as well stay down here and watch more TV." Making such a statement requires attention to three or four logical links that a child with attentional problems may have difficulty making. She may simply announce, "I want to stay up later!" To help such a child practice more logical thinking and at the same time develop her attention span, you can encourage debates and "lawyer-to-lawyer" discussions. "Why do you want to stay up later?" you could ask in a friendly tone. "Give me two good reasons and maybe we can work something out."

As you challenge your child's debating skills, you also help your child connect her emotion, or desire, to her ability to string

together many ideas logically. There is nothing that motivates a
child's desire more than a good, healthy debate in which she is
trying to point out that she is right and you are wrong! Such
emotionally based discussions, be they over bedtime, food, manners, choice of clothes, or any of a hundred topics that create
friction between children and parents, are far more effective for
improving attention than any emotionally empty, contrived task.
Through these long emotionally driven sequences you are also
giving your child general practice in sequencing ideas and behaviors, an important aspect of motor planning.

During the next stage of development, when children are
naturally more interested in triangular relationships, you can encourage more complex thinking by helping a child consider the
implications of her behavior for other people. For instance, if she
is trying to get her mother to let her stay up late, the mother
could ask, "What do you think Dad would think of you going to
bed an hour later?" You are helping the child to think in terms of
a three-person system, where she is considering the feelings or
ideas of the person she is dealing with, as well as someone else.
Similarly, if your child wants to invite her "best friend" over but is
ignoring her other "best friend," you could ask (not in a negative
or critical way), "What do you think Claire would think if you
invite only Alicia over?" Now your child is attending not just over
a period of time but is attending to more intricate details in a
complex pattern. She is learning to consider not only what happens to the person she is dealing with directly but also to a third
person who is involved in the relationship. Attention now involves
not simply how long one can ponder, study, or concentrate on
something, but how well one can take into account all the *different*
parts of the pattern.

Attention is especially important, and can be severely challenged, during the next phase of development when the child's
world comes to include other children. The child's ability to plan
sequences of behavior or action, or to absorb auditory or visual
information is now being called upon in a much more challenging arena—the "politics of the playground." A child with poor
motor sequencing ability doesn't automatically "work the

crowd." Each step, each hello, each "can I play," each smile or frown has to be consciously planned. What others do on automatic pilot becomes a tiresome, anxious, effortful task. A child with weak auditory-verbal abilities, for example, can't perceive tones of voice easily. She has trouble telling when other children are angry, teasing, or happy. She can't figure out how to deal with them when they reject her because she's never sure whether they are serious. Such determinations depend on extremely rapid assessments of other children's words, vocal tone and rhythm, subtle sequences of words, and emotional emphasis. When many children are talking rapidly in a group, the child with poor auditory-verbal processing easily feels overwhelmed and confused. If the child also is highly sensitive to auditory stimuli, the volume of noise by itself can be extremely overloading, leading to confusion and distortion. Trying to make sense out of this confusion will lead some children to try to pay attention to one detail after another: listening to a part of what Julie is saying, a piece of what James is saying, Stephanie's giggle, and Molly's angry tone. The overall result is a very distracted youngster. If the child chooses instead to give up and tune into her own inner thoughts, she now appears less distracted but is inattentive in a self-absorbed way.

If such a child's visual perception is strong, her parents can help her use visual attention to focus on other children's facial expressions to pick up the emotional cues she needs and to make better sense out of what she is hearing in their voices. Conversely, a child who is weak in visual perceptions can be helped to use auditory and verbal skills to comprehend other children.

Often children are inattentive during this stage because they get overloaded. The child who is highly sensitive can easily be lost in the details of life and may need help in seeing the big picture. Say she comes home from school claiming that "Bart's mad at me. He hates me!" You might ask her how Bart has felt about her each day over the last week. Let's assume that she describes how Bart is angry with her one day and nice to her another day and ignores her on another day. You then might ask her how she puts these pieces together. She could conclude, "Well, I guess he doesn't know how to make up his mind." That's big-picture thinking and quite a different conclusion than she had before. Similarly, when reading a story to a child who needs help in focusing on broader concepts, rather than asking, "Now, what did the bear do after he got out of bed in the morning?" you could ask, "What's this story about? Is this a nice bear?" If the child is good at grasping the overall scheme but has difficulty with details, you might ask, "How do you know the bear is a grouchy type of bear?" The child who can see both the big picture and understand how the details support the picture has achieved a high level of attention. She has what most adults wish they had— big-picture conceptual attention and subtle-detail nuance attention over a period of time.

Keep in mind that children who have difficulty attending to the vast array of communications involved in relating to other children often need *more* practice with other children, not less. Many parents whose child is having difficulties with distractibility in their relationships tend to let their child shy away from other kids, or, out of embarrassment, they themselves avoid other children and families. Instead, parents and teachers need to help that child get more involved in the group—perhaps by arranging play dates, getting her involved in team sports like soccer or softball. In that way, she becomes involved in many interactions and has many opportunities to learn to read and attend to other children's verbal and nonverbal communications.

As a child gets older, her attentional capacity becomes more complex. In the stage when she begins forming her own inner values, her capacities for paying attention reach a new dimension. At this point, we observe children beginning to plan more, actually taking responsibility out of an inner desire of their own (for example, to study "because I really want to learn French. We may be going to France next year," or "I need to learn math so I can get a good job").

Discussions about a child's values or goals and the way her plans meet or don't meet those goals will help her elevate her attentional capacities to this new plane. Discussions about the "why" of behavior, rather than saying "Do this" or "Because I told you," are especially important at this stage. When a parent talks about the principle underlying a particular behavior (asking, for example, "What do you think is fair in this situation?"), he is supporting a child in her emerging capacity to abstract or form a general sense of self based on inner principles. Attention is needed not only for the here and now, but for planning the future. The child's ability to base her planning on inner goals and values helps her sustain her attention over long periods for such endeavors as research for a paper, building an engine, and practicing music or gymnastics.

Self-Observation and Self-Cuing

"Self-observing" and "self-cuing" capacities are abilities that children develop during the school years between ages five and twelve. By the time children are in the stage of "the world inside me," they are developing this ability to observe themselves. Not only is this a developmentally advanced form of awareness (paying attention to one's own thoughts and feelings) but it can also enable a child to overcome most of the routine difficulties of attention. For example, consider a very sensitive child who is easily distracted by every sight and sound around her. She can hardly pay attention to the teacher when the older boy she has a crush on is whispering to her friend just to her left and the boy on her right is talking to another child about a plot at recess. She gets completely overloaded. Add the roar of an airplane outside or a few kids talking in the hallway, and the child may not only be inattentive and distracted, but may be jumping out of her seat as if her body were being pulled in a hundred different directions. But she can call on her self-observing ability, saying to herself, "Here I go again. Listening to everything and everyone except the teacher. I'm not going to know how to do my homework later unless I tune back in to Mrs. Rodriguez." Her ability to make this self-observation will be greatly enhanced by prior problem-solving discussions with her parents and, possibly, her teachers or counselors in which she has imagined herself in precisely this situation. Most young children don't have this ability, which tends to emerge during the school years. Like all skills, it can be harnessed and refined by use and practice.

Self-cuing has to do with reminding oneself to pay attention and forming a strategy to do this. A child might take notes or ask herself every few minutes: "What did she just say?" At first, this may seem almost silly. But an internal dialogue, a form of pinching yourself to take notice, is just what can help an easily distracted person. It creates an active, internal process where information is consciously pursued. Many children, and many adults, don't need this process: they can listen passively, attend, and automatically register the teacher's words. Other students require this active, internal voice—this investigative stance—constantly asking, "What in the world is she talking about?"

Self-cuing is also useful to the child whose inattentiveness takes the form of what is sometimes called an "organizational learning problem." This problem manifests itself when a student forgets to bring home her books or remembers the books but forgets the homework assignments. Or, if she remembers the books and assignments, she forgets to hand in the homework the next day! This common difficulty is often related to a larger problem with sequencing. Parents and teachers become enormously frustrated with this child. They lecture her, punish her, yell at her, but to no avail. They often assume that she doesn't care. What they do not see is that for this child, creating these sequences of behaviors requires a great deal of conscious thought and effort, unlike other children for whom bringing home books or homework assignments is as routine as putting on shoes and socks in the morning. Interestingly, upon reflection these parents often remember that they also had trouble learning the sequences involved in such daily routines as getting dressed, getting ready for school, and bringing home assignments.

For this organizational learning problem, self-observation and self-cuing skills can be extraordinarily helpful. For example, through prior practice the child learns to associate seeing the door that leads out of school with a big sign that says "Do you have your homework?" For the child who has difficulty creating this image that will cue her up and remind her to ask whether she has her homework assignment for each class, one can go a step further. She could arrange to have a "homework pass" signed by her homeroom teacher in order to get on the school bus. She gets it signed by showing her teacher that her assignments are written down. These types of self-cuing strategies are used by the many adults who put notes on the refrigerator to remind themselves of chores or who rely on lists to keep organized.

PROFESSIONAL THERAPY AND THE QUESTION OF MEDICATION

When a child who finds it hard to concentrate and attend is labeled as having Attention Deficit Disorder, and, as is often the case, medication is suggested, parents are frequently unsure about what to do.

In making a decision, they need to be aware that a number of factors can be first overlooked in diagnosing and treating these children. One factor is the difference between how a child attends and thinks in an *optimal* setting—for example, how does she behave with one supportive, encouraging adult, as opposed to how she behaves in a noisy, busy classroom of twenty-five children and an overworked teacher.

Another question to consider is whether or not a child's attention problem can be related to aspects of her development. We need to look at how a child reacts to and processes different sensations and motor patterns. Is she over- or undersensitive to sounds or words, sights, smells, and so on? Does she have difficulty comprehending sounds or spoken words or designs, letters, or written words? Does she have difficulty carrying out complex motor patterns? Does she have difficulty with motor planning? All these questions are vital in planning treatment.

Still another factor is whether a child is experiencing stress at home. Is he or she worried, preoccupied, frightened, or overstimulated?

Before a proper diagnosis can be made and treatment recommended, all these factors must be considered. Also, professionals need to think about how a child functions at home, school, and with his or her friends, as well as the boy or girl's own thoughts and feelings and family history. A proper evaluation often takes many meetings with a highly trained professional.

The following guidelines might help you as you decide what is the best approach for your child:

• When a child can attend and think in an optimal setting, such as a one-on-one relationship, but can't easily pay attention in a large group, this suggests that the child has the basic *ability* for paying attention. So you can try to tailor your child's learning environment to her learning capacities and gradually help her develop more flexibility as she matures.

• If a child has difficulty with under- or overreactivity to any of the sensations that we have discussed, a great deal can be done to help your child improve the ability to attend, think, and learn. A speech and hearing therapist, for example, can help with auditory processing difficulties. An occupational therapist can help with motor or sensory reactivity and processing difficulties. Special educators can also help with processing difficulties. Therapists can show a child new coping strategies, such as helping her "see the big picture," rather than getting lost in the details of life.

• Emotional difficulties within a child's family often can be helped by appropriate types of therapy, such as counseling.

Before considering medication, I recommend—in addition to a complete evaluation—that the following conditions be met:

1. A child has difficulty attending and organizing her thoughts in an optimal one-on-one setting.

2. Working with a child's unique processing abilities has not helped much.

3. Family problems and emotional factors have been fully explored and addressed.

4. After a reasonable attempt at therapy (lasting at least eight to twelve months), there has been insufficient progress. This therapy should be aimed at helping a child develop constructive coping mechanisms and at helping her understand and deal with

her patterns of avoidance and escape, as well as the feelings that she has about those patterns.

If medication is tried, it needs to be accompanied by regular therapy so that the child can continue to work on developing improved coping mechanisms that may enable her to learn to pay attention, concentrate, and think logically without medication. Therapy will also help the child who must take medication deal with her feelings.

LOUISA'S STORY

Nine-and-a-half-year-old Louisa Maxima came to see me because her parents and teachers were extremely worried about her progress in school. She was a restless, dreamy child—she looked out the window, wandered around the classroom when she was supposed to be seated at her desk, went to the bathroom up to a dozen times a day—who did anything except focus on her schoolwork. Her grades were suffering: she got mostly Cs and Ds. She claimed she felt "mixed up" about her schoolwork, that she didn't understand the assignments. Even on the occasions when she remembered to bring her homework home from school, she didn't seem to be able to sit still to do it. In fact, Louisa didn't seem to be able to sit still at all—she gulped her meals and then slipped away from the table. She was constantly darting off during a conversation or slipping off in a daydream when an adult was speaking to her. She couldn't seem to finish anything that she started and had difficulty following directions or remembering specific facts. "I forgot," she said a lot, or "I'm bored."

Louisa had been diagnosed in school as having some learning disabilities—a delay in fine motor skills and an auditory processing difficulty. The same report said that she had a mild difficulty with perceptual motor skills. In other words, Louisa had trouble understanding what the teacher said, and had difficulty copying words or designs.

"It is very hard to get Louisa to focus on anything," her mother, Miriam, told me. "She will not answer my questions. She just wanders away. And she will never do what I ask of her. I always have to clean up after her and put away her things."

Miriam sat stiffly in her chair next to her husband, Raoul. She appeared to be an anxious, restrained person. She told me that Louisa, if asked to do simple tasks, such as fetching silverware, would "forget" and wander off on the way to the silverware drawer. Louisa seemed to feel bad about herself as well, her mother said, describing herself at times as a "dummy" or as "lazy."

Raoul seemed irritated that there were problems with his youngest child. He preferred to concentrate on himself. During my session with Raoul and Miriam, Raoul kept changing the subject from his daughter to the busy, successful dentistry practice that he had built up after a difficult youth in a large, immigrant family.

"Louisa has it easy, I believe," he said, speaking rapidly in slightly accented English. He was a handsome man, with dark hair and big, soft eyes. "I spend my whole day providing for my family. I start early and go late into the night. I have a lot of pressure. But Louisa? She only has to remember fourth-grade history. When I was in school, I helped my father wax floors in restaurants at night."

Like Miriam, he sat stiffly, gesturing little, as he spoke. It became clear to me that, while they were conscientious parents, they preferred to avoid some of their daughter's challenging behavior.

Raoul, whose workaholic patterns emerged as we spoke, didn't want to deal with Louisa's behavior, while Miriam was reluctant to set limits because she, too, worked hard at Raoul's dental office. She expressed concern that this work kept her away from their four children too much.

"I know the children can take care of themselves," Miriam said. Louisa was the youngest. She also had two sisters, aged eleven and fifteen, and an older brother, eighteen, who was a senior in high school. "But I don't feel right if I am not there when they come home from school. Raoul is never home for dinner, of course, and when I get home, I hate to ruin everything by having to punish any of the children. So I just clean up the house myself if it is a mess."

I asked Raoul and Miriam about Louisa's early years. They said it was hard to remember details because there were three other children around as well. She had been mostly an agreeable baby, Miriam recalled, who liked to look around, making few demands. From an early age, she had difficulty in following directions, reacting with a puzzled shake of the head even to the simplest directions, such as "Give Mama the cup, please." She was easily distracted and would wander away when people were speaking to her.

"She never sat and played with her toys like her brother or sisters," Miriam said. Louisa would move restlessly from one toy to another, apparently unable to concentrate on one activity.

She was slow to talk, but when she did, she quickly learned to talk in sentences. However, she always seemed better at saying what was on her mind than answering other people's questions.

Later on, when Louisa was in school, she would make excuses whenever she faced a challenge that was hard for her, such as copying shapes or writing her name. She managed to learn those skills, but with difficulty, and tried to avoid them whenever possible. She would claim she had to go to the bathroom. She was constantly in trouble with the teacher for not sitting in her seat or for giggling and talking during story time or quiet time.

Over the years, Louisa's teachers had been prone to blame her learning problems on the fact that both Spanish and English were spoken in her home. "Don't worry," one teacher had told Miriam and Raoul. "When she gets older and is more comfortable speaking and writing in English, her attention span will improve." But Louisa's attention problems only worsened over the years. "Her English is excellent," Miriam told me with a shake of her head, "and she has the same problem when she speaks or writes Spanish. It is not the language."

As Louisa got older, she continued to avoid challenges at school, making up excuses to leave the room and then not returning for thirty or forty minutes. At home, when her parents grew exasperated when her homework or chores were not done, she retreated to her room and played with her stuffed animals.

Raoul and Miriam didn't recall Louisa engaging in much pretend play during her preschool years. Occasionally, when she was younger, she had worn a fairy princess Halloween outfit. Otherwise, she had tended to keep her make-believe world and fantasies to herself, although recently she seemed to spend more and more time with her stuffed animals.

My sense from meeting Raoul and Miriam was that they tended to be anxious and think in concrete terms. They weren't comfortable using their imaginations or encouraging their children to be imaginative. Miriam was close to her daughter and, in some respects, made up for Raoul's distance. But her closeness consisted of doing things for her children or nagging them rather than using imagination or empathy when talking or playing with them.

After meeting with her parents, I had my first session with Louisa, a tall, thin girl with long, thick black hair and a bright smile. She was dressed in colorful leggings and a sweatshirt. Despite her broad smile, she had a kind of "don't hassle me" demeanor—arms and legs crossed, wary eyes. She rocked back and forth slightly in her seat.

I asked her how I could help her. She frowned.

"School."

"What about school?" I asked.

She sighed, slightly exasperated. "I don't get all my work done."

"I guess it's not easy to do it all," I sympathized.

"The teacher gives me way too much work." She looked pleadingly at me. "I try, but I get these really long projects all the time. And all that writing's hard for me because English isn't my native language, you know."

As she began to relax a bit with me, I asked her to elaborate on her workload and on why writing was difficult.

"I try really hard. I really do," Louisa said, again with an air of pleading. "But my teacher writes the stuff on the blackboard so quickly and then erases it before I can copy it all. And sometimes my mother doesn't put my homework with my clothes in the morning and I forget to take it to school."

"Sounds like you don't feel that your teacher or your mom are making it easy for you."

She nodded. "And I always get in trouble with the teachers and Mom and Dad. They think I don't try hard enough. But I *do* try! There's just too much to remember."

"Can you think of a time when there was too much?" I asked.

"Once I left my bookbag in the library after I was talking to this new girl who was going to live near me. And this other time I went to Amanda's house after school once and she almost forgot the stop, so we had to run to get off the bus and I left my social studies notebook and then it was gone. And Leah was pushing me *just* as I was putting all my stuff in my bookbag and my English notebook got left out. . . ."

In our first few minutes, Louisa impressed me as a warm, engaging youngster with a relatively even mood. She was articulate and clear, and she could stay on one topic, such as weaving together intricate explanations of how it wasn't her fault when she lost or forgot things.

But I also sensed a bit of sadness, a feeling of being overwhelmed at times. As she talked more rapidly, telling me story after story, I could sense the level of tension rising, as though she seemed to realize that the logic didn't fit together. She leaned forward as she sped through explanations and excuses. A flat, tense quality crept into her voice.

During the remainder of our first session, Louisa gave me additional examples of getting confused and overloaded and how people like her mother and teacher made it hard for her.

In her second session, Louisa filled me in on what had been going on since our first meeting. Louisa began elaborating further examples about other kids, teachers, or parents causing her to forget things. When I asked her how it felt when things like this happened, she quickly reiterated, "It's not my fault." I empathized with her worry that someone would blame her and how she was obviously fearful that things were her fault. I could sense that behind her many excuses, there was a harsh inner voice ready to pounce on her for any mistake. She needed to defend herself against this critic.

I said to her, "I can tell how important it is that people know that you are trying your hardest and that they don't blame you."

She looked almost tearful for a second and told me about her gym teacher—Mr. Stone—who would sometimes yell at her for being slow in tying her sneakers. She was holding up the class, he told her. When I asked if anyone also yelled at her at home, Louisa gave me a knowing look. She began talking about her father for the first time. She first talked about how he sometimes just yells at everybody. Then she described situations where he would come in and scream at her and her mother when Miriam was trying to help Louisa with her homework. Raoul would angrily lecture that "it wouldn't take you so long if you didn't daydream so much or play with those stuffed animals so much."

I asked what seemed to make her father the most angry. She described her family heading out for church on one recent Sunday. Louisa couldn't find her nice shoes "because Mom put them in the wrong place and Daddy got really mad and slammed the door so hard that a picture came flying off the wall."

We then talked about her mother and her siblings. The theme of Louisa always worrying that people would blame her continued. It was also clear that, while her mother sometimes overprotected her in a dutiful and concrete way, her father often got annoyed with her. He certainly did not treat her as a little princess, a status that youngest daughters in some families enjoy.

Louisa was obviously bright (her elaborate explanations and rationales showed me that), but I wanted to see what her academic abilities were. So we played a few quick games. I observed her auditory short-term memory by reciting a few numbers and asking her to remember and repeat them back to me forward and backward. Her skills were about average for a child her age, but they were far below her general level of intelligence.

I then observed her perceptual motor and fine motor skills by asking her to copy a design drawn on a piece of paper. She was significantly below average in this area; she had real trouble recalling the design and drawing it.

This profile fit with her academic performance in school. She had a hard time with tasks that required seeing and copying (such as writing down what the teacher had written on the blackboard) and with subjects in which much of the information given out was spoken (such as social studies). No wonder she was easily distracted and forgetful at school. Like many children who are relatively weak in these skills, the elementary school years were hard for Louisa. This explained why she shied away from a lot of school tasks and why her teachers reported that she didn't listen well. She did much better on tasks that required some thinking, reasoning, and creativity, such as making up a story or creating a science experiment. But those skills really aren't stressed until high school or college. The lower grades are tough for a child like Louisa; in fact, they can be the hardest years, more daunting than college or graduate school.

Louisa talked some more about school. She kept giving me examples of times when she had forgotten something, but how it was not her fault.

"Let's look at how you forget," I suggested. "Let's take it step by step."

Louisa ran through a series of scenarios in which she forgot things. She described her household chores and rather formidable homework assignments (she went to a school that gave a lot of homework). At first, she said simply that there was too much to remember.

"It kind of builds up and builds up and then I have this whole mountain of stuff I have to do," she said.

I empathized about her workload: "Boy, that does sound like a mountain of stuff," and then I wondered what she did when it got so big. A big smile suddenly spread across her face. With a hint of pride, she said, "Sometimes I just pretend it's not there."

When I asked how she did this, she said, "I just sort of forget about it. I make it like you can see right through it. Like it's invisible."

I could picture hundreds of pieces of paper, homework assignments, notes from teachers, and reminder messages from her mother and dad all of sudden becoming invisible and maybe going to Neverland.

"I think you may have just put your finger on it," I said. "Making it invisible. That's the key." Making it invisible—forgetting or minimizing it—was Louisa's way of coping, but this strategy only made her schoolwork load more onerous.

As Louisa described more situations where she just made things invisible, she smiled and her tense look lifted. "I'm good at making things go away," she said.

I nodded in agreement, and I wondered aloud whether she did the same things with feelings. She volunteered, "Sometimes when I'm mad at someone, I pretend they're invisible so I don't have to look at them."

When I asked about other situations where she made feelings invisible, she said, "Well, the teachers at school, they like the boys better than the girls. Like, my teacher calls on the boys more. And she doesn't get as mad at them when they don't do their homework. Sometimes I make her invisible, too."

I wondered about what happens in her family.

She said, "At home, my sister Alicia bosses me around all the time, and Mom takes her side."

Louisa described the alliance between her mom and her sister as being almost as if she had two moms, both overwhelming and dominating her. It angered her.

"What about Dad?" I asked.

"Oh, I guess he's fairer, but he's not there a lot." Then she added quickly, "But that's all right. He's working hard for us. That's what Mom says. So it's no big deal." She smiled. "*No importa*," she said in Spanish. I inquired whether she made any of these same feelings invisible at home. She said that she sometimes goes to her room and pretends that there are only ghosts in the house and she can't see anybody, just her stuffed animals. She seemed to do this mostly when she was having angry, jealous, or lonely feelings or when she was missing her father.

I empathized with how she might find it easier to make all these things invisible—her homework, strong feelings that felt unpleasant. She nodded.

Many children who come to see me because of their difficulties in school use coping techniques similar to Louisa's. Because of their particular vulnerabilities, they are overwhelmed by the demands placed on them. Their way of dealing with it all is by forgetting or escaping (either physically or mentally) many situations. This approach leads to continuing problems. If these children aren't aware of what they're confronting (and most aren't), they tend to see themselves as more and more passive and victimized ("unfair" things happen to them).

I sensed that many of the important elements of Louisa's personality were where they needed to be for a girl her age. She could relate to, engage with, and focus on other people, and she could read other people's gestures and expressions. She could picture her feelings and build bridges between different emotional ideas as a basis for reality testing and impulse control. But at the same time, she showed little emotional flexibility. She avoided, for example, dealing with anger, competition, or sadness. She also avoided the feelings of ineffectiveness, overload, or incompetence associated with lots of homework or learning challenges. When her frustration with her friends, her siblings, her mother, or her school built up, making her angry or sad, she just made it all invisible. This kept her from learning more appropriate coping methods, such as trying to master the challenges piece by piece or learning to verbalize (at least to herself) some of her feelings. Sometimes children her age try to deny their feelings—by blaming the other person or by changing an angry feeling into one of justified disrespect (instead of "I hate him," it's "He's a jerk," or instead of "I can't do my homework," it might be "The teacher doesn't know how to teach and gives us too much to do!"). In these instances, however, the child is at least aware of a problem and of her feelings generally—even though that awareness is marked by some rationalizations and selective changes, she is coping in her own way.

Because of her particular challenges, some of the activities in school—and the homework assignments that involved a sequencing of verbal information, such as reading assignments—required extra energy and attention from Louisa. But Louisa did not put in that extra effort. She didn't initiate the "self-cuing" that would help her compensate for her difficulty. Instead, she exaggerated the difficulty. Whatever aspects of the homework she did remember, she made "invisible." You could say she went with the flow—exaggerating her natural tendency to be forgetful by making mountains of information invisible.

Is Louisa unusual in her tendency to exaggerate her vulnerability? Not at all. Most children turn their natural tendencies into coping strategies. When the going gets rough, they cling to that coping strategy, even when it is a negative one.

Like the rest of us, children with attention problems do what comes naturally. Consider an adult with an amazing memory for sequences of verbal information. She can't forget them if she wants to. She is so tuned in, so alert, and so responsive to every verbal nuance, so aware of sequences of information that she often gets annoyed, reminding everyone in the family of what they have to do! She can't help having such a terrific memory. Sometimes such a person will complain that when she gets overloaded and anxious, she becomes even more vigilant about details in her and her family's lives. She, too, is a victim of her nervous system. She would like to relax and make things "invisible," like Louisa, but she can't. Both the person with a weak memory for verbal sequences and the person with a strong memory for verbal sequences are in the same boat. Each one exaggerates her natural tendency under stress. That's because, under stress, people are their own worst enemies until they learn a more adaptive coping strategy. The goal with the Louisas of the world is to help them learn how to go against their natural tendency.

Our task was to teach Louisa how to hold information in her mind even when her inclination was to make it more and more "invisible." She had two closely interrelated challenges. One had to do with the way her nervous system processed information. The other had to do with the way she coped with her own nervous system, exaggerating the vulnerability rather than compensating for it. We, therefore, had to work with Louisa on both fronts. Working on her coping strategies, which exaggerated the problem (and were derived from the problem), had to come first. When you don't face the coping strategy and only try to deal with the underlying processing problem, it is like trying to roll a stone uphill. The child is trying to escape and avoid the very exercises you are doing to reverse the underlying difficulty! Therefore, you need to work at both levels.

FLOOR TIME: MAINTAINING AN EMPATHETIC PRESENCE

The first challenge for Louisa's parents was to become more involved with their daughter beyond the day-to-day issues of clothing, feeding, and schoolwork (tasks that both parents were doing quite well). The relationship between Raoul and Miriam also needed work, so that a greater feeling of relaxation and warmth could be present in this large, busy family. A more nurturing atmosphere was needed in order to allow Louisa to tackle the learning issues that were causing her attentional problems.

I always spend at least part of my time with the parents of the children that I see, stressing the importance of improving their relationship with each other at the same time that they work on their relationship with their children. In my sessions with Raoul and Miriam, we talked about why Raoul didn't return home until eight o'clock or later.

"If I am home earlier," Raoul said, nodding his head in the direction of his wife, "she becomes angry because she says I do not help with the children or that I am ignoring her." Raoul felt he kept peace in the family by staying at his office late. By the time he did get home, Raoul said, Miriam was "too tired to bother me."

Miriam was surprised by Raoul's assertion. "I have all the responsibility for the children, the house, and everything else," she said. "And I cannot do it alone, as well as help you with your business. So, of course, I come right at you when you come home, because you are never home!"

At my suggestion, after the children had gone to bed, Raoul and Miriam tried to focus on each other's needs and wants, instead of on their children's issues. Surprisingly, many families find it hard to spend time together without an agenda. Raoul and Miriam tried to make that time a period of relaxation with no agenda—a time to listen to each other empathetically. In other words, they planned a "floor time" for themselves.

After a while, they began to realize that the more Raoul avoided Miriam, the angrier she got at having to cope with all the home responsibilities herself and the greater her need to dump on him when he came home at night. These patterns meant that neither Raoul nor Miriam was as relaxed and warm in their family life as they would like to be. So we negotiated. Raoul stopped taking evening appointments and came home instead, and Miriam put off any criticism until a half-hour "business meeting" they held each night after the children went to bed.

With this renegotiation, Raoul was able to begin enjoying hanging out more with his children, especially Louisa. But that took a while.

"I am not good at this," Raoul told me after a few attempts at floor time. Raoul and Louisa simply didn't know what to do with or say to each other.

I reassured Raoul. "Even feeling uncomfortable and tense is an experience of closeness," I told him. "Try to tolerate it, and sooner or later something will happen that will help the two of you feel more comfortable."

Sure enough, during another awkward time, with Raoul sitting stiffly in Louisa's room, Louisa began poking at a lump of modeling clay for a school project in which she was supposed to sculpt an animal that she invented. As the silence grew, Louisa got more and more absorbed in what she was doing—and Raoul found himself watching with growing interest.

"What do you think it is, Dad?" Louisa asked.

"A dinosaur?" Raoul guessed.

Louisa giggled and shook her head.

"I know," Raoul tried again. "It's a big dog with a very long tail!"

Louisa giggled some more and shook her head in mock disgust. "No it's not, Dad. Can't you see? It's a . . ." She threw back her head, her eyes closed, thinking. "It's a Hoospa—sort of like a dinosaur but with long legs like a horse. He can run really fast and run away from anybody who's bothering him."

During the next few weeks, Louisa continued to make different kinds of animals—each one faster or more elusive than the former. The theme of escaping from danger kept recurring. She was now putting into her play images of her own escapist coping capacity. However, this was critically different from her day-to-day tendency to escape. Now the escapes were creative fantasies and the person whom she likely viewed as her harshest critic and the one she most had to avoid—her father—was a friendly, supportive, empathetic person listening to her every word.

Parents are often unaware of the wondrous things they can do for their children by simply being a calm, empathetic presence, letting their children play out the fantasies they develop of themselves, their parents, and their relationships. These pictures are often distorted by young children's vivid imaginations and poor grasp of reality as well as their tendency to create extreme images based on the feelings of the moment. The calm presence of an empathetic parent allows a child to rework some of these images on her own. The parent need not even be aware of what's going on and certainly needn't play psychotherapist and try to interpret the dramas. The parent's warmth works by simply taking parent and child out of the negative patterns they may have gotten stuck in. Raoul, for example, had often ended up in the role of unavailable, harsh critic. But an attitude of warm understanding puts the parent into a new pattern, allowing the child the freedom to explore new psychological territory.

As we have discussed, Louisa favored an escape pattern as a way to cope with her problems. She would make her books, assignments, or people she was angry at "invisible." In her initial play with her father, her animals often escaped on their especially fast legs. With Raoul watching and commenting only on how fast or how amazing Louisa's different animals were, Louisa slowly changed the personalities of her animals. One day, instead of having a creature run away, Louisa said, "He's got big, mean teeth to eat up animals that chase him."

Over time, Raoul and Louisa grew to enjoy their game. Louisa made shapes in the clay and Raoul had to guess what they were. Louisa especially enjoyed sculpting more creatures and making up stories about how big and scary they were. She explored not only "big, mean teeth" but also huge claws, poison bites, big beaks, and massive stingers. The fantasies helped her picture aggressive feelings. This eventually would give her the flexibility to reason and think about such feelings. Just as important, they showed that Louisa was beginning to use her imagination, with which she hadn't really been comfortable before.

The play with her father and the "creatures" also had effects in Louisa's other relationships. She was gradually becoming more assertive and less escapist with friends and in her overall attitude toward daily events. She started to be more demanding in her own viewpoint in arguments and debates with friends.

When Miriam began floor time with Louisa, she also ran into some obstacles. Like Raoul, she initially had trouble finding things to talk about or to do. Since she hated silences, Miriam tried to fill the void by asking Louisa about her homework or by talking about objects that interested her in Louisa's room. These conversations inevitably turned into lectures by Miriam on the importance of school or of keeping her room neat. Louisa would retreat to the backyard or to watch television in the family room. Miriam began to realize that floor time wasn't going to be successful if she focused on what she herself was worried about. She began to notice that she constantly pushed and nagged her children, intent on ensuring that they would succeed in life to become doctors, lawyers, and scholars. Her family and Raoul's had come so far in America, and Miriam was determined that her children not slip back. But during our talks together, Miriam began to realize that her obsession with success probably came up so strongly also because she was feeling emotionally empty in her relationship with Raoul.

One day during floor time, Miriam didn't rush in to fill the silence, and Louisa spontaneously started telling her about a boy who lived around the corner. She suspected that the boy, Josh, might have a crush on her.

"He doesn't pay attention to me at the bus stop," she told her mother, "but he and his friends always look at me the whole ride to school. And he chased me on the playground yesterday." Louisa seemed pleased by the idea.

Miriam was initially amazed that Louisa opened up to her

in this way. But as we talked later, she realized that she and Louisa had always been close. "I guess it makes sense that she would talk to me about these boys if I just let her," Miriam said.

Louisa's little confidences convinced Miriam to try to tolerate periods of silence in their time together. Miriam learned that it was important to give Louisa some space—some time to say what she wanted to say or just to let her thoughts unfold. Louisa and Miriam began to look forward to the time after dinner when they could talk: Louisa mostly told Miriam about the kids at school. Miriam had assumed that Louisa didn't have many friends. But Louisa began telling her mother who was nice to her and who was mean to her, and whether this boy or that boy had a crush on her.

Miriam worked with her daughter on using her imagination by building on Louisa's interest in telling her about the kids at school. "I think Josh likes me," Louisa told her mother once. "He told Adrian. And Adrian told Santiago, who told me."

"What do you think might be going through Josh's mind?" Miriam asked her.

Louisa enjoyed making up stories about what these boys might be thinking. "I bet Josh likes me because I like animals," she told her mother. "He makes all these animal noises when I'm around—he moos and meows and barks. He is very funny! I think he wants to go to the zoo or a place like that!" With Miriam, Louisa pretended that she was a kitten and that Josh was feeding her dinner.

Miriam had learned something very important—that when she intruded and controlled the conversation, her daughter avoided and escaped. When she created a listening, loving, and accepting presence, her daughter shared her most intimate confidences and began using her imagination to include the warm, caring side of life.

Interestingly, Louisa worked out aggressive feelings when she was with her father. This made sense because her father had been the angry critic in the family. With her mother, Louisa worked out loving and caring feelings, as well as feelings about boys. With both parents, Louisa was switching from a pattern of avoidance and escape into one of assertive sharing. The escapist pattern, as I noted earlier, was in part fueled by Louisa's learning style—the way she processed information—and made it easier for her to avoid unpleasant situations or make things invisible. Now, through her new relationship with her parents, she was learning a new psychological approach—one in which she could assertively create pictures of her feelings and wishes.

In their conversations with Louisa, Miriam and Raoul also began to be mindful of Louisa's tendency to get lost in her own thoughts. Because of her auditory processing difficulties, she found it easier to listen to her own thoughts than to make sense of words coming in from the outside. This often gave her the appearance of being inattentive even while her parents were very available and compassionate. They often complained to me that just when they were asking a question or commenting on what Louisa had said, trying to be empathetic, Louisa seemed to drift off into her own world. She didn't seem to be paying attention to them. For example, when Louisa was sculpting clay with her father, he noticed that when he was talking, she would "float away from me" into her clay and "not listen to anything I am saying. I might be commenting on how fast the animal looked that she was making, but she will look at her clay and then say something about the purple color of the animal's face."

Similarly, Miriam would get frustrated when Louisa started talking about a boy at school. Miriam would try to ask the boy's name, but Louisa would seemingly ignore her mother's question and talk about the boy's "cool T-shirt."

I felt these were indications that, because of Louisa's auditory processing problem, she had a hard time opening and closing circles of communication. I helped her parents patiently and persistently assist Louisa in opening and closing every circle of communication. When she drifted off into her state of inattentiveness, her parents would not simply give up and withdraw, as they had in the past, or take over and structure the conversations with a series of questions. Neither strategy helped Louisa. Instead, Raoul and Miriam let her know that they had "lost" her and that they were confused. In the most gentle and sympathetic tone of voice, they said, "Where did Louisa go?" If she didn't get back on the topic with that gentle reminder, they pushed a little further. "You were just talking about . . . ," they would remark, or "I asked a question and now I'm a little lost!" Sometimes they used their own imagination and Louisa's interest in animals. "I'm a little lost dog who cannot find his way," they said. They encouraged Louisa to close her circles of communication. Initially, it sometimes took ten or fifteen minutes of gentle persistence on their part for Louisa to complete her thought or answer a question. But they were careful to make sure they didn't close the circle for her. She had to rescue them, even if it took all evening.

Over several months, Louisa became fairly adept at maintaining the extra concentration that was required to process information coming from her parents, an effort that children who don't have her processing difficulties would not have to bring to bear. She developed a nice give-and-take with them. Along with the change in her fantasies from themes of escape to coping with aggression and closeness, she was also able to bring a new level of assertiveness to the way she communicated and organized information. Louisa was learning to *compensate* for her processing difficulty rather than exaggerating it.

PROBLEM-SOLVING TIME: HARNESSING A CHILD'S STRENGTHS

After a sense of engagement and warmth was established, we added problem-solving time. As you'll recall, this time involves a more logical give-and-take between parent and child, where they size up various troublesome situations together and then collaborate on finding realistic solutions. It doesn't have to be done at any particular time or place. Miriam used the time after she picked Louisa up from school. Raoul arranged to drop Louisa off at school in the morning so he would have some time then.

I encouraged Miriam and Raoul to take a broad look at the challenges Louisa faced and to begin talking with her about how she dealt with difficult situations in general. In Louisa's case, the goal was to help her see how she retreated from or avoided situations that embarrassed or frustrated her.

The idea of getting a child to see her own character patterns and then resolve them may seem impossible. Parents may feel stymied. But making even a little progress will be less frustrating than making no progress at all.

The first step in problem solving is to help a child *anticipate* situations that are challenging, *anticipate* the feelings that come up, and then together look at how she usually deals with them. This means taking a respectful, appreciative attitude toward the child's particular coping strategy, even if you disagree with it, because it is the child's way of avoiding some uncomfortable feelings. With a child with attention problems that arise from learning challenges, you can use problem-solving time to help her see her strengths as well as her weaknesses. She can learn to observe herself, figuring out what she does easily and what takes more work. Once she can do this, she can find useful strategies, such as "self-cuing"— creating reminders for herself. She could, for example, leave herself a note on the top of her desk at school listing which books she needs to bring home. At a more sophisticated level, she could mentally associate the tree outside the classroom with remembering to ask her teacher at the end of the day what the homework assignment is. Or she could learn to associate her impulse to wander away from a situation or lose her concentration to "there must be something I feel uncertain or insecure about."

Louisa was great at avoiding tasks, people, or situations that overwhelmed or frustrated her. And she was pretty good at making herself feel helpless and overloaded. So during problem-solving time, Miriam and Raoul commented on how she liked to get away from situations that made her feel uncomfortable.

"I think you are a good escape artist, do you know that?" Miriam told her one day.

Louisa smiled. She found it amusing to be cast as an escape artist, but she played dumb. "What do you mean?" she asked.

"Well, you know," her mother responded, "when a boy or a girl is sitting in class, they might look out the window at the clouds and escape from having to look at the teacher, who is trying to embarrass them with work they can't follow."

Louisa readily acknowledged that she was a good cloud watcher; she could do it during spelling and reading and history. She gave some examples.

"We were learning about the Civil War," she said, "and Mrs. Cutler gave us all these names of generals—so many generals!—and I forgot to write them down because I was looking out the window."

Mindful that she needed to respect Louisa's ways of coping, Miriam asked, "What do you see in the clouds?"

Louisa thought for a moment. "Shapes and things. Circles and squares and even clouds that look like people and animals. I saw one yesterday that looked like a tree with beautiful, long branches that reached way out in the sky." Clearly, she had paid a lot of attention to the clouds. She then said she would like to sculpt some of the shapes.

In this empathetic conversation, Louisa's parents were encouraging her powers of self-observation. She identified her "bathroom" trick—another way to get out of class. Or the "my foot fell asleep" trick when she pretended that her foot had fallen asleep and she had to walk around to "wake it up again." Then there was the "feed the fish" routine, when Louisa would suddenly decide the fish in the classroom tank looked hungry and needed to be fed. After hearing all these tricks, Miriam and Raoul began to wonder if Louisa ever sat in her seat at school! Of course, Louisa knew very well that her foot wasn't asleep and that the fish weren't hungry, but by jumping up from her seat, she was avoiding whatever situation embarrassed her—such as not being able to do the spelling and penmanship drills.

With these revelations, Louisa's parents were able to take problem solving further—to help Louisa think about situations from which she would probably want to escape, to anticipate how those situations made her feel, and to predict what she was likely to do. When Miriam and Raoul first walked through potentially difficult situations with her, Louisa said she didn't know how she felt.

"Then let's pretend," said Raoul. "I will be the teacher and I am explaining the five spelling words you need to learn today." And Raoul began talking rapidly in English and pantomiming writing out words on the chalkboard while Louisa, looking more and more confused, watched. After they had played out this scenario four or five times, Louisa looked at her father.

"I am afraid you're going to make fun of me because I don't know those words and all the other kids will laugh at me," she said. Although Louisa had been speaking English as well as Spanish since birth, her language difficulties in both English and Spanish made her even more acutely aware of her difficulties. Embarrassment and humiliation were two feelings that Louisa—like many grade-schoolers—desperately feared.

"Has the teacher ever done that?" Raoul asked.

"Well, no," acknowledged Louisa. "But she might someday!"

In discussions with me, her parents had learned that at this point the goal wasn't to *get over* the feelings, but to help Louisa see what feelings she was experiencing.

Raoul slid down on the floor next to Louisa. "Frightening feelings can be like frightening people," he said gently. "If you get to know them better, they may not frighten you as much."

Later, when I discussed these emotions with Louisa, she talked about how angry she got when she felt embarrassed and then she remarked that "volcano" feelings would emerge. A pattern came to light: anytime the class was studying a subject with which Louisa was uncomfortable, she would begin to feel embarrassed and experience "volcano-like" sensations. To avoid both the discomfort and the rage that accompanied the embarrassment (hence the image of the volcano), she needed to get herself out of the situation through one of her escape routes.

As Louisa identified numerous difficult situations, she began learning to anticipate them. Her escape attempts were no longer something that "just happened" to her but part of a clear pattern that she could easily describe. This greater self-awareness in itself brings progress. Usually a child won't use the same avoidance techniques once she is aware of what she is doing. Of course, she needs to see the behavior for herself; her parents can't simply "make" her see it.

Louisa and her parents then began to imagine other ways she could act in those difficult situations. How could she avoid discomfort without setting herself up for worse problems by escaping more and learning less?

It's important to remember that any alternative coping strategy has to meet the objective of the original behavior in some way. In other words, if the original behavior was designed to avoid pain and embarrassment, then the new strategy must also allow the child to avoid embarrassment and pain. Otherwise, the child simply won't use it.

In many cases, the best approach is to find something that the youngster is good at and takes pride in and apply that particular skill to the challenge that is making the child feel humiliated. That's not as hard as it sounds. In Louisa's case, she felt proud of her talent for drawing, sculpting, and creating forms and shapes. She felt awful about her difficulty with language and writing.

"Why not help her bring her wonderful ability for picturing shapes to her language problems?" I suggested to Raoul and Miriam.

"How is drawing pictures going to help her learn spelling?" they asked.

I suggested that they explore this with Louisa. After a number of brainstorming sessions, Raoul, who recalled that he had had similar problems when he was younger, came up with a solution. He suggested that Louisa use drawings as notes. For example, if the teacher was reading a story that the children would later have to answer questions about, she could draw the main elements of the story. Louisa then decided on her own that she could draw the story with little animals, playing characters in the story. If a boy was having a conflict with his sister, for example, Louisa might draw a picture of two cats who were mad at each other. She preferred the animal forms to human forms and found them easier to draw. Later on, Louisa found that she could begin drawing pictures in her mind without even using markers and paper. Soon, Louisa was using her strong capacity for visual imagery to compensate for her difficulty in remembering words and sentences. Once she translated words into picture form, she also found that her comprehension improved as well. She could discuss the stories and debate how the different characters might feel, because she visualized various scenarios—in the way some-one else might picture dramas unfolding on TV or in a cartoon strip. This success in comprehending the information helped Louisa feel confident and secure, far more pleasant feelings than embarrassment and the wish to escape.

This approach can take many months, sometimes years, for a child to master. But parents should realize that even when it takes years, the child has mastered a lifelong coping capacity. Many adults still rely on some not-so-helpful coping techniques, such as avoidance or becoming fragmented and disorganized, strategies that they devised during school years. We also use some of the more helpful approaches we may have been fortunate to learn in those early years. When you begin identifying challenges at a relatively early age, time is on your side. It is better to strive for slow and gradual, but substantial, progress than a quick fix that may be ephemeral.

Because Louisa still found it easier to tune into her own thoughts instead of other people's words because of her auditory processing difficulties, her parents continued to offer her practice in closing circles of communication. If Louisa didn't answer a question or complete a thought, they acted confused. They would ask Louisa to help "unconfuse" them, using the imagery of lost little animals who needed to find their way. Each time a conver-sation got off on a tangent or went from a discussion of some-thing at school into an escapist fantasy, Louisa's parents emphasized how lost they were.

Raoul and Miriam also encouraged her to use her capacity for fantasy constructively. For example, when Louisa talked about feeling "dumb" and went into a fantasy on how it made her feel like a snail stuck in sand and then returned to talking about her "dumb" feeling, she was using fantasy to elaborate and solve the problem at hand. On the other hand, if she started to talk about the lost snail but then moved on to talk about a friend who found pretty shells at the beach and then wanted to know when she could go to the beach again, that was an escape fantasy. Her par-ents would say, "Gee, I want to talk about the beach, too, but I feel like your little snail—I'm lost. What were we talking about just before? How did we get here?" Even if it took ten or fifteen minutes and only a few circles were closed, they persisted. As a foundation for constructing good coping strategies, the circle closing always came first. Naturally, as conversations began to stay on course, it was easier to talk about the content—that is, Louisa, her friends, and her school.

REPLACING CRITICISM WITH EMPATHY

As you will recall, parents find it useful to try to see the world from their child's perspective; this aids them in helping their child to identify the basic assumptions that cause her to feel and behave a certain way. During their problem-solving time with Louisa, Miriam and Raoul learned to empathize with their daughter's feelings, rather than criticize them.

Louisa, they learned, had assumed that it was wrong to feel vulnerable. So when a particularly difficult challenge came along, she "made it invisible" and ran away from it rather than feel weak. To Louisa, feeling vulnerable meant she wouldn't be loved and connected to her family. When her parents had criticized her inattention, they only compounded her sense of helplessness.

Being compassionate about lonely, lost feelings and vulnerability was a new experience for Raoul and Miriam—as it is for many parents. An accusatory voice inside them seems to whisper: "Well, if you were a better father or mother, your child wouldn't have these feelings." But *all feelings* are part of the human drama. The bad feelings come along with the good feelings—love, pride, joy, happiness—and their presence in our children shouldn't diminish us as parents.

It was particularly important for Raoul to recognize those vulnerabilities in himself—a difficult task for a man from his culture. "I guess I sometimes am not comfortable as a father," he said during one of my sessions with just him and Miriam. He crossed his arms tensely as he talked. "I am a very good dentist—that I know. But as a father? I feel . . . ," he searched for the right phrase, his lips moving and a band of sweat forming on his forehead, ". . . awkward. I do not know what it is to be a good father. My father was very busy when we moved to this country. I did not see him very much. And so I do not know if I am doing things right. Should I hug my children more? Should I discipline them? I am never sure if I am doing the 'right' thing with them."

Miriam talked about how she often felt that she wasn't giving enough to each child. "With four children and my job at Raoul's office, I always feel that I do not have enough to give," she said. To deal with these feelings, Miriam focused on the day-to-day concerns with her children—making sure that they got their homework done, their clothes were clean, their lunches were made, and their bedrooms were neat. As a result, she appeared critical toward her children. She was constantly telling them to do this or that and had little time for cuddling or imaginative play. And her concrete attitude kept her from thinking about what she really felt bad about—that she wasn't nurturing each child enough.

"The children don't need you in the same way that they did when they were babies," I told her. "But they *do* need you to spend some time with them empathizing with the feelings they are having and with their new experiences and concerns at school. This is just as important as the time you spend making their lunches or helping them with their homework."

In time, Miriam came to recognize that her relationships with her children could be better balanced. And Raoul came to empathize with Louisa's vulnerable emotions instead of feeling that this meant that he wasn't a good father. This led them both to spend less time being critical.

INCREASING ATTENTION—ONE STEP AT A TIME

By breaking a child's challenges into small steps, the parent can help a child who has attention problems resulting from learning challenges to master even hard areas of learning. Remember, learning needs to be fun and pleasant for this child, and parents and teachers can't expect too much progress too quickly. Again, the goal is to harness strengths to compensate for weaknesses.

Our first goal with Louisa was to help her start in a small

way to use her interest in shape, form, and even color to picture feelings that interfered with her work. Raoul and Miriam began with simple feelings, such as disappointment or embarrassment.

"If you wanted to draw this feeling," Miriam and Raoul would say, "how would you draw it? What color would you want to make it? What shape?"

Louisa decided that mild embarrassment would be sort of orange-pink. "And very big embarrassments would be very bright pink," she suggested.

"What shape would embarrassment be?" Miriam asked.

Louisa gave a small smile. "It could look like the amoeba in my science book," she suggested. "Sort of round and with little things poking out. And it would grow, like embarrassment." Over time, Louisa identified other feelings and gave them shapes and colors: anger was bright red and had a spiky shape with lots of sharp edges and corners; sadness was soft blue and round; happiness was yellow and cloudlike; fear was dull brown and rectangular.

The next challenge was to help Louisa identify some of those feelings, such as mild embarrassment or humiliation, as they were happening. During the first few weeks of these exercises, she came home from school talking about having some of those "pink" feelings or some of those "red" feelings. She enjoyed giving her feelings color and shape.

We also began to work on verbal concepts to enhance reading and comprehension. That was hard. How do you change a verbal concept into a form, a shape, or a color? To a child with Louisa's challenges, a story read in class was only a series of words. Since she couldn't retain the sequence, the story had no plot or real meaning for her. Louisa gradually learned to attach colors and images to each element in a story.

If a story was written skillfully enough to include vivid descriptions, Louisa pictured them in her mind. One day the teacher read a story about a girl who gets lost looking for shells on a beach. When the girl was mad because her mother had walked off in the opposite direction, Louisa gave that part of the story the color she used for rage—bright red. Then when the girl grew frightened over her predicament, Louisa imagined that she turned a brownish color. She remembered that the tale contained a beach and a girl who first turned bright red in anger and then dull brown in fear.

Her teacher asked, "What was the chapter about, Louisa?" She answered at first, "A red girl on a beach who turns brown."

Her teacher looked puzzled. "I don't understand. What was the theme of the chapter?" she asked.

Louisa thought for a moment and then put it back into terms that her teacher and the class would understand.

"The chapter was about a girl who got lost on the beach and couldn't find her mother. At first she was really mad and then she was afraid."

Her teacher smiled. It was the first time that Louisa had shown much of a grasp of her reading assignments. "Louisa, I'm really impressed."

Louisa's parents and I continued to work with Louisa, as did her tutors in English and handwriting, to build a foundation for future learning. Her strengths (imagining and recalling images) were used to compensate for her weaknesses (rote memorization, reading). It was obvious that Louisa could think clearly and be quite attentive once we had figured out a way for her to retain and reason with the information at hand.

To make this kind of progress, each task must be divided into small enough segments so that the child feels a sense of success and enthusiasm after mastering each step. That supplies the encouragement a child needs to continue. If she experiences too many challenges at one step, then break up that step into even smaller chunks. For example, if Louisa hadn't been able to grasp the idea of using colors and images to remember her story about the girl on the beach, then we might have worked on simply helping her remember *one* color for one emotion (such as the bright red, angry girl) and then later work on remembering other colors.

If progress seems agonizingly slow, take heart. I've often found that a child's progress speeds up after she masters the first few steps of a particular challenge and gains some confidence.

Each step, however modest, should be seen as an important accomplishment.

SETTING LIMITS: HELPING THE CHILD STAY FOCUSED

As we have seen with Louisa, children with attentional problems tend to construct many manipulative strategies and escape routes over the years. The structure that comes with limit setting helps such a child stay organized and focused.

Despite her wonderful progress, Louisa's habit of avoiding and "making things invisible" reappeared at times. Limit setting for Louisa rarely involved dealing with aggression, as she was sweet and unaggressive. Rather, it meant being very persistent when she got into her escape pattern, or left open circles of communication. Specifically, it often meant not permitting Louisa to escape from lengthy homework assignments that involved a lot of writing.

Louisa's parents continued to play to her strengths and let her use a tape recorder to elaborate her ideas quickly without the barrier of her fine motor difficulties. Then her parents would help her copy from her own tape recording. As she got older, her parents worked with her to become a good typist on a word processor so she could transcribe her own recordings.

While her parents were flexible and supportive, they nonetheless were very structured in the expectation that she not avoid her challenging assignments. Her parents, for example, decided that she could not see some of her favorite Saturday night TV programs unless she completed her homework assignments during the week. If she needed extra time, she could catch up on her assignments on weekends. But no amount of whining, complaining, or excuses ("My hands hurt!") would get her more TV time. At first, she would escape into playing with her stuffed animals and daydreaming, and the TV never went on. Her parents mentioned how much they wanted to take her to a movie that had recently opened. But if she preferred to play with her stuffed animals, her mother said, then "I guess that movie will have to wait." During problem-solving time, her parents helped her anticipate some of the ways she sabotaged her own good times with her escape routes.

Slowly but surely, over many months, Louisa used this firm structure to motivate herself to get her assignments completed. Her parents' flexibility in suggesting things like using the tape recorder enabled her to see that they were really on her side. But she also learned that she couldn't easily outfox them! Raoul and Miriam's refusal to get drawn into power struggles and the ever-increasing floor time ritual they maintained when the negotiations around limits got intense kept up a positive working relationship even about difficult tasks like homework.

As I have pointed out in previous chapters, setting limits should always be accompanied by extra floor time because it helps to maintain the nurturing and collaborative spirit that is so necessary for overcoming learning and attention challenges. You yourself may even appreciate an increase in floor time, so that you feel secure and less guilt-ridden when you stick to your agreed-upon limits.

Limit setting shouldn't deteriorate into a power struggle. A child, particularly one who faces special challenges in learning, needs to have a sense that she has the support of her parents. She mustn't feel that her learning problem is also an emotional defeat. During warm, unstructured time together with their parents, children can feel affirmed for their strengths and experience a secure, unqualified sense of belonging in the family.

In general, when confronting a child with attentional problems or any other challenge to focusing or learning, the following principle may be useful: try to find a way for the child to enjoy and achieve a sense of satisfaction from the work involved in mastering her vulnerable area. It's a bit like someone telling you that you have to write your name backwards with your left hand one hundred times. It's not going to be fun because your nervous system will not accomplish this easily. But if we make it a game, where writing one little letter with your left hand wins you a chocolate and writing ninety-nine more words wins you a car, somehow the pain and agony are less noticeable. Not every learning challenge can have exciting jackpots but the general principle applies. There is a natural physical tendency to avoid activities that our nervous system tells us are difficult. Similarly, there is a natural tendency to repeat activities our nervous system tells us are easy and fun and that result in a continuing and quick sense of mastery. The natural reader or jump shooter needs little encouragement to practice. And even the long-distance runner or a child who can study eight hours in a row does not find it terribly hard to intensify an effort in an area of natural competence. If you want to put pressure on a child in the traditional sense, it will work only in areas where the child is naturally gifted. I don't recommend that approach in any case, but children do have much more flexibility in their areas of natural strength. Build on this strength, with patience and support, and slowly but surely you will see your child find ways to focus and learn.

7

THE ACTIVE/

AGGRESSIVE CHILD

THE IMPULSIVE, AGGRESSIVE CHILD IS CONSTANTLY on the go. He runs instead of walks, acts instead of talks. These boys and girls jump headlong into new experiences—diving in first and looking later. If they learn to use their considerable energy in constructive ways, they can be energetic, creative, enthusiastic, charismatic—they may become athletes, pilots, soldiers, business entrepreneurs, or politicians, perhaps. At school, such a youngster could be the class rabble-rouser, throwing his pencils and books around and enticing all the other children to yell and scream, particularly when the teacher wants everyone to sit down. But he is also easily frustrated and angered and might resort to hitting, punching, and pinching to get what he wants or to express anger.

There is probably no greater challenge for a parent than coping with an angry, aggressive, frustrated child. When a child gets mad, he challenges our own emotional reactions; we become upset and irrational ourselves. A lot of that reaction occurs simply because we are human. When we are upset or angry, it's easy to forget everything we know. I don't know any parents or educators who would deny that they sometimes yell or say things that they later wish they hadn't. We have a running joke about this in my house: my children tell me, "Daddy, you're getting that killer voice again." As much as I try, at least once a week that voice comes out of hiding.

Anger and aggressive feelings are unavoidable for all of us— children and adults. These emotions play a big role in early development and cannot be swept under the rug. Anger is an essential part of the human drama. It is as important to psychological growth as love and warmth. As long as angry and aggressive feelings are balanced with feelings of closeness and empathy and are well regulated, they can do us an enormous amount of good. They can energize us and motivate us to do more than we thought possible. They fuel our ambitions, spur us to set goals for ourselves, encourage us to achieve and accomplish. They even help us define our sense of self—who we are and what our boundaries are. My colleague Peter Neubauer, mentioned earlier, has observed that angry and rivalrous feelings often help us differentiate ourselves from others. When you're upset or feeling competitive with someone, you certainly know where you stop and the other person begins. Children need to acknowledge the full range of feelings, including the angry ones, so that these emotions can become part of their evolving sense of themselves. Then they can become integrated people capable of being competitive as well as nurturing, assertive as well as loving.

Children who tend to be aggressive, just like children who tend to be sensitive or withdrawn, vary considerably. Some may be aggressive because they are frustrated and highly sensitive. Other children may be aggressive because they crave lots of sensory input. Whatever the cause, aggression in a child can tax us to our limits. But if we can understand the underlying physical and emotional reasons, we can use it as an opportunity to help the child grow and develop emotionally.

THE SEVERELY ANTISOCIAL CHILD: A FAMILY AND SOCIETAL CHALLENGE

When a sensation-seeking, daredevil child has a family that isn't equipped to provide the child with adequate nurturing, communication, or limits, there are potentials for real problems. Nurture compounds nature, and such a child is prone to dealing with his feelings by acting out physically. The less warmth and nurturing this child gets, the more difficulties he may face. If a child's family is under stress, for example, because of a father who drinks and has an explosive temper, the child's rough-and-tumble nature could easily turn mean and bullying. He could become the type of child who beats up other children, defies teachers and parents, and, later in life, runs into trouble with the law.

The more the impulsive, aggressive child's family life is filled with emotional neglect or physical abuse or both, the more potential there is that the child will become violent. Children who are very aggressive and lack any regard for other human beings, while representing an extreme, have become a pressing societal concern and, as we shall see later in this chapter, need an intensive long-term approach if they are to be helped.

While some of us may consider such cases utter mysteries, in fact we now have the ability to understand more fully just how anger, fear, and violence are fostered in children. Here are some characteristics that many of these children share.

• *They can't care for others because no one has consistently cared for them.* The process of forming an attachment to someone—which should begin in infancy and continue throughout childhood—is an essential foundation for developing a sense of shared humanity, a feeling of compassion, and concern for others. Without loving contact in infancy and early childhood, a sense of human connectedness may never materialize. The child may view other people as things to be kicked or destroyed when they stand in the way.

 • *They can't purposefully communicate their desires, intentions, and feelings.* As we have seen throughout this book, learning to communicate a full range of emotions in an intentional manner—first nonverbally and then verbally—is an ability all children must master to get their needs met without undue frustration. When a distant, angry parent sees a toddler reaching out to be picked up as an aggressive demand, the parent might say, "Leave me alone!" and the child may withdraw in confusion, in his own wordless way wondering, "Is my request for love an assault?" Even a very young child has developed his own set of emotional expectations. As the child's sense of frustration mounts and his faith that his parents will meet his needs collapses, he may act out with disorganized, aggressive behavior.

Children whose constitutional makeup leads them to opt for hitting, scratching, or other physical movements when frustrated are especially likely to show aggressive behavior under these circumstances. Having received no rewarding response when they tried to communicate emotional needs in a nonverbal way, these children will have even greater difficulty communicating needs with words and symbols.

 • *They can't construct internal dialogues.* If you asked people who behave impulsively and aggressively how they are feeling, they probably won't express their feelings at all and may speak only of actions. For example, in answer to the question "How do you feel?" they may answer, "I hit him six times," instead of "I was angry." As we have seen, the capacity to form a mental picture of wishes and feelings develops between about eighteen and thirty months and keeps developing in more complex ways after that. But many young people prone to violence never acquire the ability to visualize their feelings and are thereby unable to contemplate their actions in advance. When challenged, they respond with impulsive actions—they hit, for example—instead of recognizing their feelings and making a choice.

Many aggressive children tend to crave physical input. They *underreact* to a number of sensations: they seem to need a lot of noise, sound, touch, or other sensations. But, unlike the withdrawn child described in chapter 4—who is also underreactive to sensations but who reacts by retreating into himself—this child's motor system is such that he throws himself into the world, trying to get what he feels he needs. A nine- or ten-month-old may enjoy butting his head into daddy's tummy. A toddler or preschooler may enjoy going down the slide headfirst. He wants to touch things all the time and tries to grab every object in sight— mommy's hair, daddy's nose, that expensive stereo—often knocking over furniture and valuables en route. He may break things because he is always manipulating and touching them.

As he gets older, he horses around and wrestles a lot. He may grab other children's toys, hug them unexpectedly, or constantly want to rough-house or fight. He could be less sensitive to pain than other children; he doesn't mind banging into other children because he likes the physical contact. He is a "little daredevil," his parents may say. He is on the go all the time.

Because of his craving for action and movement, he appears distractible or inattentive. He may actually share some of the challenges of the inattentive child, such as difficulties with auditory processing or receptive language. Sometimes children with these tendencies also have difficulties in sequencing their movements (motor planning). Motor difficulties often seem paradoxical to parents because of the child's pleasure, activity, and interest in trying difficult challenges, such as climbing, jumping, or running in tight quarters. But as he learns to copy shapes and draw, trouble in planning out motor sequences may appear. Can he replicate elaborate shapes or does he tend to make a mishmash? Does he have to work hard to control the pencil?

In contrast to the underreactive child with low motor tone, a very active, sensation-craving child may tend toward high motor tone. When held, he may feel more stiff than loose. Whereas the low-muscle-tone child prefers positions that involve lots of flexion (the fetal position, for example), the high-muscle-tone child may prefer positions or activities that involve lots of extensor effort, such as pushing against something. This child may want to reach out and touch daddy's face but, because his control is incomplete, his aim is poor and daddy winds up with a bop in the nose. If his motor-planning problems are severe, it is easy to misread him and assume that his flailing gestures are intentional.

Just as the highly sensitive child may become more cautious under pressure, the active child may also increase his natural tendencies under pressure. He may react to feelings of anxiety or embarrassment or being reprimanded by stepping up intrusive or aggressive behavior. (When the going gets rough, we all tend to fall back on coping skills that are easiest for us.) None of this behavior is appealing to adults. A child who uses what are sometimes called "counterphobic" tendencies (that is, he becomes more, rather than less, of a daredevil when scared) tends not to get as much sympathy as a child who becomes more fearful or withdrawn under pressure. Therefore, parents, teachers, caregivers, and professionals who work with this child need to be especially alert to the danger of getting into an adversarial relationship with the child. This is not to say that older children shouldn't be responsible for their behavior. They should. But we have to understand the mechanisms they are using in order to help them develop new and more flexible behaviors.

When this child gets frustrated, he is not quiet about it! And because he gets frustrated and enraged easily, he tends to use his motor system to change what he doesn't like. If the toy isn't working, he will want to break it. If his mother and father aren't doing what he wants, he wants to butt them with his head or push them over. If another child has something that he wants, he may pinch the child, or even knock him down, and grab the toy. Because of his enormous energy level and his strong desire to do what he wants when he wants to, he is less likely to be interested in two-way communication. He will tend to communicate one way—his way.

As I mentioned earlier, not all children who are aggressive display these physical characteristics. Another type of aggressive child, for example, is *highly reactive* to sensations. Like the sensitive child, this child is too "tuned in." His senses lack an adequate filter: sights, sounds, smells, and touches that bring other people pleasure can be overwhelming, irritating, and sometimes downright painful to him. Even his own emotions can be too much for him. In chapter 3, I described the "highly sensitive child" who reacts to all these sensations by becoming finicky, fussy, and fearful. Other highly sensitive children, out of an internal sense of self-protection and because they feel overloaded physically and emotionally, may lash out. These children have more fears than other children—they may be more scared than usual of robbers, wolves, or monsters. They may also be much more afraid of other children's aggression. In situations that overload them, they bite, hit, pinch, and push—perhaps in a crowded classroom.

This sensitive/aggressive child might also be bossy and controling, trying to manipulate his environment because he is so sensitive. He wants his fork lined up right next to that spoon and he demands that his friend stand exactly three feet away. He wants that truck right here and he wants you to talk in just the right tone of voice. He can be very tyrannical and if you challenge him, he will be frightened, but might react physically—by hitting or biting, for example.

PARENTING PATTERNS TO AVOID WITH THE ACTIVE/AGGRESSIVE CHILD

Lack of nurturing can lead to aggressive behavior in any child—whether or not he is sensation-seeking. The active, sensation-seeking child simply has a greater likelihood of such a pattern. Other children who are deprived of love are more likely to show their trauma in other ways, such as apathy and withdrawal or self-destructive behavior.

Some parenting patterns inadvertently support aggressive behavior in more subtle ways. Certain parents who are warm and caring may have a lot of difficulty setting appropriate limits. They may also be confused by their child's active, sensation-seeking manner and find it difficult to teach their child how to communicate his intentions and feelings.

We have found that youngsters who have good control over their aggression, whether it is at school, at the daycare center, or at home, tend to have lots of little interactions with adults in which they receive *nonverbal* messages about limits. Normally, when a child is becoming mischievous or aggressive, there is plenty of warning—a twinkle in his eyes, a devilish look, a grimace, a scowl, a clenching of the fist, a stamping of the foot. A parent looks back with a warning look in his or her eyes or may even say, "No, you can't do that." The child backs off or, at least, gives the parent some indication of what is to come. But, in some families, there are no such warnings. When the child and parents begin to get frustrated and angry, neither the child nor the parents show it at first. They are expressionless, poker-faced, their bodies stiff. For example, a child is playing nicely, talking, and pushing his car around the kitchen floor when, suddenly, he pinches his mother in the leg. Parent and child suddenly explode, screaming and hitting. There have been no nonverbal "cues" and warnings exchanged between parent and child. Instead, they both leap right to physical actions. Even a child who isn't generally overly active and sensation-seeking can have problems with aggression when nonverbal interaction is lacking.

Another common mistake that many parents make with a child who is active, assertive, and quick to anger is to vacillate between being "nice guys" and then exploding in rage, before swinging back to being "nice guys" again. Parents, of course, like to be nice guys. They don't like to get angry. So they may say in a calm tone, "Oh, come on, Maurice, please don't touch that plug! I don't think you're listening to me, Maurice. Please listen to me. . . ." Meanwhile, the child just smiles and continues reaching for the plug. Reluctant to get angry, the parent may continue pleading with the child in the same tone of voice until, utterly frustrated, she blows up, frightening the child, who wasn't prepared for his parent's explosive anger. Then the parent feels guilty for the out-of-control rage and tries to make it up to the child by overindulging him. The child experiences an unpredictable, chaotic environment—first nice-nice, then out of control, and then nice-nice again.

A child who can't understand nonverbal communication because of a lack of practice with his parents (or because of difficulties with processing what he hears or sees) gets confused and misreads situations. When the teacher looks serious, the child may think the teacher is fooling around and react by keeping up his provocative behavior. Or, conversely, when the teacher looks a little annoyed, he may be frightened that the teacher is furious and may seek to defend himself by lashing out. Wrestling with a friend, he might not understand when the friend tells him he wants to stop and keeps wrestling. Or when another child approaches to offer him some candy, he may throw a punch because he mistakenly thinks she is trying to take something from him.

The trouble can mount as the child reaches the stage when he is supposed to begin learning emotional ideas. Having been discouraged from developing a vocabulary of gestures to communicate emotional needs, he will have even greater difficulty expressing needs with words and symbols. Teachers and parents of an active/aggressive child are often so busy setting limits that they forget to give the child extra practice in using ideas instead of actions.

Parents who don't encourage pretend play (which fosters the development of emotional ideas) or who don't support emotional ideas when it comes to coping with aggression only compound the challenges. The child doesn't progress beyond the physical and behavioral manifestations of aggression and learn to elevate his feelings to the level of ideas, in the form of make-believe play and narrative. The child doesn't learn how to construct an internal dialogue that connects his emotions and his language. He never acquires the ability to picture his feelings and is thereby unable to fully contemplate his actions in advance.

Some parents, because of their own upbringing, may equate thought and action. "If I think it, I will do it." They, therefore, believe that it's best not to have any aggression emerge in either pretend play or verbal description. When the good soldier starts shooting the bad guy, the parent may respond with "Don't do that," or try to change the scene to one of nurturing: "Hey, let's make those soldiers become good friends and like each other!" While our desire to have our children think only nice and loving thoughts is understandable, we need to be more aware that all of us, by the very fact that we are human, experience the full range of feelings—assertiveness and anger as well as love and warmth.

We, as parents, have a choice. We can continue to let the child express anger at the level of behavior. But then the child can only either act out the anger or anxiously try to inhibit it. Alternatively, we can help our child to elevate anger and other feelings to the world of ideas and let him bring the feeling into pretend play (with soldiers fighting, for example) and into his words ("Mommy, I'm mad!"). Eventually the ideas will be accessible to his reasoning ("Boy, am I mad. I'm gonna talk to Mom about why I'm mad"). When a child learns to picture and verbalize his feelings, he has the opportunity to reason and make intelligent choices. If we don't help our children learn to raise their feelings to this level because we are worried that saying "it" will mean doing "it," we actually increase the likelihood that our child will act out rather than talk out his feelings. Helping a youngster through this transition can be exceptionally challenging for parents who were brought up to believe that thinking and doing are the same. It means changing their own way of coping with feelings at the same time they are trying to help their son or daughter.

In addition to helping children use ideas, parents sometimes have difficulty fostering self-observation. Encouraging a reflective attitude toward emotions is also difficult for parents who are either too strict (they have lots of rigid rules) or parents who are too permissive (they simply give in on every front). When parents believe in a very concrete, law-and-order approach, and the notion of pausing, reasoning, or putting feelings into ideas has no meaning for them, they go head to head with a child who is already very intense. The resulting power struggles and conflict may only make the child more aggressive.

It's not unusual to have a punitive father and a permissive mother in the same family. But parents who are too strict and

parents who are too permissive have something in common; neither one is fostering a truly reflective attitude. Neither one is
helping the child observe his own behavior and try to understand
it. For example, when the child insists on going outside when it's
raining and icy, the strict parent may simply say, "Not now—and
you'd better stop squawking." The permissive parent may simply
say, "Well . . . yes, but put on your raincoat." The parent who is
fostering a reflective attitude toward emotions will say something
different. "What is your hurry? Why do you want to go out in the
rain? Do you remember how slippery it was? And what are you
going to do out there anyhow?" In the dialogue that ensues, the
child is thinking about and discussing his wish rather than immediately giving in to it or inhibiting it. This reflective attitude becomes part of an ability that many adults cherish in themselves:
the ability for self-observation—the ability to ponder what you
are feeling and what you want to do and then analyze the consequences in advance.

HELPFUL PARENTING PATTERNS

Because of his energy and exuberance, the active/aggressive
child has enormous potential. But his parents need to learn how
to harness the energy, urging him to direct it toward the nurturing and caring side of his personality, and helping him learn to be
a more thoughtful problem solver. First of all, he needs extra security, warmth, and engagement. Second, he benefits from a lot
of communication through gestures in general and then words.
Third, he needs limit setting and a sense of structure. Fourth,
extra practice in pretend play shows him how to use ideas rather
than just actions. Finally, he needs to practice connecting his
ideas together through give-and-take dialogue with caregivers
during pretend play and even during heated debates. This enables him to learn how to label his feelings and take a reflective
attitude, rather than act out.

The first stage of emotional development, when a child is
learning to be calm and regulated and, at the same time, is interested and engaged in his environment, is a challenge for this child

because he needs so much stimulation to feel alive. But you can work with him to give him the sensations he needs—while helping him to channel it and modulate it. At the same time, you can help him to find experiences that give him what he needs to feel organized. If he craves touch, you could encourage him to carry around a lump of Play-Doh to mold or some worry beads to finger. To give him the kinetic stimulation he craves, you may want to plan physical activities every half-hour or so—jumping or running games, for example. To help him learn to regulate his motor system, games that combine slow and fast movements work well. For instance, a "Simon Says" game with commands like "Simon says run fast!" "Simon says run slow!" "Simon says run medium fast!" and "Simon says run fast again!" is enjoyable and helpful for active youngsters. Also, games and interactions that involve fine motor activity *as well as* lots of running and jumping assist an energetic child to regulate his activity, motor sequencing, and concentration. You could, for example, come up with a game that combines running and jumping with threading beads onto a string and drawing circles and squares (perhaps all part of a treasure hunt or a Power Ranger game).

For the second stage of emotional development (learning to feel close to others), caregivers need to make an extra effort with an aggressive child to maintain the nurturing part of life. Children learn empathy through a warm, deep, joyful relationship. Since such an active child may be busy running around, you need to work harder to catch his attention, pull him in, and let him know that he is special. That can be done in many little ways. If you're talking to another child when he comes up to speak to you, put your hand on his shoulder so he knows you are aware of him. When you are busy on the telephone, pull him up on your lap and give him a hug while you're talking. When he is intruding between mom and dad, let him know he has to wait, but do it with an arm around his shoulder, so he feels your warm, loving presence while he is learning to be patient.

Give him floor time before you get involved in other activities. After he has had at least half an hour of floor time, where you followed *his* interests, he will be more able to empathize with your need to follow *your* interests. When he is excited and enthusiastic, hang in there an extra minute to respond to his words and happy expressions. When the two of you are talking, let *him* break off the communication, leaving *you* hanging, rather than breaking it off yourself to do something else while he is still trying to maintain his connection with you. Keep the especially joyful moments going. Put other things off.

What I am talking about here could be described as bringing a "floor time" approach to daily events. A hurried, overly controlled, rigid stance or rejection or withdrawal, you will probably find, isn't very helpful with the active/aggressive child. He needs warmth, love, attention, and the comforting knowledge that you are present for him. This child also needs *consistency* in his care and love. If he is in daycare, for example, or if a caregiver comes into the home, he should ideally have the same caregiver for the first three or four years of his life.

As this child grows, he would ideally benefit from having the same teacher over a number of years, providing another source of emotional consistency in his life. Alternatively, mentors who, over time, are a constant part of his life and can work with him on a day-to-day basis on one skill or another provide yet another opportunity for supportive relationships.

Almost all our clinical experience and studies of children with aggressive or antisocial tendencies point in one direction: the most important ingredients for raising such a child are *nurturing relationships* from which he can learn caring, empathy, and respect. Loving support from his family, consistency of babysitters, daycare, teachers, and mentors gives this child opportunities at each stage of development to form and sustain special relationships over a period long enough to allow him to develop a sense of compassion and security.

When it comes to two-way communication, it's especially important for a child with a tendency toward aggression to learn how to read the body language and facial expressions of others. To help him do this, because the active and aggressive child may also be inattentive, you need to be quite lively. Gesture animatedly (act almost like a mime) and make your voice very clear. He may also need a lot of practice in opening and closing circles of communication.

For example, when trying to get an active/aggressive boy to dinner, you say to him, "Evan, we need to sit down. We're getting ready to eat." Evan ignores you and continues playing. Refrain from grabbing him and saying "Sit here!"—that doesn't help him learn to read your gestures and your voice tone. You could perhaps say instead, "Evan, Evan, don't you hear me?" *First,* you need to get his attention, *then* you need to get him engaged emotionally with you. You might talk about what's for dinner, mentioning some of his favorite foods. Then, to get him interacting with you so you can convey your real message, you may pretend to be hiding something in your hand that he might find fun to eat. You might put your closed hands in front of you and say jokingly, "Bet you can't guess what I have in here." Or perhaps you could ask him to guess which hand has something in it. Now you have him attentive, engaged, and interacting with you. There is a much stronger likelihood that he will understand your request to sit at the table for dinner if all *three* systems (his attention, emotions, and ability to interact) are engaged. You can continue the "flirtation" a little longer, if you want, and let him know he can discover what is hidden in your hand by coming and sitting at the dinner table. This way, you have embedded your message into a playful dialogue that operates on a number of levels at once.

The key point is to recognize that your child communicates with you at different levels—attending, engaging, and interacting. To engage a child who is prone to using aggression to express himself, it is best to work your way *up* the developmental ladder. Getting his *attention* comes first; *engaging* him comes second; *interacting* with him, then giving him your message comes third.

Voice tone is an essential signal in helping the active/aggressive child inhibit his behavior. Children understand your meaning by perceiving the tone of your voice. They also notice your facial expressions. Sometimes you'll need to go "up the scale" of emphasis, starting with a soft voice and reassuring facial expressions. If you don't get a response with a low-key approach, you can slowly increase your intensity until you have the voice tone, expression, and body posture of an army sergeant getting the cooperation of his unruly recruits. Always gradually work your way up the scale of emphasis, even with a child who seems only to respond to the "sergeant" level. This gives your child a chance each time to respond to the gentler tone.

To help him learn to develop emotional ideas, which give him the capacity to put his feelings into words and ideas instead of straight into action (hitting and shoving), an active/aggressive child will benefit from extra practice with the concept of word over deed, idea over act. That is, you want to help him learn to *label* and *anticipate* his feelings and think about them, rather than immediately acting them out. Give him extra help in being aware of his wishes and intentions.

Helping an active child foster a reflective attitude can be done very subtly. When your child seems ready to move into action (he *has* to go out on his bike or he *has* to have that toy right now) don't fall into the trap of giving a concrete, yes or no answer. Neither yes nor no helps your child pause and reflect. The yes merely lets him get what he wants right away. The no simply inhibits him or leads to a tantrum. "What's the hurry?" in contrast, helps him reflect and ponder. Even if he just hesitates for a few seconds and then says, "I gotta go outside right away!" or "I gotta have that right now!" and then tries to grab it, you still have a victory. You have helped him think things over for five seconds. That is five times better than a one-second statement on his part and a shift into action.

Over time, you can ask the impatient child not only "What's the hurry?" but "Where do you want to go on your bike?" and "What do you want to do there?" in a curious, not critical, tone of voice. You may even talk about all the things that sound like fun on his way somewhere or what game will be the most fun to play with the toy. Through these discussions, you help him to develop a capacity to reflect on his wish—what makes it fun, what makes it exciting—rather than putting the desire directly into action.

Eventually, this practice will help your child to consider his aggression and anger. Sooner or later, he will be able to ask himself questions like "Why am I so angry?" and "What will happen if I push Jamie off the slide?" A healthy adult certainly feels anger, but he is generally able to use his own fantasies and thoughts ("Boy, I'd like to tell her off!") to let himself know what he is feeling and then, strategically and rationally, decide what actions would be most appropriate. Such thinking enables children and adults to be aware of their feelings, provides them with an outlet through thoughts and fantasies, and helps them to select behavior that is in the long-term interest of themselves and others.

Pretend play is also invaluable. Through pretending, youngsters learn to express feelings verbally and use ideas, rather than just relying on angry behavior. For example, many opportunities arise during make-believe to help a child describe his feelings or the feelings of the characters in his drama.

As you can see, family tendencies can play a crucial role in helping the sensation-seeking, potentially aggressive child. If the family can support warm, trusting relationships, communication, and the concept of ideas over actions, our aggressively inclined child can become an energetic, enthusiastic, creative contributor to society. On the other hand, if the family doesn't furnish such a child with trusting relationships and employs fragmented, intrusive, neglectful, or abusive interactions, and if they either directly or by default support acting out (rather than *talking* out) feelings, the risk of dangerously aggressive behavior rises.

HELPING THE SEVERELY ANTISOCIAL CHILD

With children who are in danger of crossing the line and getting into trouble with the law, society needs to step in. A successful preventive effort needs to be built around the same philosophy described earlier that emphasizes personal relationships and nurturing patterns of care. Such an approach might begin with initiatives that help the most vulnerable parents become better caregivers to their kids—a tall order, certainly. But results of a fifteen-year study by the Syracuse University Family Development Research Program are promising. In the low-income families visited by child development trainers every week for five years to work on individualized parenting skills, only 6 percent of the children in the study group went on to have probation records as opposed to 22 percent of the control group. Pediatricians and other health care providers need to be as aware of the emotional state of the infants, children, and families as they are of physical well-being. While the American Academy of Pediatrics has recognized the importance of a child's psychological development in the guidelines it prepares for health care professionals, focusing on the details of the emotional lives of children during routine health care is still an unmet goal.

As I discussed earlier, we also need to increase the continuity of relationships between adult caregivers and children. This is especially true when the children are at risk. For example, daycare administrators should consider letting staff stay with the same children throughout their infancy and early childhood, instead of changing each year for efficiency. Under ideal circumstances, the same schoolteacher might work with an at-risk child for all seven grade-school years to form a relationship that the child might never get at home.

If a severely aggressive child requires foster care because of his family circumstances, special training and incentives should be made available to the foster parents so they will remain his caregivers throughout his entire childhood, unless, of course, he can return to his biological family. And if he requires repeated foster care placements because of an unstable family situation, ideally he should return to the same foster parents each time. With support and training, his foster parents can learn to work with him successfully.

Creating a mentor relationship with a child from this background can make an enormous difference in his life. Studies of families found that a key factor in the children who survived deprived or abusive backgrounds is a nurturing, supportive relationship—sometimes with a family friend or relative, or a mentor in an intervention program. We also need to create programs for children at critical points in childhood and adolescence—for instance, once a pattern of absenteeism from school is established or after the first criminal offense—that foster relationships with mentors. Many years ago, a Newton, Massachusetts, program run by Milton Shore and Joseph Massimo worked with young delinquents immediately after they dropped out of high school. The program significantly reduced the incidents of criminal incarceration and mental health difficulties. In follow-up studies twenty years after the program ended, 80 percent of the group that did not have mentors were in the criminal justice or mental health system, while 80 percent of the group that had mentors were doing well in terms of work, family, and general well-being.

The main point is that, at any age, children can be helped. But the key ingredient is a relationship that can be used as a vehicle for shifting these children's values and rebuilding the emotional milestones they may have missed.

SCOTT'S STORY

By the time Deborah Konrad came to see me, she was close to the end of her rope. Her eight-year-old son, Scott, was turning her life into chaos. Teachers at his school and his after-school daycare program complained that he beat up other children—pushing them down, yelling at them, and punching them. He had been sent home from school several times in the previous six months for fighting, and the director of his after-school program was threatening to kick him out if he got into any more trouble. At home, Scott and his thirteen-year-old brother, Brad, fought constantly.

"I talk to Scott about his behavior, and he always says he'll try to be better," Deborah told me. "Then I get a note from his teacher that says he hit another child."

Deborah was a tall, elegant woman with dark hair. She sat stiffly in her seat as she talked, her eyes guarded. Divorced from the boys' father, Tom, for three years, she was the busy executive director of a trade association. Deborah and the boys lived in a large home in the suburbs of Washington, D.C. After the divorce, Tom, a corporate attorney, had moved to Chicago. Deborah worried that Scott was becoming too much like his father, whom

Scott and Brad saw one weekend a month. The divorce had been difficult, and Deborah believed that Tom bad-mouthed her during their sons' visits. Deborah described her former husband as a man who loved his sons very much, but who had an explosive temper. It was clear, she told me, that Scott got his bad temper from his father.

Deborah also told me she was seeing a man, also an attorney. They talked about getting married at some point in the future.

Scott Konrad had always been a precocious child, Deborah recalled. He sat up, walked, and talked earlier than most children. From her description of Scott's early years, I could tell that Deborah and her son had once connected well emotionally.

"He was pretty active," she told me, remembering her son's early years with a slight smile. "I was always chasing after him." Scott had been constantly on the go, grabbing, throwing things along the way. He loved to be swung through the air. As he got a little older, he enjoyed wrestling with his older brother and his father.

"He had enormous energy," Deborah said. "I felt like I could never keep up with him."

Deborah had worried for a while that Scott was hyperactive and had considered taking him to get evaluated. She noticed that he liked to touch everything. When he fell, he invariably jumped up, even when he hurt himself, and didn't seem to be affected by scrapes and bruises. She saw that he seemed to want a lot of stimulation in other areas, as well. He seemed to enjoy rather than avoid loud noises. He sometimes turned on the radio full blast, for example.

Along with his vast supply of energy, Deborah recalled, Scott also had been "kind of a clumsy boy. He was always bumping into furniture, people—you name it. And he tripped over *everything.*" She grimaced slightly. "Tom gave him a hard time. I think he thought Scott was doing it deliberately." Deborah said she found herself constantly defending Scott and probably "overindulged" her son because of his father's strictness.

Deborah couldn't remember Scott using imagination or

make-believe in his play. "I think he was too busy just running all over the place," she said. "He was such a physical kid, I don't know if he ever had much interest in pretend games."

The first signs of trouble for Scott appeared when Deborah and Tom's marriage began to fall apart. They argued constantly, and the arguments almost always ended with Tom storming out of the house. As tension between his parents mounted, Scott, who was then about three, began to get more belligerent and combative. He threw noisy tantrums at the least provocation. He grabbed toys from other kids and reacted strongly to any sign of aggression from them. From what his mother told me, I guessed that Scott had difficulty reading other children's gestures and body language, probably mistaking a playful push for a sign that he was being attacked. He hadn't moved into what we would expect to be his next stage of development—learning to communicate with ideas. The lack of interest in make-believe or pretend games suggested that he was not yet using ideas to communicate his aggression, as well as other emotions.

"He was pretty tough to deal with, but we managed for a while," Deborah told me. "In the last couple of years, though, it's started to cause trouble." Deborah and Tom had separated when Scott was five, and Deborah, who had gone back to work part-time when Scott was six months old, then returned to work full-time. She threw herself into her job and was eventually promoted to executive vice-president of the organization, which meant late nights and some travel, along with a demanding work week.

"I don't have time for Scott to be in trouble," she told me. "It's exhausting and incredibly stressful, of course. And I can't leave work all the time to go visit teachers."

Deborah described her everyday life with her sons, which seemed very hectic. There wasn't much time for in-depth talks or playing together. Deborah dropped the boys off at school on the way to work and they attended after-school programs until 6:00 P.M. The after-school program sounded rather chaotic. Scott's group consisted mostly of older kids, and they usually played outside without much supervision. I suspected that Scott spent much of his time defending himself. Deborah had told me that Scott was a tall kid, and I got the feeling that he was probably an easy target because he was younger than the others. Scott had a number of casual friends in school and at the after-school program but, unlike many other kids his age, he had no close friends. A babysitter picked the boys up at 6:00 and drove them home for dinner. Deborah usually arrived home about 7:00 or 7:30—unless she had a late meeting. After a hurried dinner, the boys did their homework or watched TV. On weekends, Deborah usually caught up on paperwork for part of the time, while the boys either watched TV or played outside with their skateboards or rollerblades. They flew out to visit their father once a month in Chicago. On the other Saturday nights, Deborah usually took them to a movie or out to dinner. Paul, the man she was seeing, often came along.

Deborah struck me as a well-organized, concerned parent, although she was overwhelmed at the moment with survival issues—running her busy career and raising her boys by herself.

Deborah described Scott and his brother as fairly self-sufficient. "They really take care of themselves," she said. "I don't even give them a bedtime. They just go to bed when they're tired—sometimes as late as eleven or midnight. I guess they don't need much sleep."

She said Scott never turned his aggression on her. Most of the time, she could get him to do what she wanted. But Scott and Brad fought constantly, with Brad complaining that Scott "bugged" him all the time and "picked fights" with him.

Along with his difficulties, Scott was struggling in school. He was getting Cs much of the time, and teachers said that he didn't seem to hear or understand what they were saying. He had, however, shown special abilities in math and science.

With that background, I was now ready to meet Scott. He came in by himself while his mother stayed in the waiting room. He was a tall, skinny boy with warm brown eyes. He moved quickly, almost charging in the door, and slid into a chair opposite me. He smiled nervously, looking around the room, moving restlessly in his seat. I had the sense that it was difficult for him to sit still.

I welcomed Scott, as I do each child who comes to see me, with a smile and "How's it going?" Because I like to let the youngster make the first move, so that I can see how he reacts to me and his new surroundings, I waited for Scott to speak. After a short silence, he said, "I don't know what I'm s'posed to say."

"I can imagine that it must feel funny—not knowing what to say," I said.

Scott looked around my office and shifted nervously in his chair. His foot tapped on my carpet. I usually have my office set up with toys or games appropriate to the child's age. For Scott, I had set out a few balls, a couple of games, and some action figures. He glanced at them briefly and then began talking.

"I guess my mom told you I get into trouble a lot," he said.

"When does that happen most?" I asked.

He grinned shyly and shrugged.

Clearly, his aggressive behavior troubled him because he had almost immediately brought it up. I continued, "How do you end up getting into trouble?"

He shrugged again. "I dunno. I—it just kind of happens."

I asked him to describe what happens, and Scott told me about a boy at school who "pushes" him. "I push him back, and he yells, and then I get into trouble with the teacher."

The same theme emerged in other stories he told me. At home and at school, Scott was under attack. But when he tried to defend himself, the teacher or his mother caught him rather than the true perpetrator. At home, when he and Brad argued, Scott told me, Brad invariably started the battle by shoving or kicking his younger brother. But when Scott retaliated, Brad would yell for their mother, and Scott ended up in trouble again.

I wondered aloud to Scott about why he kept getting provoked by these other kids and then ending up in hot water himself.

"Well, when they bug me, I need to get even," he said.

"If your goal is to get even, how come you don't delay and think about things?" I asked curiously. "Instead, you're telling me that you need to act so quickly that you get into trouble yourself." I wanted to see if he was aware of his tendency to dig himself into a deeper hole, so I probed gently a little further. "How come you set it up so the other guy doesn't get caught?"

Scott shook his head. "I'd have to wait too long to get the other guys caught."

In our discussion about school, we explored some of his academic skills. He related that it was hard for him to remember things he read or figure out what stories were about. We tried a few exercises involving auditory processing, such as remembering numbers or a series of words. And, in fact, he did have difficulty with auditory processing. Yet at the same time, he showed me that he could concentrate, reason, and think on his feet and even solve mathematical problems quite easily. He clearly had a gift for reasoning with numbers.

I also asked Scott to draw some pictures for me—a request I make of most of the children I see. That way, I can observe their fine motor skills (how well they can hold and manipulate pencils or crayons) and how they use spatial relations (how well they use the space on the paper). Also, some children simply communicate better visually than they do with words.

The pictures that Scott drew were interesting. He did not have good fine motor control, holding the pencil awkwardly and frowning slightly as he drew. And his pictures were rather empty. He drew animals, as well as lots of people engaged in activities like driving cars and airplanes. But the animals and the people did not have facial expressions. The pictures seemed hollow, devoid of emotion, and lacking in the exuberance that fills most kids' drawings.

Then Scott wrote a story for me. It took him some time. "One day Eric went to the basketball court. He played some basketball by himself and then he saw a kid and wanted to play with him. He was so glad he brought his basketball with him. And they played for a while. Then they went home."

I asked him whether anything else had happened between the kids. He looked sad. "No, they didn't see each other again."

"Did they want to?" I asked.

Scott didn't answer. Abruptly, he changed the subject, telling me in great detail about a wrestling match he had seen on TV. He seemed to need to tell me about the gory parts—the bloody nose, the broken arm. Every time I tried to bring him back to the theme of loneliness in the story, he only intensified his description of the aggression in the wrestling match. It seemed as though, at least with me, he ran away from his lonely feelings, conveyed by the boy who never saw his new friend again, and quickly substituted aggressive themes for the lonely ones. I wondered how much this contributed to his aggression generally.

We also talked about his father. Scott told me he liked visiting his dad even though "he yells at me sometimes." I sensed from Scott's description of his father that Tom probably was also overwhelmed by Scott's energy. Unlike Deborah, who reacted by letting Scott do basically what he wanted, Tom reacted by trying to clamp down on Scott.

One of Scott's favorite activities was going to Chicago Bulls games with his father. He started to tell me about the time he had seen Michael Jordan play.

But then he stopped talking. After a pause, he asked me if I ever saw wrestling matches and, with a lot of fidgeting, started again describing some of his favorite wrestling moves, such as when a wrestler jumps off the ropes and lands on his opponent. I commented that I could tell that the wrestling was exciting, but that just before the wrestling he had been talking about going to Bulls games with his dad. He stopped talking again.

"When I have to go home, I feel sad," he said suddenly. His brown eyes filled briefly with tears and he blinked. "We only get to see him one weekend a month."

"I'll bet you want to see him more," I said.

He nodded. "Maybe one whole week a month. It would be even greater if he still lived with my mom, or if they lived real close together."

This was the only time Scott was able to describe his feelings to me. Otherwise, when feelings of sadness or loss came up, Scott immediately switched to describing some violent struggle or a wrestling match that he'd seen on TV or a fight that he had had with a kid at school.

After a couple of sessions with Scott and his mother, the

following impressions emerged. From his mother's descriptions, he appeared to be underreactive to a number of sensations, which meant he needed a lot more stimulation than other children—even to the point of physical pain. So the physical discomfort of, say, getting punched, wouldn't discourage Scott from getting into tussles as much as it would other children.

He was able to focus and engage with others. He communicated clearly with gestures, ideas, and words but sometimes had difficulty understanding other people's intentions. He seemed to misread situations quite frequently and assume he was being attacked when he wasn't. While he showed some ability to use emotional ideas, there were limitations. He avoided using ideas that conveyed emotions dealing with aggression, vulnerabilities, or sadness and dealt with aggression more through physicality than thinking. Outside of these areas, he could do some logical thinking. He appeared to have progressed into the world of triangular relationships, having some grasp of the rivalries and intrigues that can swirl around relationships, and he had also delved into the world of the peer group.

In the "politics of the playground," however, Scott showed limitations in his approach to others. Whenever he felt vulnerable or sad in complicated group situations or in competitive triangles, he resorted to aggressive behavior rather than thinking out the situation or expressing his position in words. He wasn't able, for example, to wait long enough for his tormenters to get themselves into hot water or for the teacher to observe that he wasn't the only culprit in a fight. Rather than diagnosing the relationships between the teacher and the peer group and planning his own strategies appropriately, he felt compelled by his own feelings to hit before being hit. This betrayed not only his poor impulse control, but also an inability in certain situations to reflect and comprehend how the relationships worked.

Like many of the children I have seen, Scott had progressed in some areas of his development, but remained limited and therefore vulnerable in others. His need for sensation, for activity, and his lack of sensitivity to pain all worked to intensify his general tendency to *act out* anger rather than using reflection and words. Auditory processing challenges further contributed to his sense of confusion and, at times, to misreading of situations.

But my gut reaction was that, despite his reputation for being hot tempered, he was a friendly, likable child. Much was being demanded of Scott. He had a busy mother, a father in another city, and he spent most of his day in school and in an after-school program where he constantly had to deal with other, often older kids. I suspected that, because of his size, his teachers and after-school supervisors weren't helping him out much. Even though he was still a child, Scott was being expected to act like an adult. I sensed that he had a deep loneliness inside, as well as a lot of anger at having to be on his own so much. That inner loneliness and anger, combined with several factors—the marital tension between his parents earlier in his life, the usual peer group challenges at his age, and the rather rambunctious atmosphere at his after-school program—created difficulties for Scott. He felt that he needed to, as he put it, "defend" himself.

This reaction is fairly typical for children who have some problems with aggression but who nonetheless have good potential. They may have mastered many developmental challenges but are unable to turn to emotional ideas in dealing with important feelings.

Even though Scott and his mother loved each other very much, there wasn't much emotional satisfaction between the two of them. And Scott simply wasn't getting enough of his mother or his father.

Some children growing up in overly busy families face the same issues as Scott. They spend long days in programs where children of many ages may be thrown together. If the setting is inadequately supervised, the child can easily feel scared and vulnerable. If his parents are too busy, they may not be able to provide him with a sense of being protected from these stresses. As I indicated earlier, Scott's difficulties were exacerbated by his uneven mastery of certain emotional milestones, by his physical tendencies, and by his family dynamics—a permissive mother and a punitive father.

Our first step with Scott, as with other children in his

situation, was to work to improve his most important relationships and, within their framework, help him renegotiate, or negotiate for the first time, the stages of development that he had not fully mastered. We needed to deepen Scott's relationships with his mother and father (although it would be more difficult with his father). As we worked on Scott's challenges, using the steps outlined in earlier cases, Scott progressed through a number of the emotional milestones needed for developing viable coping capacities.

FLOOR TIME: DEEPENING RELATIONSHIPS

When I first explained the concept of floor time to Deborah, tears came to her eyes. In the stress of her divorce and her new job, Deborah realized that she had missed a lot of the pleasure of being a parent. She began by reserving a half-hour a day for each of her sons after dinner. For an hour each night, she devoted herself to Scott and Brad. They could talk, they could play, they could be together.

At first, finding an hour simply to be with her sons was difficult for Deborah. It meant leaving work a little earlier than normal and turning down the heat on her career a notch. That decision was a struggle for Deborah. She was a dedicated professional, and the idea of doing less than her best on the job every day was uncomfortable.

Floor time also presented her with another challenge—how simply to "hang out" with her sons. Like many parents, Deborah was accustomed to planning very structured time with her children. Floor time didn't come easily. When she sat down with Scott in his room during the first of their floor time sessions, Deborah wasn't quite sure what to do. Scott wasn't either. But it was clear that he valued the special half-hour because he had a big grin on his face whenever Deborah spent time with him.

At first Scott showed her the basketball cards that he had collected at school. Some of them he had obtained by tricking other children into trades. Deborah disapproved of Scott's efforts to trick his classmates, but I suggested that she simply focus on his perspective and respond with warmth and understanding to the pride he obviously felt.

It's important to realize that you can show interest in a child's perspective without agreeing or supporting what the child is doing. Taking the attitude of "I know there must be a good reason why you get some pleasure from what you're doing" doesn't convey approval; it simply tells a child you're trying to see things from his view. A supportive response like this may help a child eventually convey his reasons for his behavior and then you will be in a better position to help the child figure out other ways to feel good about himself. Obviously, if Scott had told Deborah that he had been doing something illegal or dangerous, she would respond differently. If your child crosses that line, you need to place strict limits on his behavior. At the same time, however, you need to maintain empathy and try to understand the child's behavior from his perspective.

As the daily floor time sessions continued, Deborah noticed two themes emerging: Scott needed to feel that he could outsmart people and he needed to feel powerful in his mother's eyes.

"He's really just a little kid trying to be a bigger man," she told me in wonder during one of our one-on-one sessions. That realization helped her become aware of Scott's insecure feelings, as well as his drive to be "top dog" at school, at home, and at the daycare center.

A subject that kept coming up during Deborah's and Scott's floor time was Scott's brief weekends with his father. Scott told his mother what he had told me—that he missed his dad very much and wanted to see him more often. Deborah preferred that her sons spend as little time with Tom as possible. She felt Tom was too strict and punitive, particularly for Scott. Despite her fears, I still felt that Scott needed to see more of his father.

"Why is it so important?" Deborah asked. It was clear that she didn't think much of the idea.

"When someone is a parent, he's a parent for good and for bad," I explained. "He's important to his children no matter what. In fact, children may be influenced *more* by the parent that they see less frequently. That's because they don't know him well enough and tend to idealize him."

Deborah reluctantly agreed to let Scott and Brad see their father more frequently. After a few stiff, awkward phone calls between Deborah and Tom, Tom agreed to arrange his business travel so that he could regularly come through Washington. He stayed in a local hotel and had the boys join him on weekends. Happy to see so much of the boys, Tom also offered to extend their monthly weekend trips a day or two when school schedules permitted and to take them for six weeks each summer. The boys were delighted. A side benefit for Deborah was that she gained some extra time to get caught up on work and to see Paul. Scott responded well to seeing his father more often: he was better able to connect with his father emotionally, and he gained another strong adult figure to relate to.

It's important that a child have a relationship with both parents if possible. His feelings of security, his sense of being cared for, derive from his relationships with each parent, even if the exchanges between his mother and father are less than cordial. Children are observant: they know the difference between an available relationship that is being undermined (for example, when a father or a mother refuses to grant the other parent generous visitation rights or strives to estrange a child from the other parent) and an unavailable relationship (say, when a parent lives a great distance away or is no longer living). Obviously, if one parent is abusive, the other parent must do everything he or she can to shield the child.

After several months, Scott and his mother were experiencing real rapport during floor time, and Scott was reaping the benefits of a masculine presence in his life.

PROBLEM-SOLVING TIME: LEARNING TO ANTICIPATE AGGRESSIVE FEELINGS

Problem-solving time can be especially helpful for children who get into trouble because of their aggressive behavior. It helps them learn to think and talk about their feelings, in other words, to put their feelings in the form of *emotional ideas*. It also helps them anticipate situations that are particularly difficult. Done at a separate time of the day than floor time, problem solving allows a parent and child an opportunity to work out challenges together.

Scott's first challenge was learning to open and close circles of communication. Because of his difficulties with auditory processing, he tended to listen more to himself than to others. It was harder for him to decode ideas coming in from outside than ideas emanating from his own mind. He also tended to misread situations. If a group of children was laughing together on the playground, Scott tended to think they were laughing about him. If a friend playfully tried a mock karate kick on him, he was apt to think it was an attack and responded by getting into a fistfight. When his teacher frowned at him and asked him to sit down and pay attention, he had a tendency to chuckle and keep tossing pencils in the air, convinced that "she's just kidding."

Deborah began problem-solving time by simply asking Scott to tell her about his day. It wasn't easy at first. The dialogue went something like this:

DEBORAH: What did you do in school today?
SCOTT: Nothing.
DEBORAH: Nothing?
SCOTT: Well, it's the same old stuff.
DEBORAH: Same old stuff? What's that?
SCOTT: Well, you know, regular.

I told Deborah not to get discouraged. First, she needed to keep in mind that the child who doesn't talk very much may communicate with posture—sitting stiffly with arms crossed or with shoulders and head slumped. She could comment on what she observed. And she needed to remember that Scott's difficulty with word retrieval made it hard for him to find words to describe ideas or things. Sometimes when he said "Nothing" or "I can't remember," he needed a little help or cuing. It could go like this:

DEBORAH: Sometimes it's hard to remember all the stuff that goes on at school.

SCOTT: Yeah. After school it all leaves me.

DEBORAH: Well, let's see. Normally you play with Tony at recess. Did you do that today or something else?

SCOTT: Oh, yeah. We did, but he was kind of mean. He pushed me when I was kicking the ball.

Sometimes, a few cues from Deborah got them off and running. But sometimes she had to work a little harder.

DEBORAH: Well, usually before lunch on Tuesdays you have gym. What did you do in gym today?

SCOTT: Kickball. I scored twice!

DEBORAH: That's great! How did you do that?

SCOTT: I don't know. Just kicked the ball, I guess.

DEBORAH: Well, you're a pretty fast runner. Did you kick the ball and then run fast?

SCOTT: Sort of.

DEBORAH: Who did you kick the ball to?

SCOTT: Denise.

DEBORAH: Then what happened?

SCOTT: Oh, I remember. It was pretty funny! Denise tripped when she tried to pick it up, and then she threw the ball to Matthew and it hit Mr. McCartney on the head.

Deborah had to keep in mind that Scott might say only a few words at first and that it could be six weeks or longer before he came up with a few sentences. But that was considerable progress. When Scott added a word or two at a time, he might achieve as much as 50 to 75 percent progress!

Deborah was so squeezed for time that she used breakfast and the time in the car as she drove the boys to school to hold problem-solving conversations. It wasn't perfect, but she made good use of the morning and also tried to carve out a little extra time several days of the week for some one-on-one problem-solving chats with Scott.

Once Scott was more comfortable with carrying on a logical dialogue, Deborah was able to move to the next challenge. Like many children exhibiting aggressive behavior, Scott found it tough to talk about his feelings and how he coped with emotions. He couldn't identify the situations that got him in hot water and thus wasn't able to come up with strategies to cope with them.

If you look at people who cope successfully with difficult situations, they often automatically think ahead and anticipate the circumstances. They envision how they'll feel in those situations and how they are likely to behave, which gives them the chance to work on various responses. An adult going into a job interview, for example, might anticipate the questions he'll be asked and how he will feel about those questions. Then he can figure out the appropriate answers beforehand.

Children, and adults, who have trouble identifying and anticipating difficult situations usually charge into them with their eyes closed. Because they are unable to hang onto a thought or feeling long enough to consider dealing with challenges through different behavior, they instead rely on reflexive responses, such as aggressive physical behavior. This is especially true of physically active, underreactive children like Scott who have a tendency to misread other people. And, like many parents of overactive/aggressive children, Deborah had been so busy setting limits or just giving up that she had never offered him extra practice in using ideas instead of action.

We recall that Deborah started by simply asking Scott how the day had gone, patiently cuing him. After a while, Scott began to describe scenarios where he had ended up in trouble. His mother listened carefully but refrained from criticizing her son's behavior.

After several days, Deborah said, "Let's see if we can figure out what kind of situation comes up a lot that makes you hit or push somebody."

Initially, that was very difficult for Scott.

"I can't, Mom," he said in exasperation. "It just kind of happens."

"Well, let's look at when it happened the last two or three times," his mother said. "Maybe we'll see something that keeps happening and we'll be able to predict what will happen the next time."

Scott grudgingly agreed but warned his mother, "Mom, these things are never the same." But he described a recent event that had spurred him into taking a swing at a classmate. "One time, Mom, Katherine tried to take this pencil I was using when I needed it. I was just sitting at my desk, Mom, and she tried to grab it right out of my hand."

Gradually, as he described similar episodes in which he was attacked or provoked, Deborah saw two patterns emerging. First, when he anticipated some threat from another child, Scott couldn't wait for the situation to develop but instead would strike early. If he and another boy argued over who got to use the soccer ball first during recess, for example, Scott would cut the discussion short with a quick punch.

The second pattern that emerged was that Scott reacted strongly when he felt he was being treated unjustly: if his teacher called on another when Scott felt he should have been chosen, for example, or if a classmate whom he wanted to pal around with was friendly with someone else. The feelings of unfairness were always associated with something that he wanted, some longing that he had, some wish for closeness, camaraderie, or approval. Rather than focusing on how he felt, Scott focused on the inequity—how unfair it was that another kid got the teacher's attention or that some other kid got the pal he wanted. And those feelings of injustice made Scott look for a fight.

Deborah tried to help Scott identify these types of situations.

"What happens when you think somebody wants to fight with you?" Deborah asked. "It seems to me that you like to get that first punch in before they do anything to you."

Scott smiled proudly. "I sure do. I don't want to get hit."

Deborah kept going. "Are there any kids you think want to get you into trouble?"

Scott named three kids with whom he had constant problems. His mother wondered aloud about how he felt when he was getting ready to launch one of his "defensive missiles" at an alleged aggressor.

That was a big challenge for Scott, of course. He didn't like to picture feelings. So Deborah suggested that they imagine what would happen if another kid took his pencil or tried to bump him during soccer.

"What would happen next?" she wondered. Scott took to this fantasy game and came up with some interesting tales. He imagined a monster who disguised himself as a kid to attack an earthling. The game allowed Scott to talk for the first time about feelings of fear and danger. He described a tensing of his muscles and a tightening in his arms and in his stomach and a momentary flash of fear. As one of Scott's monsters was about to tackle the earthling, Deborah asked, "I wonder, how is the monster feeling?"

"Oh, he's really mad, Mom," Scott answered.

"What about the earthling?" Deborah asked. "I wonder what he's feeling?"

"He's feeling really scared," came the reply.

"I wonder why?" Deborah mused aloud.

"He thinks he has to get even with the monster or everybody will laugh at him," Scott said one day.

"I wonder why everyone would laugh at him," Deborah said softly.

Scott paused. "Because they'll think he's too scared."

"What's wrong with being scared?" asked Deborah.

"Then everyone thinks you're a jerk," he replied in such a low voice that Deborah could barely hear him.

Scott's admission that feelings of fear caused him to lash out reminded Deborah of her former husband's quick temper. She was tempted to throw up her hands and blame all of Scott's problems on his father and do nothing else.

"This is why I don't want the boys going to see him more often," she told me in frustration. "All they learn is how to get mad, how to yell, how to pound tables."

Upon reflection, Deborah was able to see that the critical issue for Scott wasn't visiting his father, but learning to size up his own feelings. By doing so, he would more easily be able to form an accurate picture of his father as well. Deborah realized she had to keep working with Scott, and not give up and blame her former husband.

Slowly, Scott improved in identifying the emotions of the characters of the stories he told, including scared feelings, which often underlie angry ones. In his conflicts with his brother, Scott realized that he often tormented him when he was feeling lonely. So Scott and his mom began to consider other things he could do when he was feeling scared or lonely instead of trying to banish the uncomfortable feeling by taking a swing at somebody.

Gradually, during their discussions, they talked about the fact that Scott always seemed to be the kid in trouble. "Like yesterday, when James pushed me into the wall when we were going to assembly, and I pushed him back and Mr. Naughton only saw me," he said. It began to dawn on Scott that he always ended up being seen as the guilty one, while his tormenters never seemed to get caught.

"Can you think of another way to deal with the kids who pick on you?" his mother asked.

Being a good Nintendo player, Scott understood the advantages of reacting quickly but, at the same time, thinking two or three moves ahead. But he'd never thought of using such strategy with another child. Pausing to think ahead would also give Scott time to experience and reason about his feelings: "I'm mad because Mae took my book" or "I'm scared that the other kids will think I'm a jerk if I don't punch James after he pushed me." Then he could think of a way to react that would help him get what he wanted without getting him into trouble.

Scott didn't necessarily come up with a definitive course of action to take whenever stressful situations erupted. But he was at least acquiring the ability to consider alternatives to lashing out physically. His main accomplishment was developing an ability to ponder the situation, including his feelings. This skill would be a lifelong asset. Often we mistakenly assume we have to provide a child with an immediate solution to his problem. It's far better to provide a child with a *method* of approaching the problem. In this case, Scott was learning to substitute reflection and thinking for impulsive action. In time, this would lead to some good solutions as well. But, in the meantime, in thinking rather than doing, he was learning that he could buy some time and, at least in the short term, stay out of trouble.

Once again, this progress could be seen as a step up the ladder of emotional development. The critical issue for Scott, and many other aggressive children like him, is to move from an *action* level to a *thinking* level. Instead of going immediately from feeling an emotion (such as anger) to acting on it, Scott was learning to pause and think. Although it may seem critical that Scott *know* that he was covering up feelings of vulnerability or sadness with aggression, the more important lesson for Scott was the emotional skill of thinking instead of just acting. Eventually this ability would enable him to understand many of his deeper feelings. For now, however, simply being able to delay, ponder, and explore his feelings and motives was an excellent first step for Scott.

EMPATHIZING WITH THE VULNERABILITY BENEATH THE ANGER

When parents try to see the world from their child's perspective, they help the child identify the basic assumptions that are causing him to feel and behave a certain way.

During their time together, Deborah sympathized with Scott's fear that another kid would get the best of him and empathized with his feelings on those rare occasions when he talked about being lonely. One day Scott told her the teacher had picked someone else to lead the class out to the playground for recess when Scott had very badly wanted to do it. He had waved his hand in the air "really, really hard," he told his mother later, and hadn't "yelled or shouted or anything. I was really good."

But when he hadn't been chosen, he had acted up, throwing pencils at another boy's head, and had been forced to spend recess inside as punishment.

"Mr. Naughton said I could lead the class out!" Scott said. "He *promised!* It's not fair!"

Fortunately, Deborah had spent enough one-on-one time with her son to pick up on the fact that when he complained about something not being fair, he usually meant that some basic need or deep longing was not being met.

"You must be really disappointed," she said sympathetically.

Scott looked sad for a moment. "I really wanted to be the class leader. You know what?" He turned to Deborah. "Mr. Naughton *hates* me."

As Deborah listened to the emotional message behind Scott's words, it became clear that he was longing for approval from his teacher. So Deborah looked past the "he hates me" message and was able to hear Scott's sadness and disappointment. "It's really hard when somebody promises you something and then doesn't come through, isn't it, honey?" she said. It would have been all too easy for Deborah to get caught up arguing with Scott over whether the teacher really was unfair. In the past, she might have pointed out how many other students there were and, without intending to, empathized more with the teacher than with Scott. This time, however, Deborah sidestepped the outer reality. She didn't lecture Scott that he should be less demanding and, instead, helped him recognize that behind his annoyance and his perception of injustice were feelings of disappointment and perhaps even some sadness.

Those of you who have inadvertently sided with the teacher or the other kid, even though your main goal was to point out reality to your child, have probably noticed that there is no better way to fan the flames of anger and frustration. It's easy for parents of an aggressive child to find themselves constantly in an adversarial position. But by empathizing with your son or daughter's feelings, you can take yourself out of that stance, at least for the moment, and be more like a good friend saying, "Gee, that's a tough way to feel." But it's important not to be patronizing or contrived. Be compassionate in a way that seems natural.

Scott's conflicts with his brother, while fewer, continued. Deborah empathized with Scott's difficulties. She recalled some of the battles she had had with her older sister when she was a child. "It's hard to have a big brother sometimes, isn't it?" she remarked.

Often Scott accused her of favoring his brother. "I didn't start it!" he repeatedly said. "He took my rollerblades when you were at work and hid them and still I get in trouble 'cause I kicked him!'"

Instead of arguing with Scott or giving in, Deborah listened to his complaints that she favored Brad. She noticed that his conflicts with his brother seemed to be triggered by the feelings that he was alone in an overwhelming situation. She realized in these discussions that Scott had some rather definite assumptions about the world. He believed that the world was a dangerous place and to protect himself, he felt that he should never have to be lonely or scared. Deborah believed that this outlook came from his father; she knew that Tom had great difficulty facing these emotions. And she suspected that in her rush to appear in command of the family as a single parent, she had hidden some of her own feelings of loneliness and her fears about bad qualities the children might have learned from their father.

One day, Scott asked Deborah about her fears, pointing out that she never showed them even though she had tried to acknowledge that sometimes she was afraid too. He smiled and said to her, "I'll bet when you get scared you just act bossy." Scott seemed to have learned a valuable lesson—that sometimes one set of feelings can camouflage another set.

CUTTING DOWN ON AGGRESSION ONE STEP AT A TIME

Earlier, we saw how Deborah gradually helped Scott learn to communicate better. It was like pulling teeth to get him to talk about school, friends, teachers, conflicts, or almost anything other than his own interest in getting a new toy or defending himself after hitting his brother. Deborah started by focusing on the here and now, such as asking him about the TV show he was watching. Then she moved to asking him about events that had happened in the immediate past, such as at school that day. Then she began to talk to him about feelings. She only expected Scott to close one or two circles of communication at first, then three or four, then five or six, and so on—but the first ones were the hardest. The same gradual process will be needed to help a child become less aggressive. While Scott had made enormous strides in opening and closing circles of communication, he was still getting in trouble at school. "I sometimes don't know what happens," he tried to explain. "It just sort of comes out."

Threats and punishments very often succeed in scaring an aggressive child into changing his ways. But this approach does nothing to change his basic perception of the world. In fact, it just reinforces his view of the world as a dangerous place. Instead, we must concentrate on changing this basic assumption and, just as important, help the child learn new ways to obtain what he wants. Then we need to motivate him to use his new skills.

It would have been unrealistic to expect Scott to stay out of trouble all the time because he usually faced it every day. The playground was an especially difficult place for him. He felt more vulnerable outside, running around with the other kids, with only one adult watching from the sidelines. In the classroom, where there was more structure and supervision, Scott felt safer.

So Deborah and Scott had a talk. They discussed some realistic goals, agreeing that Scott would try to have one good day a week—no reprimands or notes from the teacher. With each success, they went to his favorite pizza restaurant or video arcade. As the one-a-week good days got easier for Scott, they added a second day, and then a third, and so on, taking care to leave sufficient time for Scott to adjust. It should be emphasized, however, that Scott's ability to achieve more "peaceful days" was supported by regular floor time, problem-solving time, and empathy—as well as firmer limits.

SETTING EFFECTIVE LIMITS

Setting limits with an aggressive child is, of course, crucial. But many parents and educators make the mistake of *only* setting limits. Limit setting, however, is effective only in conjunction with the kind of supportive parenting that I have been describing.

We always need to use the proverbial "carrot" and "stick" together. Most of us get pulled into one direction or the other.

The "carrot" can then turn into overprotective parenting that allows the child to escape the consequences of his behavior. The "stick" used alone produces, at best, resentful obedience. But if loving warmth and firm limits are increased in tandem, the child becomes motivated because he wants to behave better and understands the reasons behind the limits.

With an aggressive child, you must set up clear consequences for certain behaviors. And be aware that you need to communicate your message clearly (through body language, gestures, and tone of voice as well as words). Remember, children with a tendency toward aggression often misinterpret nonverbal messages. Be aware of the importance of using firm gestures, unambiguous facial expressions, and a serious tone of voice; you can adjust these elements so that their intensity gradually increases.

Deborah had to face the fact that she still overindulged Scott as a way of making up for his father's strictness. It was a holdover from the days of her marriage that she had difficulty shaking. Also, like many busy parents, she was reluctant to punish the boys because she didn't want to ruin the little time she had with them. So, normally after Scott was sent home from school for fighting, Deborah yelled at him and then left it at that.

To motivate Scott (and Deborah), we set up some clearly defined sanctions. The sanctions were intended to emphasize to Scott that his mother was serious about curbing his aggression. As well, they gave his mother some structured rules to fall back on whenever she felt tempted to give in to Scott or let his unacceptable behavior pass.

At the same time, Deborah increased the nurturing floor time she spent with Scott. Parents can't give their children too much of their time, and by spending it in loving interactions, they earn the right to set limits on their children's behavior. In addition, they alleviate their own guilt at having to lower the boom.

With Scott, we decided the limits ought to occur in two ways. First, he needed to go to bed at a reasonable hour to establish that he was a *child*, not a grown-up like his mother. Although he wanted to feel like a grown-up, he also resented feeling like he *had* to be one. Second, Scott and his mother discussed some automatic punishments that would kick in every time Scott wasn't able to keep out of trouble.

Deborah carefully considered the types of punishments to use. She decided that Scott's punishment would be to lose a night of television for every incident of wrongdoing. Scott hated to lose TV—especially during basketball season. Another punishment was a half-hour of household chores for each report of a misdeed from his teacher.

Fortunately, Scott was reasonably obedient as long as someone kept a close watch over him. Some children simply refuse to do what they're told, so it's hard to implement punishments, which in turn just leads to more punishments. In those cases, it's easier to keep a child from doing something he wants to do, like watching TV, rather than forcing him to do something. But Scott was willing to pay the price for "messing up." At first, he sometimes earned as many as four or five hours' worth of work and missed as much as a week of television. At the same time, Deborah set a 9:30 P.M. bedtime and firmly enforced it.

The power struggles between Deborah and Scott were difficult at first. "I hate you!" Scott would shout from the bathroom as he cleaned the sink. "You're a lousy, lousy, lousy, lousy bitch!" Sometimes Deborah had to shout at Scott to get him to do his extra chores. But she made sure she spent extra floor time with him so she could balance setting limits with intimacy, trust, and respect. Scott gradually took pride in his progress: he learned to adopt a more cooperative, empathetic attitude toward those around him, to curb his aggression, and to become more aware of his feelings. He talked proudly of how he avoided conflicts that he previously would have plunged into. He told his mother that when another kid tried to provoke him by snatching his pencil out of his hand during English, he had simply opened his drawer and pulled out another. When he did, Mr. Naughton looked up, saw the other kid with Scott's pencil, and that kid found himself in hot water. At recess, when one child tried to provoke him, Scott went over to play with another group of children. He began to take pride in using his brains to avoid trouble. His attitude of

"Look at the trouble I got into" began to be replaced with one of pride that proclaimed, "I got through the whole week without any fights."

Scott also began to form a few close relationships with other kids at school. Previously, he played with lots of kids but had few intimate friends. But now he especially enjoyed talking and playing with Joey and Amrith. They did projects in school together and shared opinions of teachers and other kids.

He also shifted his priorities: he showed more pride in his skill as a basketball and soccer player and talked less about having to be top dog.

During this time, Scott began to complain to his mother about her schedule. While that was hard on her, it was a very important step in his development.

"We never do anything or go anywhere," he told her one day. "It's not fair! You have to work all the time." While it would have been easy for his overworked mother to dismiss Scott's complaints, she was able to see them as an honest statement of how he felt. He was now dealing directly with his mother and his feelings, rather then beating up other children.

Deborah tried to pay attention to his criticisms. She acknowledged that she didn't have time for many excursions together. Parents often go through times when they can't live up to their children's expectations. But that doesn't have to mean denying the existence of their children's wishes or feelings. Empathizing with their desires and feelings, even if you can't realistically satisfy them, conveys to the child that you respect what he feels, that you are concerned about it, that you might even wish you could do something about it, and that you feel badly that you can't. Your child will probably still be frustrated and may even throw some tantrums. But he benefits greatly by knowing that you know and respect what he wants. This shared respect for his desires and hopes helps him to eventually accept what he *can't* get. His anger eventually will turn into disappointment, perhaps sadness, and, ultimately, acceptance. Denying or ignoring your child's wishes out of the understandable concern that talking about them will only make your child madder or greedier actually strands a child in his angry, frustrated frame of mind. Ironically, it intensifies, rather than ameliorates, the blocked feelings.

Deborah tried to make time for special activities with the boys. She took them to some basketball games. The boys loved the excitement and enjoyed sharing their passion for basketball with their mom. She also made sure there was as much one-on-one time with each boy as she could possibly fit in.

A more open relationship developed between Deborah and Scott. She talked more about her job and its demands and continued to listen to Scott and discuss his feelings when he complained about not having enough time with her.

Over time, Scott became more cooperative at school and at home, felt more positive toward himself, and developed some real coping strategies in terms of being able to understand and talk about his own and other children's feelings—happy ones, sad ones, and even angry ones.

8

ENVIRONMENTAL AND

DIETARY INFLUENCES

ON CHILDREN'S BEHAVIOR

So far, we have talked about how a child's physical makeup and her interaction with her parents can affect emotional development and behavior. But another set of factors influences the way children feel and behave. Some youngsters seem to be more sensitive to certain substances in their environment—such as food, chemicals, and environmental pollutants. This sensitivity can be a factor in learning difficulties and behavior problems. It can also affect children's sensitivity to touch and other sensations, their maturation level, and their moods.

To be sure, this is a controversial area. In particular, food sensitivities—whether to dairy products, sugar, additives, preservatives, wheat, or other foods—have become a hot topic in recent years, partly because of excessive claims made by self-appointed experts. Those who believe that food sensitivities can profoundly affect children's behavior report their findings with great emotion, while those who believe that food sensitivities play no role in children's behavior are equally adamant. In fact, the research on diet and environmental sensitivities is not conclusive. Some studies confirm food influences on behavior and support the notion that eliminating certain food groups may help reduce such symptoms as hyperactivity and migraines. Other studies claim no link between food and behavior. However, increasingly even these studies report that while the statistical evidence is not strong, a small number of individuals are very sensitive and demonstrate that this link indeed exists. While there may not be enough of such people to affect the outcome in any particular study, the small "very sensitive" group may constitute a significant number of individuals in the general population.

Substances in the environment, such as paint fumes, formaldehyde, petrochemical-based solvents, and cleaning fluids, have long been suspected of having an effect on children's behavior and moods. We all have either experienced ourselves, or know someone who has experienced headaches, sinus problems, irritability, distractibility, and hazy thinking when they breathe paint fumes or strong-smelling cleaning products for a while. Indoor pollution has received a lot of attention in the media recently. But, again, studies are conflicting, and more systematic research is needed for definitive conclusions.

In the meantime, how do you evaluate all the contradictory information about whether your child is affected by the food she eats and the chemicals she breathes? It's easy to believe whichever doctor you saw last or whichever scientific study you may have just read.

I suggest that the easiest and most effective way to navigate this controversial area is by paying less attention to the global issue of how widespread food or chemical sensitivities are and focusing more on your child as an individual. That way, you don't have to draw any premature conclusions about food and chemical sensitivity in general; you simply want to determine whether *your* child has some sensitivities that might be affecting her behavior and affecting her emotional development. Once conclusive studies are completed, there will be reasons to become active in preventing environmental and dietary threats to the well-being of all children, such as the clampdown on lead poisoning.

I suggest that if parents suspect a child has a sensitivity to some food or other substance, they should conduct their own "elimination diet" with her and adopt an investigative approach toward other substances that might be causing her problems. That is, take on the role of food and environmental detective: watch your daughter's behavior and keep track of what she eats or what fumes are in her environment. Sometimes parents will comment, "After a birthday party, she goes haywire," or "I noticed on days when I clean house, she doesn't do as well." Heeding those clues may allow you to pinpoint the food or chemicals that set her off.

THE ELIMINATION DIET

If you suspect that a certain food is causing behavior or learning problems, have your child avoid that particular food for ten days to two weeks. (If you are breastfeeding and suspect that something you are eating is causing problems for your baby, then follow the same elimination diet.) *Don't* look for improvements in your child's behavior or learning during this period. There may be many other factors—such as emotional or family patterns, other foods, or chemicals—affecting her behavior. But then, reintroduce the banned substance back into your child's diet for one to three days. Let her have a lot of it! If, indeed, she is sensitive to it, her behavior or learning difficulty may *worsen*. Watch for a change in attitude, activity level, irritability, sleep habits, eating patterns, mood, ability to control impulses, tolerance for frustration, or any other behavior. Some foods or chemicals can lead to negative changes even at low levels. Others require high levels for a day or two. If you're not sure that the food in question is the culprit, then you can repeat the process.

Of course, with an older child, it can be difficult to eliminate foods that she loves—such as ice cream or chocolate. (In fact, some people are sensitive to the very substances they crave most.) With an older child, you can explain the reason and point out that unless the food is clearly causing her trouble, she'll be able to eat it again. With a younger child, you may need to work with her teachers and caregivers to see that the foods aren't given to her at the babysitter's, daycare center, or in school during the elimination diet period.

The most methodical and effective way to conduct an elimination diet is to divide foods into groups. Remove a particular group from your child's diet for ten days to two weeks and then reintroduce it. If you notice changes in your child's behavior, you can break down that food group into individual components and cut those foods from her diet in order to pinpoint the culprit or culprits.

There are many ways to divide foods into groups in order to carry out an elimination diet. Here is a method that I have found effective.

First, test for foods containing *refined sugar, caffeine,* and *chemicals* (additives, preservatives, food colorings, food dyes) as a single group. You'll need to become a close reader of food labels for this category! Sugar foods include corn syrup, fructose, sucrose, honey, and syrup. Caffeine is present in many sodas, as well as chocolate. Additives, preservatives, food colorings, and dyes are present in many prepared foods, so you may find that your family's diet changes drastically during the time that you eliminate chemicals from your meals. If your child shows a sensitivity to this food group, then break it down and eliminate one item at a time. For example, just take out refined sugar for two weeks and then reintroduce it. If there is no reaction, eliminate only caffeine for two weeks and then reintroduce it. Next move on to chemical additives. If your child reacts to the reintroduction of chemicals, then break that category down even further.

A second group includes foods that have *natural salicylates.* Some children are sensitive to salicylates, which are present in tomatoes and most fruits and juices. Fruits with salicylates include apples, oranges, and berries, while bananas, melons, papaya, mangoes, grapefruit, and canned pineapples do not contain them.

The third group is *dairy products*—cheese, milk, ice cream, and yogurt. Again, you will have to read labels carefully because milk is present in a surprising variety of foods, including creamed vegetables, sauces, and baked goods. (If your child turns out to be sensitive to milk, though, she may be able to handle yogurt. Many people who are intolerant of dairy products can accept yogurt. But start by eliminating it with other dairy products and watch for a reaction when you add it back in.) Sometimes milk proteins are added to soy products, so, again, it is important to read labels.

Another food group to test for is *nuts* (including peanut butter). You may also want to test for *grains* (especially wheat) and yeast. Finally, you might eliminate other food groups that have roused your suspicions, depending on your family history and observations of your child's natural response to different foods.

This process, of course, is a painstaking one. And changes in diet alone usually won't dramatically alter your child's behavior. But if your child is sensitive to certain foods, eliminating or reducing them might make a significant difference when combined with the other steps that we have discussed in this book.

SEARCHING OUT CHEMICALS: THE DETECTIVE APPROACH

Certain chemicals in the environment, such as cleaning solvents, volatile organic compounds (found in new carpets), natural gas, pesticides, paint fumes, polyurethane (used to finish wood floors or furniture), and other petrochemical-based products can cause some children (and adults) difficulty. But if you suspect that an environmental chemical is causing your child problems, you usually can't simply eliminate the product and then reintroduce it, as you can with food. In this case, you need to be a detective to ferret out substances that might be affecting her behavior. Look for patterns—good days and bad days for your child—and see whether those patterns are affected by the types of substances that are used around the house on those days. For example, if you notice that your child is irritable and grumpy every Monday, and Monday is regular house-cleaning day when a lot of ammonia-based cleaning products are used, you might try other cleaning materials or only water a few times to see if she does better. Or if your child suddenly misbehaves a lot when the house is being painted, you should be suspicious.

If you are able to identify food or chemicals that negatively affect your child, don't assume that they are "allergies," although allergies may be present. In many cases, children are simply overly sensitive to certain foods or odors, just as some adults react strongly to, say, caffeine or paint fumes.

Once again, let me emphasize that the issue of how food and chemical sensitivities affect mood and behavior still needs full scientific research. Your immediate concern is whether *your* child is potentially affected: Does she benefit from eliminating, say, dairy products, or does her mood improve after, say, milder, less volatile cleaning products are used in your house? Then you can do what's best for your child while you await further research to clarify the important questions about the relationships between foods and chemicals and behavior.

9

IDENTIFYING YOUR CHILD'S
PERSONALITY TYPE

WE HAVE TALKED A LOT IN THIS BOOK ABOUT HOW each child is born with certain physical traits that underlie his basic personality and how many children become difficult because their "equipment" just isn't working right. As they struggle, they can become fussy, irritable, negative, or self-absorbed. We have also seen how the final shape of a child's personality is determined partly by how his parents and other caregivers relate to these physical traits. Challenging children *can* become more pleasant, flexible people. They can become easier to live with—

less at odds with the world, more trusting and secure. Life with a difficult child, as you have seen in this book, doesn't have to be a perpetual battleground.

This chapter provides a quick guide to figuring out your child's personality type and your reaction to it. It should help you identify which pattern your child most closely approximates, even though most youngsters won't—as is always true in life—fit neatly into one category or another.

Keep in mind that challenging children may vary greatly in day-to-day moods and outlook. One moment, they appear mature, respectful, empathetic, compassionate. Later that same day, they are crawling under tables, whining, clinging, throwing tantrums, and bossing everyone around. So don't take any one piece of behavior as a way of labeling your child. Look for patterns over a period of time. And, above all, don't be discouraged if your child appears to be making no progress at all! In time, he will. Sometimes it can just be hard to see.

THE HIGHLY SENSITIVE CHILD

Behavior Children who are *highly sensitive* (chapter 3) tend to exhibit several types of behavior. Among the most common patterns are *fearfulness* and *caution*.

In infancy, a sensitive baby dislikes new routines and is especially clingy in new situations. He restricts his range of exploration and avoids being assertive. In the early years, this child may be plagued with excessive fears and worries and display shyness when trying to form friendships and interact with new adults. In late childhood, he may feel anxious or panicky and have mood swings. He may become depressed. In general, he tends to be inhibited, reactive, and detail-oriented. He becomes easily overloaded by emotional or interpersonal events.

The highly sensitive child also tends to be very perceptive. He senses every nuance and subtlety of his world and is also quite sensitive to the feelings of other people; he can "read" other people through their expressions, body language, and voice tone.

Because sensitive youngsters are so attuned to the world, they tend to focus on the details of what they see, hear, and experience.

Physical Makeup Sensitive children may overreact to touch, loud noises, and bright lights. Sights, sounds, certain smells, and tactile experiences that bring other people pleasure can be overwhelming, irritating, and sometimes downright painful to them.

Some sensitive children face difficulty in dealing with "spatial" concepts (that is, they have trouble processing information in terms of the space around them). For example, they might get lost easily. They may not be able to figure out distances (when mom leaves the room, for example, they haven't an emotional sense of where she went—to the next room or across the country). As a result, they feel less secure than other children and may panic when their parents leave them.

In addition to spatial difficulties, the highly sensitive child may also exhibit motor-planning challenges—that is, he lacks the skills that are required to carry out a series of motor sequences, such as putting on socks, kicking a soccer ball, or writing a sentence. So if your child is very verbal but seems to get lost when he has to do anything that involves a series of behaviors or movements, be aware that his difficulty may be linked to a motor-planning problem. He could be very organized when he is operating in an area of strength but might appear disorganized when dealing with a vulnerable area.

Sensitive children may be overstimulated by internal forces as well as outside events. Their own emotions are experienced very intensely. The child may throw himself down sobbing with disappointment, jump up and down screaming with joy, or shriek and pound the walls with rage. This emotional sensitivity extends to the physical realm as well. He may complain of muscle aches, stomach aches, and other internal pains. Puberty may be especially scary because of its new sensations.

How Parents Respond The patterns described here may be inadvertently intensified by parents or caregivers who respond to the child by vacillating—for example, by being overindulgent and overprotective some of the time and punitive and intrusive at other times. The best approach is for parents and caregivers to provide consistent empathy; very gentle, but firm, limits; as well as gradual and supportive encouragement to explore new experiences.

THE SELF-ABSORBED CHILD

Behavior The *self-absorbed* child (chapter 4) may appear *apathetic*, easily tired. As an infant, she may seem quiet, perhaps even depressed and *uninterested* in exploring people or objects. She may not respond quickly to touch, sound, or other stimuli. As a preschooler, she may sit passively rather than exploring her world. More than most toddlers, she may appreciate familiar routines. As an older child or a teenager, she may appear self-absorbed and disinterested in the world. However, her powers of fantasy and capacity for independence may become assets as she matures.

Physical Makeup Unlike the highly sensitive child, the self-absorbed child needs a lot of stimuli: a great deal of sound before she takes notice, stronger touch before she feels pressure, plenty of movement before she perceives kinetic pleasures. The loud slamming of a car door, a roaring vacuum cleaner, noisy older siblings—these noises don't attract her attention as easily as they would other children. Parents of a baby with this self-absorbed temperament find that it takes twenty or even forty seconds of energetic talking to get her to take notice. They may find that she craves bright lights, loud sounds, lots of motion and speed (big swings, exciting carnival rides) because she simply isn't sensitive to subdued activity.

The self-absorbed child may appear to prefer her own thoughts and fantasies to the outside world. Given her lack of reactivity to outside stimuli, it is much easier for her to tune inward and become self-absorbed.

Low muscle tone and poor balance and concentration may make this child work harder to crawl, push a toy, reach out, jump, and climb. Difficulties arise with skills that require sequencing physical movements (motor planning). This can include drawing a picture, tying a shoe, climbing a ladder, or getting through the kitchen without knocking anything over.

This child may also have difficulties with auditory-verbal processing and expressive language (the ability to put thoughts into words). She may be slow to talk, and later finds it difficult to express herself. It is hard for her to find the words to describe what she did, felt, or wants.

How Parents Respond It is all too easy for parents to neglect or give up on a self-absorbed child. She requires intense input from them and other caregivers and teachers to attract her interest and capture her emotional engagement. If people close to her are low-key or laid-back in voice tone and speech rhythm, this child is likely to tune them out. Parents and others need to reach out energetically, responding to her cues (however faint) to help her engage, attend, interact, and explore the world.

THE DEFIANT CHILD

Behavior The *defiant* child (chapter 5) can be *negative, stubborn, controlling.* He often does the opposite of what is expected or asked of him. He faces difficulty with transitions and prefers repetition or slow change. He tends to be a perfectionist and compulsive.

As an infant, this child may be fussy, difficult, and resistant to changes in routine. As a toddler, when negative behavior is common to all children, he may be even more angry, defiant, and stubborn than most children his age. This child, however, can show joyful exuberance at certain times. A defiant older child or adult may be argumentative and frequently engage in power struggles. He may use passive defiance as a coping strategy or he may try to avoid difficult situations. In contrast to the fearful, cautious person, he doesn't become fragmented when overwhelmed, but reacts instead by trying to control his world as tightly as possible. When moderated, this child's perfectionism and boldness may well help him as a student or in later work.

Physical Makeup The defiant child may have many of the same sensitivities to touch, sound, sight, and motion as the highly sensitive child. But, unlike the highly sensitive child, the defiant child tends to have relatively better "visual-spatial" abilities. That is, he can organize in his mind what he sees and hears better than many other children. He uses this strong ability to help keep himself from getting overwhelmed by what he is experiencing. This means that he becomes very controlling about his environment, hence, his demanding, stubborn behavior.

How Parents Respond It is tempting to respond to the defiant child by becoming angry, intrusive, and punitive. While this is an understandable response to infuriating behavior, it is likely to intensify the defiant child's behavior. Caregiver patterns that are soothing, empathetic, and supportive of slow, gradual change (and that avoid power struggles) tend to enhance the defiant child's flexibility.

THE INATTENTIVE CHILD

Behavior The *inattentive child* (chapter 6) has difficulty staying in one place at a time, paying attention to one thing at a time. *Restless*, seeming to flit from place to place, from toy to toy, from activity to activity, she is often misdiagnosed as having Attention Deficit Disorder. She may also appear *forgetful* and uninterested in conversation. It may be difficult to carry on a conversation with her because she shifts from subject to subject.

Physical Makeup There are different underlying physical reasons why children have difficulty paying attention. Each of these physical patterns has its own type of attentional challenge. Some children have difficulties because of the way that they process what they see or hear, others because of how they move or use their bodies, and still others because of the way their bodies react to the world. Both children who underreact and those who overreact to sensations find it difficult to tune in and concentrate. For instance, children who underreact visually need vivid, compelling imagery to command their attention or else they remain absorbed in their own thoughts.

How Parents Respond When children do not pay attention, parents sometimes focus exclusively on this irritating characteristic. Rather than helping the child develop strategies to compensate for her difficulty, they tend to deal harshly with the youngster, using lots of "do's and don't's" and avoiding debates. A better approach would be to urge the child to ponder her behavior so she can figure out ways of concentrating on one subject. Parents and educators can help children with difficulties in processing information through one mode by encouraging them to use some of their strengths in other modes to compensate. Once they learn to focus, the other skills and abilities of inattentive children begin to blossom.

THE ACTIVE/AGGRESSIVE CHILD

Behavior The active/aggressive child (chapter 7) is highly impulsive and apt to react physically to many situations. He is often on the go, a doer, not a thinker. He jumps headlong into new experiences—diving first and looking later. At school, he may be the class rabble-rouser. This child is easily frustrated and angered, and resorts quickly to hitting, punching, and pinching to get what he wants or to express anger. At his best, he can be enthusiastic and creative.

Physical Makeup An overly impulsive child tends to have poor motor control (which can be misinterpreted by parents and others as aggression). He may be underreactive to touch (as well as to pain) and thus crave tactile experiences and other physical contact. Because he is underreactive to sound, he may enjoy loud noises. Sometimes he has trouble sequencing a series of movements (motor planning).

How Parents Respond Parents and other caregivers sometimes intensify this child's behavior patterns by alternating between being "nice guys" and exploding in anger. (Often, the

father lays down law and order, while the mother is permissive—
but the child perceives their differing approaches as vacillation.)
The less warmth and nurturing an aggressive child gets, the more
difficulties he may face. Parents who provide firm structure and
limits as well as *lots* of opportunities for consistent, warm engagement can enhance this youngster's positive qualities. As well, they
need to encourage the use of his imagination to help him learn to
express feelings verbally and use ideas to get what he wants,
rather than just angry behavior. Parents and other caregivers
should provide warm, trusting relationships and try to instill self-
observation and responsive communication. Once this child
learns to be reflective and exercise some restraint, his energy and
charisma can become powerful assets.

Keep in mind that many children won't fall neatly into one category or another. Your child may be a blend of two or more of
these characteristics, or may, in fact, display different characteristics at various times. The principles of parenting outlined
throughout the book and summarized in the next chapter, especially empathy and patient listening, will help you form a profile
of your child's personality and learn how best to respond to your
son's or daughter's challenges and to elicit his or her individual
strengths.

10

MEETING THE CHALLENGE

THROUGHOUT THIS BOOK, I HAVE PRESENTED BOTH A general philosophy of parenting and some specific suggestions for each challenge your child may have. For a child to reach her potential, she needs her parents to understand and work with her unique traits and also support her progression from one stage of emotional development to the next. Of course, these principles apply to *every* child, not just challenging ones.

Why do some parents seem to do this more successfully than others? Some parents have an approach, style, or attitudes that help children grow in a healthy, robust manner, even when they have considerable challenges. Other approaches, styles, and attitudes are, more often than not, associated with children who continue to have difficulties and acquire even greater challenges as they move through childhood. In this chapter, I want to summarize some of the approaches and attitudes that parents can bring to family life that will enable their children not only to overcome challenges but also to become warmer, more nurturing, positive, flexible, assertive, and creative as they grow older.

Principle 1: Be Realistic about Parenthood

Sometimes the best you can do is less than your "best." One of the first challenges that parents face, especially parents with more than one child, is how to find enough time to keep their children and spouse emotionally nourished, meet their own needs, contribute financially to the family—and still get some sleep! For most busy families, time is the enemy.

Parents who have achieved a measure of career and material success often are confronted with a shocking realization. For the first time in their lives, they face a situation where it is suddenly impossible to get an A or A+ in every subject at home *and* on the job. Just a few years earlier, in college or at their first job, the harder they worked and the more they strived, the better they did. Praise from their families, their bosses, and even their spouses, reinforced their own sense of accomplishment. Getting an A on a Shakespeare exam, after pulling an all-nighter, was a cause for celebration and pride. A brilliant marketing report that took time that otherwise would have been spent on a weekend at the beach but drew the admiration of their colleagues was also a source of enormous satisfaction.

But now let's shift the scene: that marketing report is due, but you have three children, all under age ten, who are clamoring for your attention. Your husband or wife is complaining that there has been little time for talk or real intimacy. As you look ahead at the next forty-eight hours, you realize that there is no way you can have special time with each child, take some relaxed time for intimacy with your spouse, and win an A+ on the marketing report. You face what seems to be a harsh choice: you can elect to get an A+ on that report, but get an F from your spouse and children. Or you can get an A+ from your children and your spouse, but rate an F on your marketing report and perhaps even run the risk of getting fired. Let me suggest a third alternative: you can try to fit everyone into some kind of reasonable balance and get Bs from your children, spouse, and boss.

What? Deliberately strive for only a B?

Most people, as they enter the excitement of marriage and the fulfillment of parenthood, rarely confront this reality. Yet if a parent is to be fair to everyone, and not end up neglecting either children, spouse, or employer, she may have to consciously strive to do only a good-enough job—perhaps for the first time in her life. In real life, being a healthy, nurturing parent to our children sometimes means that, depending on family and work circumstances, you may have to deliberately stop short of your best in order to ensure that your spouse and children get their fair share.

In many families, this is not the issue. Instead, parents may need to put family life and work life in some reasonable priority in relation to hobbies and relaxation. Or the pressing issue may have to do with reducing wasted time or becoming more efficient in work or household chores. Sometimes the issue is simply finding ways to spend time alone with each child and one's spouse. Do you drill your second-grader on his spelling so he'll get into Harvard? Or do you enjoy the castle he's building and leave the spelling until the weekend? You know what I recommend!

Similarly, after a busy week, do you and your spouse go to the big party given by an investor in your firm? Or do you steal a few hours to be alone together?

Whether these kinds of decisions about the use of time are simple or complex, the key challenge here is to anticipate, to look at the true opportunities of parenthood, which include opportunities for real closeness. That requires time and consistency. You need to take an honest look at that, alongside your other responsibilities and pleasures. Anticipate and plan, and don't shortchange the very reason for much of your hard work—providing your family with what they need.

Principle 2: Give Your Child the Most Precious Gift of All—Your Time (Floor Time)

Real nurturing, which has nothing to do with money, presents, books, or expensive schools, involves a much more distinctly human commodity—your ongoing supportive and empathetic availability. Not only is *being there* the essence of parenting, but it is also the foundation on which you can build all the rest—the skills you teach, the expectations you build, the limits you must set. By "ongoing," I mean *daily*—not weekends only, or two nights a week—but *every day* (with an exception here and there).

The best way to spend this time together is what I have described earlier as *floor time*. As you recall, this is the special unstructured time that you set aside for yourself and each child. During this time, about thirty minutes a day at a minimum, you get down on the floor with your child, trying to "march to your child's drummer." Obviously, with an older child, you might not literally be on the floor. But the goal, no matter where you are or what you are doing, is to follow your child's lead and tune in to whatever interests your child. The idea behind floor time is to build up warm, trusting relations in which shared attention, interaction, and communication are occurring on your child's terms.

Sometimes when I explain this concept to parents, they insist that they are already providing a great deal of nurturing. Twice a year, or sometimes even as many as four or five times a year, the family goes on a wonderful vacation where they spend a lot of time together and have great fun. Countless families, when I have asked them about the daily "chicken soup" nurturing part of life, respond with descriptions of idyllic vacations and the closeness they achieve. When I inquire further, I find that sometimes the mother and father's relationship can indeed be sustained by these interludes. But when I talk to the children in such families, I usually hear a different tale.

"We had a great vacation," they say, "and Mommy and Daddy were both relaxed and we all had fun. But I never see them when I need them—when I'm frustrated with my schoolwork, when my friends are mean to me, when I get scared and worried, when I feel lonely. That's when I need them."

One child said, with a sigh of resignation, "I guess I can learn to live without them." Interestingly, this child's mother was insistent about the extraordinary amount of nurturing in the family. She described the fact that they had dinner together as a family at least one night a week and did a weekend activity on

Saturday and Sunday. But she also described a very busy week, during which she got home at about 7 o'clock at night and her husband got home at 8:00 or 8:30. There was time only for some brief help with homework, a quick bite to eat, showers, and bed. The mother proudly pointed out that this was far better than all her neighbors, who didn't have even a single family dinner together during the week and didn't do things together on weekends. Further, she noted that many of the other fathers traveled during the week. She and her husband were home—albeit late— almost every evening. This mother also remarked that perhaps the standards had changed since when I was growing up—in those days, people expected there to be some family time each and every evening. But now that just wasn't the norm anymore. Yet her son still felt lonely and depressed, resigned to "living without them."

Some children, perhaps, can cope with this apparently changing standard, which seems to occur most in fast-paced, expensive cities, where many families have two working parents who arrive home past dinnertime. Our challenging children, however (and even many children who don't have these challenges, I should add), can't get along in this new schedule. We need to make sure we listen to them as we as parents redefine our expectations for ourselves.

In recent years, there has been a tendency to downgrade that part of parenting that children need most—a parent's nourishing availability. Depending on their personality and particular challenges, some children need this to an exceptional degree.

A touching experience I had with one family speaks to this point. Both parents were busy professionals, and their daughter fit the description of a self-absorbed child. Her motor tone was low and there were slight receptive language problems. Thin and frail, she was a sweet, almost angelic little girl who could easily become withdrawn—repetitively playing with some toys and hardly uttering a sound. She rarely made any demands. I saw her initially because of her language delay and tendency to withdraw from other children. With a rigorous and energetic program of the type described in chapter 4, she quickly became more outgoing, happy, verbal, and showed that, behind her apathy and tendency to become self-absorbed, she was a bright and creative child.

She made steady progress until her parents decided to move. With her parents absorbed in the packing and unpacking, she began to regress. They brought her in to see me, alarmed that she had retreated so severely. When I saw her, I was also very concerned. All our progress had been undone. She was turned inward, muttering to herself—now it was hard even to get her to look in my direction, let alone talk to me. Her parents reported that, at home, she was moping, hardly speaking, and seemed only to babble incoherently at her dolls.

I asked the parents to participate in a "family vacation" in their new home. The father was about to go on a three-week business trip. I asked him to cancel the trip, even though it would be very difficult for him to rearrange his plans. He needed to provide a consistent and a high degree of floor time to woo and reengage his daughter, intensifying a pattern that we had used originally to pull the little girl back into the world. I asked her mother to ignore the unpacking and her professional work for a few weeks to participate in this "family vacation."

The family followed the suggestions and, three weeks later, returned to my office. I was amazed to see their daughter not only back to her sparkling, enthusiastic new self, but also being even more verbal and assertive and sophisticated in her language than she had been even before she had regressed. Her parents beamed with pride, relieved that their daughter's regression had only been temporary. But now they faced a real dilemma. They saw the power that they had in their hands and within their own nurturing capacities. The father was confronted now with taking the trip that he had put off. The mother was planning on getting back into her own professional activities as well as fixing up the new house. But they both said that they had never thought that their daughter could go this far so fast. "She's learning at a faster rate than she was even before the move," said her father. "We don't know what to do now that we see how she responds to more time with us."

This father's job still called for frequent travel, and the family was going to have a difficult time deciding whether to resume their old ways and risk slowing down their daughter's progress. They wondered whether they should somehow try to maintain this rather exceptional growth spurt they had created with their own warmth and availability.

What would you do in their situation?

The point of this story is that when children have special challenges, choices are not going to be easy. While a family vacation can't go on forever, parents must become aware of the potential power they have and the choices that are possible. In that way, they can weigh all the factors and make an intelligent choice.

Principle 3: Be Sensitive to Your Child's Physical Makeup

Each child, as we have discussed, has a unique physical makeup. This constitution, in and of itself, doesn't determine your child's personality. But it is an important contributor to her behavior and how you may react. How you react and interact with your child *will* play a large role in determining the type of person she is. The more you can identify your child's unique physical traits, the more you're able to relate to your child in a way that creates the warmth and spontaneity and sense of mutual regard that is likely to build self-esteem and security in both of you. You need to understand your child's sensitivities, characteristic reactions, weaknesses, and strengths so that you can empathize with her feelings and find ways to communicate and enjoy each other.

See if you can draw a mental picture of your child's unique sensitivities. As I have discussed throughout this book, a child's reactivity to touch, sound, sight, smell, and her response to movement can play a big part in determining how she relates to you and the rest of her world. For example, some kids respond better to firm pressure—such as in rough-and-tumble play. Other children prefer light, soothing touches. I encourage you to experiment. Try different intensities of sound and different rhythms. A child who is highly reactive to loud noises may respond well to humming or soft music, for example. Another child may respond well to more dramatic sounds—such as a louder-than-usual voice. Some children like low-pitched sounds, while others prefer high-pitched ones. Watch how your child reacts; if she looks annoyed, frightened, or confused, that will tell you a lot. A child who has difficulty processing what she hears may need simpler words and sentences than a child who is more gifted in this area.

You can also experiment with sights. The level of brightness or dimness in a room, the intensity of the colors and even the amount of animation in your face can affect a child who is sensitive to sight.

You can also try different physical activities with your child. Some like slow, rhythmic movements—such as swinging or being rocked gently. Other children do better when moving rapidly— running or racing down a slide. A fussy baby who is sensitive to movement might be soothed by resting her on her stomach, over your knees, while you apply firm pressure on her back and gently move her back and forth. Another child may do better in an upright position, resting against your chest with her head in the crook of your neck. Similarly, some older children focus best when moving around, while others do best when still. Some children, for example, can only learn while *doing*. They seem to be able to attend and focus better while involved in large-muscle activity—jumping and skipping. For some children, jumping on a bed or a trampoline may foster their ability to attend and engage. Other children, on the other hand, can best attend while sitting still.

Many children who are highly sensitive to touch, sound, light, or movement may be able to focus best when they are in charge of the interaction pattern. The more they are in control, the better they can regulate and monitor all the sensations coming at them, so that they aren't overwhelmed.

It's also helpful if you can draw up a mental picture of your child's muscle tone and motor-planning abilities. As I discussed in chapter 6, high or low motor tone or difficulty with planning action sequences can make it difficult for youngsters to pay attention to the world that surrounds them. A baby with high tone may have difficulty getting her hand to her mouth, for example. As a toddler, she may knock over things while trying to grab something.

A child with low motor tone may tire easily, which means that it requires a great deal more effort for her to do routine activities. Exercises, such as having the child lie on her stomach and pretend to be a boat (rocking back and forth while arching her back) or playing the "bird game" (the child wraps her feet around her parent's waist, arches her back, and flaps her arms as her parent spins around), increase tone, strength, and stamina.

Motor planning can be supported by simple games involving a sequence of actions. For example, you might play "copy cat" or "Simon says" or a game of putting objects in certain places or taking them out. Games that require a child to change direction rapidly, such as a chase game, are also helpful.

If you have a mental picture of your child's way of reacting to sensations, ways of processing sensations, and ability for planning and sequencing her actions, it puts you in a position to find the types of interactions that will foster mutual pleasure and joy, a sense of mutual competence as well as pride and respect. Also, you're then less likely to overly personalize your child's traits ("She's just nasty and stubborn," "She doesn't like me," or "She's just like her father/mother").

Instead, you will be better able to understand and empathize with your child and (when necessary) create structure and limits. These abilities will become the basis for real progress and family harmony.

Principle 4: Work toward a Problem-Solving Orientation

You want to help your child *anticipate, practice* and, slowly but surely, *master* behaviors and activities that she finds difficult. Children with sensitivities, that is, "regulatory difficulties" in any of the areas we have discussed, need extra anticipation and practice in the vulnerable areas. If they are sensitive to touch, sound, smells, or movement patterns, those are the very areas where they need gentle, loving practice.

As we have seen in the stories of challenging children and their parents in this book, daily problem-solving discussions between parent and child are enormously helpful. For example, when the two of you discuss what will happen the next day in school, you can help her *anticipate* the feelings she is likely to have, and how she usually *behaves* in response to those emotions. You can then ask her to *picture* her feelings and usual behavior as a way of figuring out what she might expect in the future. This reduces the sense of surprise or shock and helps her feel prepared, even for uncomfortable situations and sensations.

Many parents, teachers, and mental-health professionals carry out this exercise, but they focus only on the situation and the behavior ("When it's circle time, you tend to sit in a corner by yourself"). But they forget to account for the child's feeling ("When you are in circle time, you feel . . . how?"). The child who can talk about feeling scared ("Like I can't breathe" or "Like my brain doesn't work") will have a big advantage over a child who discusses only the situation and her behavior. Her ability to understand and verbalize how she *feels* in a situation gives her much more flexibility in coping with that situation. Helping a child picture her feelings is not easy. We often want the child to feel as we do or as we wish she felt: "Don't be mad, be appreciative," "Look on the bright side." But it is far more useful to help your child express what's really on her mind. For example, when Molly missed her daddy at night while he was on a trip, it was much more helpful to picture what daddy was doing and how much she missed him (with a big hug from mom), than to tell her to think about "something else" or to reassure her too quickly how much he loves her.

One child built a little block design of where her father was going and would fly in her pretend airplane to visit him and imagine what he was doing. In addition, dad called every night and talked to each child in the family. The security of their father's real voice coupled with the pretend visits, which included feelings of missing and even jealousy, created the elements of successful problem solving. In addition to mental anticipation, actual practice can be helpful. Trial runs of the tough test—the difficult confrontation on the playground, the fast-moving soccer game, speaking out in class—can really help a child. For example, a preschooler who has difficulty being in groups because of the noise and physical contact needs some careful preparation. She may benefit from first being comfortable with one child through lots of play dates. Then expand her contact to two children, then three, and finally the larger group. In this way, she can get used to the jostling and noise of numerous children. Practicing with a small group in the security of her own home, with a parent present, will help her anticipate the situation. Having a few children actually sit in a circle at home and listen to a story will be helpful. Then, when she has to sit in a group of children at school, without a parent, she may feel more comfortable because she has had a chance to practice and anticipate the challenges. She can even practice in nursery school with a small group of children before joining the bigger group. The eight-year-old who looks confused and lost on the soccer field because of all the movement and large, overwhelming spatial expanse may require lots of practice with dad or mom in a much smaller backyard with only one or two other players.

As a general rule, in helping children with this problem-solving preparation in both fantasy and reality, always make sure to follow the axiom "Infinite patience and practice in an area where your child is challenged." For the child who has difficulty spelling, infinite patience. For the slow reader, infinite patience. For the awkward basketball player, infinite patience. And for the child who tends to space out and be passive (who also may have a low motor tone and thus looks like she isn't trying), be even *more* patient. If you have always expected a lot of yourself and can't stand it when your child doesn't seem to be trying hard enough, ask yourself that critical question—is she naturally gifted in this area or is this an area that involves some of the challenges that we have been discussing in this book? If it involves the challenges, turn your desire for perfection into a new kind of perfectionism— a drive for perfect empathy and patience. Patience does not mean that you let your child avoid challenges. It means that you find creative, enjoyable ways to challenge your child to practice what is hard. If you create pressure and tension around your child's challenges, she may become more, not less, unsure of herself and may tend to become self-absorbed, passive-avoidant, disorganized, impulsive, fearful, sad, or defiant. On the other hand, if you *inspire* your child with enjoyable challenges and a patient approach, you may see cooperation and mastery. In short, if you need to put pressure on your child, do it in areas where she is naturally talented. If you want your children to overcome challenges, *you* need to be supportive, patient, and help your *child* practice, practice, practice. Remember the three Ps!

Principle 5: Empathize with Your Child

If you don't have the same sensitivities, it can be hard to imagine how overwhelmed, disorganized, or fragmented a child who is experiencing sensory overload may feel. When a child feels overwhelmed, she often develops fantasies about her sensitivities. When voices are too loud, she may assume that people want to hurt her, for example. If she has difficulty interpreting words and gestures, she may feel that people are trying to manipulate or trick her. It is important to let your child sense that you can understand both her fantasies and also the fact that she feels overwhelmed.

You can display understanding not only with words, but also with gestures. That is especially helpful with a baby or toddler. A reassuring "I know it's scary" look can convey a lot of reassurance to a frightened child. That doesn't mean you aren't exceedingly firm when your child is aggressive. But, even here, you try to balance your firm limits with empathy for the underlying feelings—for example, "I know you're feeling like everyone is being mean to you. And you want to be mean back. And I know all that noise doesn't help. But you still can't hit or hurt anyone." At times, obviously, limits need to be backed up with restraint or sanctions. It's easier to identify with a child's desires for closeness or her fearful feelings. It is harder to be empathetic with anger and rage. And it is especially difficult, as indicated, to put yourself in the shoes of a child whose physical experiences are very different from yours. But over time, by listening sensitively to your child and observing her facial expressions and gestures, you can get a sense of what her internal world feels like. Not only will this allow you to be more helpful to your child, it will also deepen your relationship.

Principle 6: Take It Step by Step

A child with sensitivities requires many tiny steps. She needs to put one toe in the water at a time. If the first step is not manageable, it can be broken down into ten smaller steps. The critical challenge with a challenging child is to overcome her sense (and, often, your sense) that she is standing still or even moving backward and to dispel the idea she has to accept feeling inadequate, incompetent, or overwhelmed. You want to help her achieve some forward momentum, no matter how small it is, so she can feel a sense of mastery. It doesn't matter how small the steps are, so long as she moves forward. The harder the challenge the smaller the steps have to be. The skill of a parent is to turn a seemingly insurmountable challenge into small enough steps to begin forward progress. Whenever step A seems too big, don't give up—break it down into even smaller steps.

Principle 7: When Necessary, Use the "Carrot" and *Firm Limits*

In general, most challenging children need both warmth and nurturing (the "carrot") along with structure, responsibility, and discipline. With challenging children, it is especially important that discipline always be gentle and respectful, while also being firm.

Most families tend to move to one extreme or another. If they are emphasizing discipline, anger and annoyance are more in evidence than nurturing and support. If they focus on the "carrot," there is often little structure and discipline. Typically, as one increases, one decreases. This occurs not because it benefits the child; we do this because it is very hard to be nurturing when we are angry, and it's very hard to be firm and disciplined when we are feeling loving or guilty. Yet most challenging children require more of *both* the "carrot" and firm limits. Because of the nature of their challenges, they need extra experience with both of these crucial emotional experiences.

Increasing support and nurturance and structure and discipline *together* is no easy task. It requires consistent effort and self-reminders. Whenever you feel like you have gone too far in one extreme or the other, remember this important principle and try to increase your use of the other method as well. It also helps to remember that the more challenging your child, the more you are asking of her. And the more you ask of your children and expect of your children, the more you should be prepared to "give" them. Giving, in this context, means empathy and warmth and flexibility *as well as* discipline and structure.

In the principles we have just reviewed, as well as in the suggestions throughout this book, you have no doubt seen that I believe that each of a child's challenges, however difficult, also presents a wonderful opportunity. By addressing the challenge, parents can nourish their child's sense of humanity and unique personality traits.

My approach, which sets out to do more than simply help a child over a particular hurdle, is based on the notion that children are not made up of a series of isolated traits, sensitivities, or behaviors. A child is not simply aggressive *or* impulsive *or* scared *or* sad *or* overwhelmed *or* inattentive. These are individual features that are part of a larger and more profound growing person. All the efforts recommended here seek to enhance children's warmth and relatedness, sense of calm and security, capacity to use their imaginations, the ability to experience a wide range of age-appropriate feelings, and the ability to be logical and thoughtful and use good judgment.

My understanding of mental health and mental illness, in fact, derives from this broader sense of a growing person. The person who can engage in age-appropriate relationships, thoughts, and activities, and can embrace all of life's important feelings— from love and warmth to assertiveness—is emotionally healthy. Sometimes particular traits—such as being introverted or extroverted, cautious or inhibited, or bold and risk-taking—are mistakenly viewed as signs of mental health or illness or as ends in their own right. When we think in this way, we lose sight of the larger experiences and abilities that define mental health and our humanity, such as our ability to be loving and empathetic, or our ability to experience the full range of human feelings, or our ability to switch neatly back and forth between fantasy and reality. If we zero in on limited traits, we tend to develop intervention strategies that seek to work only with isolated kinds of behavior or we resign ourselves to lifelong limitations. We lose sight of the fact that a person can be cautious and thoughtful in some situations *and* exuberant and active in others, or that a person can be outgoing and bold *and* still be loving and sensitive to others. How well we perform as parents or how well we function in our careers will depend much more on our emotional flexibility and overall coping than whether we tend to be cautious or bold. In fact, the more flexible we are, and the better we can think on our feet, the more we will be able to call upon a range of traits, depending on the situation, even though one approach may be a bit easier for us than another.

Some psychologists have suggested that individuals who tend to be more shy and inhibited are somehow less well endowed constitutionally than those who are outgoing and extroverted. They support this thesis with the suggestion that inhibited, shy individuals experience more anxiety or depression. But they fail to look at what happens to extroverted, outgoing individuals when they grow up in unfavorable family circumstances. More outgoing individuals may, under stress, resort to acting-out behaviors, such as speeding in a car or making rash decisions in business. In addition, the individual more prone to acting out may tend under pressure to become more self-absorbed or narcissistic even while appearing on the surface to be very gregarious. They may have difficulty with intimacy and relationships.

Also, keep in mind that certain traits tend to be valued at different ages. In early childhood, the shy, reflective child who is having trouble joining the group is certainly not viewed as positively as is the seemingly outgoing, confident child. Yet, twelve years later, in college, the shy, introverted child—now a young adult—may be getting As and enjoying warm relationships because she is so empathetic and understanding of other people. She may be capable of focused contemplation and of high-level mental activity. The outgoing former leader may have difficulty slowing down, being reflective, and studying and may be insensitive in a close relationship. At this stage, the sensitive, thoughtful person is valued over the action-oriented, gregarious individual.

Obviously, I have painted some extremes in these examples, but I have done this to make a point. We shouldn't confuse individual personality *traits* with bigger and more encompassing personality *capacities*. The capacities that make us emotionally healthy have to do with our ability to give and accept intimacy and warmth, with empathy, with communicating in close relationships a wide range of feelings, and with emotional flexibility—as well as an ability to solve problems. If family and developmental experiences are favorable, shy, introverted individuals *and* outgoing, extroverted individuals can achieve these larger, healthier capacities. Unfavorable experiences place stresses on both types of individuals so that they rely on unhealthy coping strategies, such as depression, anxiety, acting out, and self-absorbed behaviors.

Interestingly, each set of traits makes certain things easier and certain things harder. And each type of person has to master what for her will be the most difficult in order to achieve optimal flexibility. For example, our sensitive and shy person, with proper experiences, can learn to operate in a relatively outgoing and confident manner, while at the same time holding on to her strong introspective and contemplative skills. Our outgoing, action-oriented person can learn to be sensitive to her own and other people's feelings and to slow herself down enough to concentrate and be involved in high-level mental activity.

Sensitivity and action orientation are only two possible personality traits. I have also described children who tend to be self-absorbed, defiant, or inattentive. For each child, there is a pathway for developing the abilities needed at home, with friends, and at school, coupled with the capacity to experience a wide range of age-appropriate feelings, thoughts, and relationships. The key is to remember that the growing person is more than any one trait and that each person has different ways of achieving her most important capacities: to attend, communicate, relate, empathize, and think creatively.

While for many, following the principles I have just suggested will seem like a formidable task, remember that we, as parents, are growing along with our children. Each challenge, each new developmental milestone, is an opportunity not only for our child's growth, but for our own growth as well. By the fact of being human, we are neither perfect nor automated. Our gift is our emotions. And our emotions will overwhelm us at times and thrill us at others. As we grow with our children through the daily trials, tribulations, joys, and pleasures of life, we can only make one simple demand of ourselves: to learn from our experiences. We need to recognize that our powerful emotions, which are the basis of many of our mistakes, are, at the same time, also the foundation of our triumphs.

Index

About the Authors

Stanley I. Greenspan, M.D., is Clinical Professor of Psychiatry, Behavioral Sciences, and Pediatrics at the George Washington University Medical School and a practicing child psychiatrist. He is also a supervising child psychoanalyst at the Washington Psychoanalytic Institute in Washington, D.C. He was previously chief of the Mental Health Study Center and director of the Clinical Infant Development Program at the National Institute of Mental Health. A founder and former president of the National Center for Clinical Infant Programs, Dr. Greenspan has been honored with a number of national awards, including the American Psychiatric Association's Ittleson Prize for outstanding contributions to child psychiatric research and the Strecker Award for Outstanding Contributions to American Psychiatry. He is the author or editor of more than one hundred scholarly articles and twenty books, including *First Feelings: Milestones in the Emotional Development of Your Baby and Child, The Essential Partnership: How Parents and Children Can Meet the Emotional Challenges of Infancy and Early Childhood* (both with Nancy Thorndike Greenspan), and *Playground Politics: Understanding the Emotional Life of Your School-Age Child*, with Jacqueline Salmon.

Jacqueline Salmon is an editor at the *Washington Post*. Her articles have also appeared in *Ms., Self, Seventeen*, and *American Baby*. She has two children.